HISTORICAL STUDY IN THE WEST

Historical Study in the West

MICHEL FRANÇOIS *Ecole nationale des Chartes*	France
A. TAYLOR MILNE *Institute of Historical Research*	Great Britain
WOLFGANG J. MOMMSEN *University of Cologne*	Western Germany
BOYD C. SHAFER *Macalester College*	The United States

With an introduction by BOYD C. SHAFER

APPLETON-CENTURY-CROFTS
Division of Meredith Corporation *New York*

TITLE IN BCL 2nd ED

Preface

This book had its inception in 1962 when its American editor asked three other historians to collaborate on a volume describing the organization of historical studies in France, Germany, Great Britain, and the United States. The editor, then Executive Secretary of the American Historical Association and Managing Editor of the *American Historical Review,* had long been concerned with the need for information about historical work being done elsewhere and found that the other historians shared this concern.

The present volume was prepared not for mature specialists but for students who wish to study history in one or more of the four countries or who wish to compare the diverse ways historical work is done in these countries. It is the hope of the authors that similar volumes will be written about historical studies in other countries, for historians, like scholars in other disciplines, learn by interchange of ideas.

All of the present authors know something of the historical work being done outside their own countries. Professor Michel François, of the Ecole nationale des Chartes, is the General Director of the International Committee of Historical Sciences and has first-hand knowledge of historical work in most parts of the world. Dr. Taylor Milne, the Secretary of the Institute of Historical Research in London, has had the privilege of knowing the many historians from many lands who have studied at the Institute. Dr. Wolfgang J. Mommsen of the University of Cologne, as his essay reveals, is familiar with not only the historical work being done in Germany and Europe but also that being done in the United States. Professor Boyd C. Shafer, Vice President of the International Committee of Historical Sciences, has discussed issues of historical study with historians of several European countries and of Japan and has visited libraries, archival establishments, and universities in these countries.

Historians in the four western as well as other countries are able to build upon rich literary traditions and critical methodological standards that have, over 2,500 years, become international, though not universal. For this reason the first essay traces the development of these traditions and standards. The four authors then describe the training of historians, the organization of historical work, the resources available to historians, and major problems of the historian's craft in teaching, research and writing in their four countries. Short bibliographies are appended to each chapter not only to note the published materials which the authors used in the preparation of their essays but also to suggest readings for students who wish additional information.

In the preparation of the essays on the four countries the authors agreed to follow a common plan suggested by the American editor, but, though there has been much exchange of ideas, each has done so in his own way, each has followed or departed from this plan as he thought desirable, and each is responsible only for his own essay. None of the authors attempts to discuss philosophic questions concerning the meaning of history.

The American editor translated the essay of Professor François on French historical study, and, with the aid of Professor E. N. Peterson and Mrs. Peterson (Wisconsin State University, River Falls, Wisconsin), that of Dr. Wolfgang J. Mommsen on German historical study. The editor has also been responsible for the editing of his colleagues' essays, always, of course, with their knowledge and consent, and he has amplified the essay of Professor François, again with the author's knowledge and consent. Professor John Higham (University of Michigan), Dr. Walter Rundell, Jr. (University of Oklahoma), Professor John Snell (University of Pennsylvania), and Professor C. Vann Woodward (Yale University) read and critically commented upon the essays on the history of historical study and the study of history in the United States, and Leo Gershoy (New York University) the essay on French historical study. Other historians, too numerous to mention, offered astute suggestions that improved the text. The editor's wife, Carol L. Shafter, and his secretary, Mrs. Wiladene Stickel, assisted in the preparation of the volume in all the ways two intelligent, sympathetic, and critical individuals can help a scholar. He owes also a debt of gratitude to his own students who have been his severest critics. The authors, of course, remain responsible for the views expressed.

Boyd C. Shafer

Contents

Part Five

Part One

A Brief History
of
Historical Study

BOYD C. SHAFER

Historical study concerns the past of men. This definition seems satisfactory until amplification is attempted. Historical study concerns itself with everything men have done, said, thought in the flow of past time. This definition is simple, too simple. Of what men have said, thought, done, only traces remain. It is only these traces in the form of records, be these physical remains, oral traditions, inscriptions in stone, or writing on papyrus or paper, that historians can study, and from which they can write history. Historical study, then, is the study of the surviving records of men. This explanation needs qualification and elaboration.

History is everything that has happened to men in the flow of past time. History as a study is the attempt to discover and understand what happened.[1] Historians have sometimes hoped to recover the past as it actually was. But the actual past cannot be recovered for many reasons and not only because past men have left only traces of their acts and ideas. The surviving records, especially of ancient times, are scanty, while the records of modern times, though partial and incomplete, are so vast that an historian can but sample them. The records were created by men; they may or may not give an accurate description, but they never give a full account of what happened. The historian himself is a product of his own times and has the biases of his own culture; and he cannot, even imaginatively, fully project himself out of his own present into the lives of men of earlier times, for they acted and thought in ways partly beyond his comprehension.

[1] In English and French the word "history" (*histoire*) is used to denote both the past and what is known of the past; in some other languages, as German, different and more precise words (*Geschichte, Geschehen, Historie*) may be used. Footnotes are employed rarely in this essay and then chiefly to note exceptions. Quoted statements usually come from the books and articles mentioned in the bibliography.

A quite different version of this essay appears in *The New Catholic Encyclopedia,* which has given permission for publication in this volume.

While an historian wishes to recover as much of what happened as he is able, he also wishes to know more than the bare record, even if it could be found, will reveal. What can be known of the past is always less than what happened, as the knowledge reflects both the incomplete and faulty nature of the records as well as the limitations of the historian. But what is thought about the past may be more than men of the past could have thought about themselves, for the historian hoping to make the past meaningful to himself, his readers or his students, seeks answers to questions arising out of his own culture, questions which earlier men of different cultures would not have asked and probably could not have answered.

Historians have defined their subject in many ways, some narrow—"history is past politics" (Edward Freeman), some broad—"the science of the development of men in their endeavors as social beings" (Ernst Bernheim). In this essay historical study is taken to mean the study, insofar as evidence and reflection permit, of all that men "have suffered, thought, and done—the entire life of humanity" (Robert Flint). The essay is devoted to the purpose, nature, and history of historical study, and more specifically to historiography. It does not consider ultimate meanings of history—theological or philosophical—nor does it cover the history of earliest (prehistoric) men for which separate and related disciplines, archaeology and anthropology, exist.

Among the major purposes of historical study, as these have been set forth over the years by philosophers and historians, four stand out: (1) to reveal the will of God (Augustine, Bossuet, Ranke); (2) to satisfy curiosity and afford enjoyment through the literary art (Herodotus, G. M. Trevelyan); (3) to obtain insights into the meanings or directions of life on earth; and (4) to learn of and benefit from the experience of men. To describe these purposes in detail is not possible here. The first and second purposes seem self-explanatory. The third and fourth are summed up in the following statements. Human nature, as distinguished from nature, has been formed by history (Ortega y Gasset); therefore, to understand man, study the past—the "past is prologue." Not to know what happened before one was born is always to be a child (Cicero), and "where experience is not retained . . . infancy is perpetual" (George Santayana). With remembered experience (history) each man need not start anew, while a tiger is always the first tiger—he has only his instincts to guide him. If men desire to understand how they became what they are now, they may gain insight from history. If men desire to understand or to control their future (Lewis Namier, E. H. Carr), the past experience of their species is one guide. History, therefore, affords "content, wisdom, and signposts" (Friedrich Meinecke). History is man's "deliverer not only from the undue influence of other times, but from the undue influence of" his own (Lord Acton).

A few commentators have disparaged the value of historical study, saying that it was not a branch of knowledge (Descartes), that it overstressed tradition (Nietzsche), that it aroused dangerous emotions (Paul Valéry), or that it was easy (Samuel Johnson). Few, on the other hand, have asserted that it can or should be the only or principal guide to life. Many present historians would probably agree with a contemporary French historian, Henri Marrou, that history's role is humbler: it affords to "feeling, thinking, acting men" an abundance of facts and ideas on which to base their judgments and will. This may be true, as the English-American poet, T. S. Eliot, has written, because

> Time present and time past
> Are both perhaps present in time future
> And time future contained in time past.

A host of other purposes for history have been put forward. For early Chinese scholars (Confucius, Liu Chih-chi) as well as ancient western historians (Thucydides, Livy, Polybius) history taught ethics as it afforded lessons through examples. They believed it a school for rulers, statesmen, generals, just as modern historians (Ernest Lavisse, Charles Beard) thought it a school subject through which ordinary men could be taught to be good citizens. Several nineteenth-century thinkers (Auguste Comte, Henry Thomas Buckle, Henry Adams) sought to determine scientific laws of history, and in the twentieth century other philosophers (Spengler, Toynbee) have formulated elaborate historical explanations for the rise and fall of cultures or civilizations.

History has also been used for more limited or less noble purposes: to support the interest of an individual (Napoleon) or a class (Marx), to inculcate narrow nationalism (Treitschke), or to attack particular religious beliefs (Voltaire). From history it is possible, indeed, to draw almost any kind of example or moral, for human experience in the thousands of years of historical time has been wide and varied. But from history alone, it is probably not possible, for this very reason, to prove or disprove any human contention beyond doubt—that, for example, man is either a peaceful or a warlike creature. Knowledge of history, it is true, enables any man to make any past man his ancestor and therefore from history he may pick out almost any kind of example he wishes. But while the opportunity this permits may be misused, it frees, as Lord Acton said, the individual from sole reliance upon his own narrow and short experience and also from excessive reliance upon one tradition. The greatest value of historical knowledge may be that it reveals potentialities and limitations of men.

The origins of historical interest may be as old as man—whenever (as Voltaire remarked) the first father, for reasons of education or enjoyment, first told his son stories about his own past, or the first son, out of curiosity, began to wonder about his parents.[2] About the origins, however, there can be only conjecture. There are no written records (though many physical remains) until recent historical times —the fourth millennium B.C.—and but few survive from ancient civilization hundreds of years later.

Once European students bound by the limitations of their own culture believed the earliest history to be that of the Old Testament Jews and the ancient Greeks. Now archaeological excavations and historical research have pushed the history of men backward (and will probably push it further because of new discoveries and the radio-carbon technique of dating). Now, too, the western world has "discovered" the ancient civilizations of the Near and Middle East which predate those of the Greeks and Jews. Inscriptions in stone or bronze (later writing on clay, leather, or papyrus as well) giving property and king lists, appear in very early (roughly 2500 to 1500 B.C.) Sumerian, Assyrian, Hittite, and Egyptian civilizations. The earliest known writing, on a limestone tablet, is a pictograph from about 3500 B.C. The early lists, and later annals and chronicles, do not constitute history in an interpretive or critical sense, but a few of the Middle Eastern scribes apparently began to separate historical happenings from natural phenomena and to realize that no two events were the same. The ancient Egyptians had no word for history,

[2] But cf. Eliade, Mircea, *Cosmos and History, The Myth of the Eternal Return*, New York, 1959 (original French edition 1949).

though they did use *gn wt* which may be translated as "annals." They developed myths about the beginning of human life but no philosophy of history. Possibly one of the earliest Egyptian historians was Manetho, of the third century B.C., of whose work only fragments survive. In China traces of written records survive from about the same time as in the Middle East. The first chronicles, the so-called "Spring and Autumn Annals," said to be edited or inspired by Confucius, cover the State of Lu from 722 to 481 B.C. The first history, *Shih chi* or *Records of the Historian,* was composed by Ssu-ma Chien (145?–90? B.C.). For the ancient Hebrews the historical books of the Old Testament probably date from about the ninth to the fourth century B.C. though behind these are oral traditions and other records. From the books of the Hebrews came the conception of human history as God working out his purpose for a "chosen people," and hence for the rest of mankind. Greek records are possibly earlier than these that survive of the Hebrews. But Herodotus, the "father of history," composed his great work on the Persians and Greeks only in the middle of the fifth century B.C. and Thucydides his interpretive history of the Peloponnesian War near the end of that century. Muslim historical study, purporting to reveal "the unfolding of divine purpose on earth," began much later, long after Mohammed and the *Koran.* It, with its Persian additions, became, with the Chinese and the Hebrew-Greek-Christian, the third independent development of historical study. In early India the study of history as such apparently did not arise; for Hindus, movements, not men, made the past and the universe changed through immense cycles of time.

Not until the nineteenth century, and then only in the western world, did historical study assume its present systematic and critical form. But, of course, not all early historians were uncritical. While Herodotus in his history hoped chiefly to preserve the great and wonderful actions of the Greeks and barbarians and has been accused of not being too careful about his sources, Thucydides in his history employed the careful methods of Hippocrates as he searched for material causes of material events in the Peloponnesian War and as he examined the accounts of eyewitnesses by the "most severe and detailed tests possible." The Greek term ἱστορία means inquiry or learning by inquiry in any field but Thucydides in the fifth century B.C. did make critical historical inquiries. So also did Ssu-ma Chien for his *Shih chi* at the court of the Early Han Emperor Wu (second century B.C.). In the third century A.D., the Christian martyr, Lucian of Samosata, in an essay on "How to Write History," thought the historian should be a fearless, independent investigator of facts who wrote "to tell the thing as it happened." And in the seventh century the Chinese Liu Chih-chi in his treatise on the same subject developed criteria for judgment as he asked for insight, talent, and learning in historians.

Roman writers carried historical study little further than the Greeks. They wrote so much history that Juvenal (60?–140?) satirized their works with his phrase, "swell to a thousand pages," and Lucian two centuries later commented, "You cannot find a man but is writing history." Of the ancient historians of Rome three, at least, must be mentioned, Polybius (205?–122?), Livy (59 B.C.–17 A.D.), and Tacitus (55?–after 117). As they wrote, chiefly about their own times, each of them attempted to teach moral lessons, to show how political policies failed or succeeded. They differed otherwise. A Greek hostage of Rome, Polybius described events for about a hundred years from the middle of the second century B.C. A widely traveled man of much knowledge, he based his forty books of history (only portions survive) upon records, the work of earlier historians, eyewitness accounts, and his own observations. Even more than Thucydides he was interested in the causes of things as he discussed in detail Rome's constitutions and wars. Livy was less critical, much more didactic as he tried to inculcate patriotism. He accepted legends and followed other historians without much investigation of his own as he wrote his rhetorical accounts. His history in 142 books (35 and fragments and summaries are extant) covers Rome's history from its mythical beginnings in 753 B.C., with great emphasis on Livy's own period. The history contains hearsay and errors, but it is almost the only source for some of Roman history. Tacitus was possibly the greatest of Rome's historians. In his *Historiae* (of twelve or fourteen books about four and a half survive) and *Annals* (nine books intact, fragments of others), this embittered aristocrat commented with insight and cynicism on the civil wars, despotism, and decline of the aristocracy as Rome changed from a Republic to an Empire during the period of the Julian and Flavian emperors. Later historians debate the amount of research he did, but he was a powerful writer, anxious "to commend the just and hold up the evil. . . ."

Ancient peoples did not conceive of time in the same way as

most modern peoples who think in terms of flow from past to the present and the future. Though their seers often attempted to prophesy the future, the past, except as story and lesson, had less meaning for them. And not only were they less aware of their past but their past was shorter and their records were scantier—Rome had no official archives until Cicero's time (first century B.C.). Their historians stressed their own times, not the distant past as they sought to teach or to provide enjoyment. Indeed, for some of their keenest minds the flow of events in time held little significance. Aristotle defined man as a "being in society" and for him the *polis,* or community, was timeless. But the ancient Hebrew prophets dealt with the guilt and punishment of the Jewish people in the past, present, and future because God had chosen them for service to mankind. For them God was unfolding his will in history through the Jews. Following them, St. Augustine discussed many questions in his *City of God,* and contemplated the histories of the heavenly city (love of God) and earthly city (self-love) from Adam and Eve and from Assyria. He saw the heavenly city slowly taking the place of the earthly as God, in history, worked through man and all things. This was basically the interpretation of history of Orosius, an Iberian priest and follower of St. Augustine, in his *Seven Books of History against the Pagans.* With variations it was for many centuries to be the dominant world historical view of those Europeans who wrote history.

Through the long ages, which later Europeans limited by their own history called the Middle, much history was written by Byzantine, Chinese, Muslim, and other historians. Here, because of limitations of space, the western work must be emphasized. But that of the greatest of Muslim historians, Ibn Khaldun (1332–1406), cannot be ignored. This historian, and in modern terms, social anthropologist, wrote history that was interpretive, critical, profound. His *Kitāb al Ibar* (universal history) recounted the history of the Berber and Muslim dynasties of North Africa, and it was preceded by a *Prolegomena* that examined fundamentals of historical method and meaning. Ibn Khaldun, however, had little effect on the historical study of either his own or European peoples.

For more than a thousand years in the west, history was chiefly written by churchmen. The "father of ecclesiastical history," Eusebius of Caesarea (260?–340), wrote a *Chronicle* of all known peoples (an important landmark) and an *Ecclesiastical History* of the early Church for which he tapped numerous sources. Many church historians imitated him as they, with St. Augustine, illustrated the will of God in history in the annals and chronicles which they compiled of their monasteries and localities. But for several centuries, little of note was written in Europe except the books of Gregory (538–594), Bishop of Tours, and Bede, "the Venerable" (673–735). Gregory wrote the *History of the Kings of the Franks* which not only told much about the Franks but church history as well. Where Gregory had first-hand knowledge his work constitutes a significant source. Bede's great *Historia Ecclesiastica Gentis Anglorum* summarized the learning of his time. Bede used and cited documentary evidence, ever taking "delight in learning, teaching, and writing." In what were to become England, France, and Russia, and in other countries as well, a few learned men maintained monastic annals which developed into more or less continuous chronicles, such as the *Anglo-Saxon Chronicle,* started probably in the ninth century, and the later *Chronicle* of Novgorod, begun in the eleventh century. But the best of the medieval histories came later.

During the twelfth century, Otto (d. 1158), Bishop of Freising, wrote his extraordinary *Chronica*. Following Augustine in the desire "to display the miseries of Babylon and the glory of the kingdom of Christ," he began his work with the story of creation. A critical and learned man, he also declared the Donation of Constantine a forgery. Some of the annals maintained by monks were little more than bare and anecdotal accounts of local happenings, though they would become primary sources of information for later historians. Others revealed wider interests and were more learned. Among these were those of three English churchmen, Henry of Huntingdon (d. 1155), who used primary materials for his *Historia Anglorum;* William of Malmesbury (d. 1143), who was the "first English writer after Bede . . . to give his details of dates and events such systematic connection, in the way of cause and sequence, as entitled them to the name of history" (Stubbs); and Matthew Paris (d. 1259), a "universal genius" who, with independent judgment lacking in his predecessors, prepared his *Chronica majora* to depict the history of mankind from creation to his own time (1259). Knowing influential people in England and western Europe, Matthew was well informed and his work supplies important information on his own times.

Of the numerous memoirs and commentaries written by laymen, from the twelfth century onward, three may be mentioned as illustrative. A courtier of Louis IX of France, Sieur de Joinville (1224?–1317) idealized his master in a remarkable biography filled with anecdotes and shrewd observations. An ambitious bourgeois, Jean Froissart (1333?–1400?), excitingly but inaccurately depicted the courts and military chivalry of France, England, Scotland, and Spain for the three-quarters of a century after 1326. A nobleman, Philippe de Commines (1447?–1511), realistically portrayed the kings and courtiers, wars, and diplomacy of the France of Louis XI and Charles VIII (late fifteenth century). Though his *Memoirs* are not free from errors, he, like Joinville, shrewdly commented on the life and manners of his time. In the interpretive and critical sense, little history was studied, written, or read, even in the thirteenth century when the study of philosophy reached a height not attained in Europe since fifth-century Athens.

Critical and systematic historical study never quite disappeared in western Europe, but from the fifteenth century it was slowly to become more critical, more systematic. With Jakob Burckhardt, the brilliant nineteenth-century Swiss historian, students of European history once perceived in fifteenth- and early sixteenth-century north Italy a sudden flowering or renaissance of culture in which scholars were sharply critical as well as creative. This flowering did occur, especially in Florence, though it was neither sudden nor a mere rebirth of classical learning. A deepening of the critical as well as the creative spirit took place in parts of western Europe from the twelfth century. Florentine humanists and political observers of the Renaissance period, nevertheless, have special significance, as a brief note on several of them will demonstrate. The humanist Lionardo Bruni (1369–1444) destroyed legends surrounding Florentine history. The versatile Poggio Bracciolini (1380–1459), and other humanists including his contemporary Niccolò de Niccoli, passionately searched for surviving manuscripts of ancient Greece and Rome and thus recovered for posterity invaluable sources for ancient history. Niccolò Machiavelli (1469–1527) and Francesco Guicciardini (1483–1540), both of whom were experienced diplomats and rejected office seekers, realistically (at times cynically) exposed the self-interested psychological motives of contemporary leaders as they wrote their histories of Florence and Italy and commented on Roman and Italian politics.

In their political views and philosophic outlooks on life, the Florentines widely differed. They might be primarily interested in classical learning or in office holding. They might think of history as a vehicle for rhetoric (Bruni), as a way of providing "wholesome instructions" (Guicciardini), or of uniting Italy (Machiavelli, in the *Prince*). But they were interested in the past as human experience, and, on the basis of classical models (Livy and Polybius) and their own personal aspirations, they subjected this past to examination. In Rome and elsewhere during the same era, humanists, e.g., Flavio Biondo (1388–1463), explored the physical ruins of classical civilizations, and this, too, by leading to an examination of sources, added a dimension to historical study.

The work of modern historians depends not so much upon their own observations and reading of earlier historians as upon research in writings and documents affording first-hand evidence about the events they describe. Much, though not all, of the best historical work until the nineteenth century had been done by historians, as Thucydides and Tacitus, contemporary with the events they described. It was also customary for medieval and early modern historians (as Pascal noted) to depend in great part upon the historians who preceded them. They could not have done otherwise, for, except by religious groups, historical materials were seldom collected, preserved, or ordered. Increasingly from the fifteenth century, the city and new national governments, and private families engaged in business as well, kept records of their affairs. And, increasingly these were systematically preserved.[3] The first major modern archives were established at Simancas in Spain in 1543. The great modern collections of manuscripts and books, so essential for historical research, were also begun about the same time. The Vatican Library was founded in the fifteenth century and the origins of the Bibliothèque Nationale in France are nearly as old.

Manuscripts and documents, it is obvious, are of little value for historical research unless they are authentic. Both may be forgeries and both, in reproduction, may be faulty. The great historical achievement of the late seventeenth and eighteenth century was in the zealous collection and erudite judgment of source materials for late ancient and for medieval history. Possibly the greatest of the erudite scholars, the Benedictine Jean Mabillon (1632–1707), noted

[3] See the forthcoming book by Ernst Posner.

that "nothing was more fashionable than critical evaluation" and he was, for his own kind of scholar, quite correct. For this work of erudition two preconditions were necessary: (1) the development of general critical attitudes of mind, and (2) the devoted, skilled labor of scholars widely versed in languages and the ways written records were created. The attitudes and criteria of Mabillon and others became the basis for later historical study, not only for medieval but for modern history.

As early as the mid-sixteenth century, Jean Bodin (1530–1596), a French political theorist, had formulated rules for judgment of historians in his *Methodus ad Facilem Historiarum Cognitionem*. But in his day, old documents were still believed authoritative if old enough and generally accepted. Outside the field of history, Galileo, Pascal, Spinoza, and others, however, had begun to apply critical methods in their pursuit of knowledge in science and philosophy, and they had situated their knowledge in historical time. And the Sieur Du Cange (1610–1688) had written splendid (still usable) glossaries of medieval Latin and Greek. Within the field of history, Jesuits, Benedictines, and others began to apply canons of criticism to the sources of late Roman and medieval history. Jesuit scholars, among whom John Bollandus (1596–1665) and Daniel Papebroch (1628–1714) were outstanding, wrote critical prefaces to their editions of lives of the saints (a work still in progress). Benedictine monks developed tests for judging documents from their study of the historical foundations of their own order. Mabillon's learned *De re diplomatica* (1681), based on his own long and arduous research, established canons (diplomatics) for judging the honesty and falsity of medieval charters. As Lord Acton said, Mabillon "belongs to the family of pioneers . . . a critic the first in the world." A little later two other priests, Le Nain de Tillemont (1637–1698) of Paris and Ludovico Muratori (1672–1721) of Modena edited magnificent documentary books on the early history of the church and of Italy. For Edward Gibbon, the secular master historian of the eighteenth century, Muratori was "guide and master on the history of Italy."

Eighteenth-century thought was long supposed to have been anti-historical in outlook because, characteristically, the best-known thinkers sought more often to discover natural laws which govern the universe and man than to learn of the varied experiences of men. These rationalists, among whom Leibniz (1646–1716) and Voltaire

(1694–1778) stand out, viewed the world partly through the lenses of physical science which had attained an immense reputation with Newton's achievements. But the century was not as opposed to history as was once believed. Just at the end of the seventeenth century, Bossuet (1627–1704), tutor of a prince of France and Bishop of Meaux, demonstrated the strength of Augustinian conceptions and the power of Old Testament accounts in his *Discourse on Universal History*. All through the eighteenth-century "age of reason," much history was written, some of it great. Edward Gibbon (1737–1794) produced a masterpiece of historical literature in his *Decline and Fall of the Roman Empire,* sweeping over 1,400 years of politics and war in elegant rhetoric. Voltaire expanded the study of the past to include not only Europe but the world and not only war and politics but civilization in two of his many books, the *Essai sur les Mœurs* and the *Siècle de Louis XIV.* The skeptical Scotchman, David Hume (1711–1776), who was primarily a moral philosopher, wrote a huge *History of England from the Invasion of Julius Caesar to the Revolution of 1688* in which he gave much attention to tracing "effects" to their "causes."

The histories of all three of these men reflected the prejudices of their age. They were skeptical, anti-clerical, anti-medieval. Their histories, too, each had defects. Gibbon, who read enormously in the sources, knew little about Byzantine history which is now known to have been culturally rich. For Voltaire, a quip could take the place of interpretation and research. And Hume was more interested in establishing the philosophic bases of skepticism and attacking religious credulity than he was in searching for primary sources. But the qualities of their histories were massive. All three men wrote history as literature. Gibbon and Voltaire wrote magnificently and their histories were read, and Hume's history, full of "solecisms, Scotticisms, Gallicisms" as it was, won much favor in Europe if not (at the time) in Britain. The rhetoric, the irony, and the vision of Gibbon's *Decline* are perhaps unequalled in historical writing. Voltaire's brilliant insights, even if he sometimes haphazardly jotted them down, pointed toward historical study concerned with the arts and customs of peoples everywhere. Hume's anti-metaphysical doubts profoundly affected the future writing of history. None of the three giants made major contributions to historical methodology but all three, in their differing ways, immensely widened the sweep and scope of historical interpretation.

Gibbon, Hume, and at times Voltaire did not share one belief of their age, the belief in progress. This belief, becoming popular in the eighteenth century, was to influence deeply the future study of history. In a famed *Discours* of 1750 the then young economist Turgot (1727–1781) spoke of the human race as marching "continually though sometimes slowly to an ever increasing perfection." A little over forty years later during the French Revolution the *philosophe* Condorcet (1743–1794) sketched ten stages of the "progress of the human spirit." If there was movement upward in history, then there was continuity in men's affairs and a framework for meaningful historical reconstruction. This continuity and framework would provide one of the fundamental assumptions of later historical interpretation.

Eighteenth-century thought was only in part rationalist. Within and without the mainstream a then little known Neapolitan philosopher, Giambattista Vico (1668–1744), wrote a discursive book, *Scienza nuova*. Vico rejected Cartesian science as the key to knowledge and stressed man as an historical being in society who made his own history and therefore could understand it. Drawing upon knowledge from the yet undeveloped social sciences, as anthropology, he meditated upon a science concerning the "nature [genesis] of the nations from which has issued their humanity, [and] which in every case began with religion and was completed by sciences, disciplines, and arts." Though his ideas had no followers in his time they profoundly influenced future historians, philosophers, and social scientists, Herder, Michelet, Marx, and Croce, for example.

As the rational thought of the eighteenth century lost its appeal, that called romantic won favor. Out of romanticism arose a new interest in and understanding of history. No two students will define alike either rationalism or romanticism, but the latter, in some ways an emotional reaction to the former, stressed the supernatural and traditional, and individual differences and folkways in contrast to reason, science, the common nature of man, and natural law. Rousseau (1712–1778), the earliest important romantic, wrote little history, but his emotion as well as his love of the primitive, were to be shared by two generations of philosophers, poets, novelists, and historians, and to become the source of persisting though differing interpretations (in the historical writings of Michelet, Carlyle, and Parkman, for example) of modern western culture. The early and influential German romantic, Johann Gottfried Herder (1744–1803), was not primarily an historian either, but his *Ideas on the Philosophy of History* portrayed all life as an organic unity and history as the continuous education of mankind. A little later Friedrich Karl Savigny (1779–1861) reached as far back in medieval law to reveal how, through continuous development, the past had led to the present. For Herder, Savigny, and other romantics the key to the present was to be found in the unique historical experiences of each people. This belief was also to become a fundamental assumption of much later historical work.

The shaking event of the age of reason and romanticism, the French Revolution of 1789, marked a watershed in historical study as distinct as that in political life. During and after the Revolution its adherents, believing in its principles and in their own reason, wrote tracts, memoirs, and histories to praise or defend what happened and their own acts. Their opponents, often romantics, believing the Revolution a crime because it broke with tradition and disrupted the organic unity of society, attacked its principles through an appeal to historical precedent. Emerging national patriotism excited the zeal of both the revolutionaries and the reactionaries, for both were usually patriots of victorious and vanquished nations who, in fear and in hope, defended and exalted their own national aspirations. Another quite different result of the Revolution made it possible to write history as never before. Many documents lost their legal value as titles to property and privilege and an enormous quantity of them would become available for later research.

For the revolutionaries the Revolution was the greatest event in history; they had created, they were certain, a brave and new society. For their adversaries, such as Edmund Burke who eloquently upheld tradition, the Revolution was tragic; it had broken the continuous chain linking the present with all the God-given past. The cleavage between the two sides, however, was not as sharp as it appeared to be on the surface, for the past appealed to both not only as vindication of their personal views but as revelation of the superior qualities of their nations. For the revolutionaries the immediate past was vital, though classical Rome offered lessons in statesmanship and oratory as well. For their opponents the historical roots of their societies in medieval and early modern times were the only valid bases for the present. In either case the appeal was to history.

Historians, revolutionaries, reactionaries, and national patriots, like other men of their times, searched diligently for justification of their ideas and for the origins of their nations and national institutions. Out of revolution and reaction, romanticism, and nationalism arose unprecedented concern for historical study. Augustin Thierry, a French historian, was not wrong when he predicted, in 1834, that history would become a mark of the nineteenth century as philosophy had been for the eighteenth. History, then as now, reflected the age in which it was studied and written. This would become vividly demonstrated in the nineteenth century as national schools of historians arose in western and later eastern Europe and in the United States, and, as historians, motivated by national patriotism, such as Jules Michelet in France, Heinrich von Treitschke in Germany, and George Bancroft in the United States, wrote voluminously on the histories of their own nations.

The streams of history coming from romanticism and nationalism did not, of course, stay within the banks of these flowing sentiments. During the early nineteenth century when romanticism was at flood tide, another current, "scientific history," was rising. This had its source in earlier traditions, but was to take a clear course of its own and, much modified, to become the mainstream.

At the end of the eighteenth century, a few philologists in Germany were evolving exacting methods for examination of languages. Among them was Friedrich August Wolf (1759–1824) who, with careful linguistic analysis, wrote his *Prolegomena ad Homerum* (1795) to prove that the *Iliad* and *Odyssey* were the work of several authors. These philologists also introduced what became known as the seminar, in which students studied together under the guidance of a master in order to learn a discipline through research and constant evaluation of their work by the master and their fellow students.

During the same years Barthold Georg Niebuhr (1776–1831), an historian and Prussian patriot, began to apply similar rules in his study of Roman history, and especially to the history of Livy. A serious young Thuringian student, Leopold von Ranke (1795–1886), much impressed by Niebuhr's work, began to employ similar methods. His *Geschichte der Romanischen und Germanischen Völker von 1494–1535*, published in 1824, included systematic criticism of earlier historians (Guicciardini in particular) who had written on the struggle of the two peoples for control of Italy. This book, in its preface, contained a phrase that was to become a motto of the coming generations of empirical historians, *"wie es eigentlich gewesen."* The complete sentence in literal translation reads, "From history one has the duty of judging the past, to serve the needs of the world for instruction concerning the future: this present investigation will not serve so high a duty; it will simply explain what really happened." In this work and in his many later books Ranke aspired to much more than just reconstruction of the past. A Prussian patriot, he was also a Protestant idealist who professed to see the "workings of God [in history] from a great distance." He wanted, through meticulous research on and intuitive contemplation of unique events (later called historicism), to write universal history, history that would be the history of mankind and that would have meaning for all men. As he himself said, he was inspired by philosophy and religion and by discovering the errors in Walter Scott's romantic novel, *Quentin Durward.*

Few people, even historians, now read Ranke, but Ranke, through his many first-rate students and his use of the seminar method (from 1830), began modern historical study. He was careful and cautious, he emphasized research in manuscripts and documents (not just the reading of earlier historians), and he had superlative students to spread his doctrines. Later historians, especially in the United States, would usually overlook his philosophical inclinations and his aspirations to universal history. Using him as a model they would stress his attempt to be objective (*wie es eigentlich gewesen*), his research in archives, and they would favor narrower specialization than Ranke himself practiced.

Independently, and for varying reasons, scholars in other countries moved in the same directions. Before Ranke's first book appeared Augustin Thierry, a romantic inspired by Scott's *Ivanhoe,* prepared his *Lettres sur l'histoire de France,* in which he also critically evaluated the works of previous historians as he pleaded for more study of the French nation. In France, too, François Mignet (1796–1884) published an objective *Histoire de la Révolution Française* in 1824, and the Ecole nationale des Chartes for the study of paleography was established in 1821 (though not well established until 1847). These were the years, also, during which monumental, carefully edited, national collections of historical documents began to be published, the *Monumenta Germaniae Historica* (from 1826) and the *Documents inédits relatif à l'histoire de France* (from 1835).

The work of Ranke and the new empirical schools of historians did not end histories written in the grand literary manner. In fact, some of the finest ones were still to be written. In 1848 Thomas Babington Macaulay (1800–1859) began to publish his well-documented and confident "Whig" *History of England* (four volumes, fifth unfinished) covering eighteen years, 1685–1702, of that nation's history. From 1833 to 1867 Jules Michelet (1798–1874) composed his poetic and patriotic *Histoire de France* (seventeen volumes) which swept over the whole history of his people. And from 1834 to 1875 George Bancroft (1800–1891) intermittently worked on his grandiloquent *History of the United States* (ten volumes and a revised edition of six volumes) to glorify his country and its democracy. History (or biography) written as narrative and in lofty or literary language would continue to delight readers, as the twentieth-century works of Winston Churchill and G. M. Trevelyan in England and Douglas Southall Freeman and Allan Nevins in the United States bear witness. But during the second half of the nineteenth century, historians would argue (as they occasionally still do) whether history was art or science until there appeared to be veritable warfare between the two approaches. The increasing numbers devoted to specialization favored the second, preferring analysis to narrative and exact reconstruction to dramatic unity. To become "scientific" became the passion of most historians who matured during the last four decades of the nineteenth century. Always, however, a few historians refused to conform and thought of history as art, as did Jakob Burckhardt in his wonderful synthesis of the life, the arts, and the values of the *Civilization of the Renaissance in Italy* (published in 1860).

The romantic Michelet died in 1874. He lived his life and found his meaning in history, seldom tried to efface himself in his imaginative recreation of the past. A year later the scholarly Fustel de Coulanges (1830–1889) began to publish his *Histoire des institutions politiques de l'ancienne France* (6 volumes). "His eyes fixed only on science," Fustel wanted the historian out of history. He was convinced that, through the minutest study of primary texts, historians could ascertain historical truth and that when historians who had done (as he had done) this kind of research spoke, not they but history spoke.

Influenced by the successes of science, especially in biology and geology, historians hoped to use its methods to achieve results as significant. If, they were convinced, they could patiently, exhaustively pile up facts, they could reconstruct the past as it really was, and "build . . . some of the countless stairs by which men of distant ages may mount to a height unattainable" by themselves (J. B. Bury). The direct sources of the new faith were the methods and work of the Rankean school, and even more immediately, the ideas of Charles Darwin (1809–1882) and Thomas Buckle (1821–1862). There were, of course, larger conditioning influences, the ancient search for God and truth, the mounting nationalism, the increasing affluence of western societies, the growing thirst for education. But the transforming factor was science, or rather the belief in it, and this belief became all the more potent because science seemed to promise progress. Ever since the seventeenth century the faith in science had been intensifying. In the nineteenth it was reinforced by remarkable technological developments and by the appealing doctrines of positivists like Auguste Comte (1798–1857) for whom scientific sociology crowned the third and highest stage of civilization. And now Darwin seemed to explain how life had evolved and Buckle to promise a "science of history" to be achieved through inductive discovery of its laws.

Few historians were well informed about science and there was no agreement on its nature or meaning.[4] For the majority of historians science probably meant only systematic, empirical search for facts and cautious, objective descriptions of research findings, for a minority the formulation of general laws through inductive reasoning from the facts. But whatever science and scientific methods were, most historians now favored them, for they believed that conscientious and level-headed men could find truth once they had systematically examined all the evidence.

In the United States the young Henry Adams (1838–1918) read Buckle's *History of Civilization in England* (two volumes, 1857–1861, unfinished) and Darwin's *On the Origin of Species* (1859) soon after they came out. Not at that time doubting that historians would follow him to create a science of history, he wrote history (*History of the United States,* nine volumes, 1889–1891), and in later life went on to try to develop his own general laws (*Degradation of the Democratic Dogma,* 1919). Not all historians read Buckle and Darwin, but their views became part of the intellectual climate and the

---

4 But see P. Lacombe, *De l'Histoire considerée comme science,* Paris, 1894.

conceptual systems of historians: evolution, the shaping effects of environment on men and societies, the probability that men, through science and education, would move onward and upward. Victor Duruy (1811–1894) who, as a professor and as minister of education, did so much to promote history in France, consecrated "his life to history which explains, classifies phenomena . . . facts under their causes." In Germany, France, Britain, the United States, and all over Europe, historians became similarly consecrated.

The idea of evolution, combined with that of progress, provided a new basis for the selection, organization, and interpretation of facts. Now, or so it was thought, it was possible to determine the causes and sequences of events, to see the unity of history. By scientific, critical methods the reliability of these facts could be ascertained and with scientific objectivity the natural biases of interpretation could be eliminated. With the resulting historical knowledge, educators could help shape future societies.

The new history of the nineteenth century took definite form in the decade of the 1880's, though it had earlier roots in Germany and elsewhere. Its distinguishing marks were not only its use of scientific methods, its stress on exhaustive research, and its claim to objectivity, but also its concentration on limited subjects or time periods and the production of analytical, monographic studies. The scholars who followed historical pursuits were increasingly teachers in colleges and universities, scholars who called themselves professional historians because they disciplined themselves and were trained to work according to accepted standards and because they gained their livelihoods through this work.

The outward manifestations of the discipline were many. Plagiarism became a scholarly felony and for younger men even to follow earlier historians a misdemeanor. Footnote citations and bibliographies as evidence of research became signs of scholarship, detection of forgeries in documents and errors in the work of other historians ways to scholarly fame. Behind these manifestations were more substantial achievements: the organization of professional societies to maintain and raise standards, the publication of scholarly reviews and of manuals for the same purpose, and the provision of graduate and specialized training so that future historians might learn professional methods and make "contributions to knowledge."

So rapid were the transformations in historical study that its practitioners thought them to constitute a "veritable revolution" (Charles Kendall Adams). What had begun in Germany with the work of Ranke, and continued with the publication of the *Monumenta Germaniae* and the founding of the critical journal *Historische Zeitschrift* (1859), now occurred throughout the western world. Here a few illustrations must suffice. Ernst Bernheim prepared his erudite *Lehrbuch der Historischen Methode* (1889), Edward Freeman his assured *The Methods of History* (1886), Charles Kendall Adams his bibliographical *Manual of Historical Literature* (1882), and Charles Langlois and Charles Seignobos their lucid *Introduction aux études historiques* (1898). Major historical journals were founded, the *Revue historique* (1876), the *English Historical Review* (1886), the *Revista storica italiana* (1884), the *American Historical Review* (1895), and a host of less comprehensive reviews such as the Japanese *Shigaku Zasshi* (1889). These reviews, which well represented the new scientific and professional interests, were often edited by outstanding historians of the new school, such as Gabriel Monod (1844–1912) of France who had been a student of Ranke, and J. Franklin Jameson (1859–1937) who was probably the first Ph.D. in history (Johns Hopkins University) trained in the United States. Historians, like their colleagues in other fields, formed national societies, commissions, and institutes for the encouragement of organized study and publication. Among prominent national societies were the Royal Historical Society (1868), the American Historical Association (1884), and the Scottish Historical Society (1886), and among the many specialized societies the Selden Society (for legal history, 1887) and the *Société de l'histoire de la Révolution française* (1888). Under the auspices of these societies historians met periodically to present scholarly papers and exchange information. Following the lead of Germany once more, history became an academic subject for undergraduates and a discipline for advanced graduate students throughout the western world. The number of historians who were teachers multiplied as students in numbers began to "take" history. The seminar method of Ranke spread to France, the United States, many smaller countries, and somewhat later and in lesser degree to Great Britain. Professional training in research became almost a prerequisite for undertaking historical study, and students, in addition, were expected to pass examinations in special fields of history and to present dissertations or theses which, in theory at least, made a contribution to knowledge.

These decades, too, were the era during which many historians, known to succeeding generations as giants, were finishing or beginning major works: William (Bishop) Stubbs, Samuel Rawson Gardiner, and Frederic Maitland were preparing thorough studies of English history; Hippolyte Taine, analyses of English literature and the origins of modern France; Heinrich von Sybel, documentary volumes on the founding of the German empire; Albert Sorel and Alphonse Aulard, big books on the French Revolution; Theodor Mommsen, monumental publications on ancient Rome; Pasquale Villari, popular histories of Italy; Ludwig von Pastor, his conscientious fifteen volumes on the *History of the Popes;* Henry C. Lea, the pioneering investigations of the Inquisition; Henri Pirenne, the brilliant economic interpretations of Lowland and medieval history; and John Fiske, James Ford Rhodes, and Edward Channing, many-volumed histories of the United States.

The big multiple-volumed histories on large subjects were becoming more and more difficult to write; the available sources, especially for modern history, were swelling as libraries and archives collected and preserved records and as the scope of history was expanding from the political and military to cover many other aspects of civilization. During the 1880's Ranke wrote nine volumes of his *Weltgeschichte* to culminate his life work, and Bancroft made his final revision of his *History of the United States.* But few individual historians would now dare to attempt work on so vast a scale. One way to attack the problem was to prepare collaborative histories. Wilhelm Oncken in Germany began to edit the *Allgemeine Geschichte in Einzeldarstellungen* which was to appear in many volumes from 1879 to 1893. Ernst Lavisse and Alfred Rambaud in France brought together many specialists to prepare twelve volumes on *Histoire général du 4e siècle à nos jours* (1893–1901). In England, Lord Acton, perhaps the most original and learned scholar of his time, began to edit the *Cambridge Modern History* which was later to appear in fourteen volumes (1902–1912). Acton expressed prevalent views when he wrote to contributors to say that, through division of labor and opening of archives, historians could "arrive at the final stages" of historical learning. The latter part of the nineteenth century was truly the optimistic age of historiography.

As if to demonstrate Hegelian dialectic the new syntheses of historical thought were challenged by new antitheses just as they were reaching definite form, and both from within and without the historical guild. Adherents of Karl Marx (1818–1883) accused historians, as other scholars, of being apologists for the dying bourgeois-imperialist society as they themselves conceived materialist interpretations labeled "scientific." In Germany, Wilhelm Dilthey (1833–1911) challenged fundamental bases of historical understanding as he, an avowed relativist, was led by "historical and psychological study" to make the "whole man in the diversity of his powers, the willing, feeling, thinking being, the foundation for explaining knowledge and its concepts." The first condition for historical understanding, he declared, was this: the historian himself was an "historical being"; he who studied history was also "he who made history." In Italy Benedetto Croce (1866–1952), both philosopher and historian, argued that all history was contemporary history, in the sense that history was not what happened but what present men thought happened. And in France, Germany, and the United States, Henri Berr (1863–1954), Karl Lamprecht (1856–1915), and James Harvey Robinson (1863–1936) pleaded for a widening of vision to all the activities of men and for the application of the hypotheses and results of social science to history. So strong did the criticism of the older scientific history become that in 1912 an American historian declared historians had abandoned its precepts. More and more historians seemed to want to know not *wie es eigentlich gewesen* but *wie es eigentlich geworden,* and some of them were willing to discard both the first and the second as impossible. As yet the European centered views of western men were basically unchallenged—Africa and Asia remained, for historians, virtually the unknown.[5] But in all else the old certainties were dissolving as Max Planck and Einstein in physics and Freud in psychology raised questions about fundamental premises of nineteenth-century beliefs. Even the then most learned of English historians, J. B. Bury (1861–1927), Regius Professor at Cambridge University, came to believe in relativism, in contingency instead of causation. The "doctrine of historical relativity," he said in 1909, "applies no less to his [the historian's] judgements than to other facts."

[5] Later there were to be impassioned attacks on European provincialism. See, for example, E. H. Dance, *History the Betrayer: A Study of Bias,* London, 1960.

During the twentieth century, two great world wars, two major Communist revolutions, two major Fascist dictatorships, and a major economic depression shook the western world. The wars and revolutions, coupled with technological advances in communication, brought Asian and African peoples into the modern world. Their political importance and their emerging nationalisms as well as a growing consciousness of the social injustices of colonialism made it essential for western peoples to understand them. Further major discoveries in biology and physics disturbed old conceptions of the universe and man, just as enormous increases in and shifts of population (to the cities) were upsetting traditional patterns of life.

Some western intellectuals thought these events, ideas, and discoveries broke the present's continuities with the past so sharply that historical studies were no longer of value, save as antiquarian pleasure. Nevertheless, there was enormous expansion in historical research, writing, and publication, in undergraduate teaching and graduate training, and in professional organization—specialized, national, and from the 1920's, when the International Committee of Historical Sciences was founded, international.

At the turn of the last third of the twentieth century, there were many approaches to historical study, leading, as might be expected, to different views of the past. Of these approaches, four, not mutually exclusive, stood out. These, in general, may be characterized as: (1) that rooted in ancient Hebrew and early Christian traditions in which history was revelation of God (Christopher Dawson, David Knowles, and Reinhold Niebuhr); (2) that sometimes vaguely called historicism, based on Rankean emphasis on documentary research, objectivity, and concentration on the unique (Friedrich Meinecke and, in some books, Lewis Namier); (3) that which accepted relativism, subjectivity, and even irrationality as inescapable (Charles Beard, and E. H. Carr), while attempting nevertheless to find meaning and achieve understanding (Raymond Aron, Marc Bloch, and Henri Marrou); and (4) that which stemmed from Marxist materialist interpretations (M. M. Pokrovsky and, much less dogmatically, R. H. Tawney).

There were new trends as well. More historians (as Marc Bloch and Crane Brinton) thought in terms of the total culture, of politics and war as but part of this total. Some would ask use of all available, not just written, evidence and themselves stressed geographic and psychological influences in history (Lucien Febvre, Fernand Braudel). A considerable number (René Grousset, John Fairbank, C. H. Phillips, Margery Perham) were beginning to concentrate on Asian and African history, and an increasing number believed, with the distinguished medievalist, Maurice Powicke, that the old impulses of race, nationalism, and class could no longer guide historical studies, that world (Arnold Toynbee and William McNeill), regional, and comparative histories (Jacques Godechot and Robert Palmer) would be more meaningful. Responding to the growing importance of science more historians (George Sarton, Joseph Needham) began to investigate and write upon its development. An articulate few (among them Ernst Labrousse) were asking for and doing statistical and quantitative studies as the basis for their generalizations. Especially in the United States a new behavioralist approach was beginning to attract historians (as William L. Langer and some younger men). Finally, there was greater interest in philosophies of history (Oswald Spengler and Arnold Toynbee) and in how meaning had been or might be wrested from history (R. G. Collingwood, Theodore Schieder, Raymond Aron, Louis Gottschalk).

So diverse, however, were the historians and their histories that they could not be placed in familiar but elusive categories, such as the romantic or scientific. Even the same historian (as did Charles Beard) might change his interests, views, and methods. A new dominant synthesis, corresponding to that represented by Ranke, had not evolved. In historical thought there was a "bed of continuity" and a "river of change" (John Higham) but no clearly defined mainstream.

That either the facts or meanings of the past would be exhausted no historian any longer thought possible. The field of history seemed to become, as Louis Halphen remarked, almost unlimited. Each generation would have to write its own history, though, on the other hand, historical knowledge could be, to a limited extent, accumulative. Again, most historians held, absolute objectivity was impossible. This did not mean that because a mountain took on "different shapes from different angles of vision," it had "no objective shape at all" (E. H. Carr), but it did mean that historians should be aware of their biases, reveal them, and strive for fair understanding. It was, indeed, understanding and not objectivity, many would think, that was most important. An historian was obligated to "open himself to all that is human" (Henri Marrou).

Beyond these generalizations it is difficult, if not impossible to go, at least in the seventh decade of the twentieth century. But the dialogues on historical study, its nature, its purpose, and its practice, will go on, for, as it was once remarked, the name of hope is remembrance. As long as men hope they will debate the nature of the past, for their differing hopes depend, in part at least, upon their differing understandings of their experience, just as the differing understandings they reach depend, in part at least, upon the nature of their differing hopes.

*Selected Bibliography**

I. Nature of historical study

BLOCH, Marc, *Apologie pour l'histoire ou métier d'historien.* Paris, Colin, 1962.

Selected Essays of J. B. Bury, Harold Temperley, ed. London, Cambridge University Press, 1930.

CARR, E. H., *What Is History?* New York, Knopf, 1962.

Lexikon fur Theologie und Kirche, 2nd ed., vol. IV, 1960, art. "Geschichte," pp. 778–783.

MARROU, H. I., *De la connaissance historique.* Paris, Ed. du Seuil, 1956.

STERN, Fritz, ed., *The Varieties of History.* New York, Meridian Books, 1956.

TREVELYAN, G. M., *Clio, A Muse.* London, Longmans, 1913.

WEINTRAUB, Karl J., *Visions of Culture: Voltaire, Guizot, Burckhardt, Lamprecht, Huizinga, Ortega y Gasset.* Chicago, University of Chicago Press, 1966.

II. Philosophies, theories, methods of history

ARON, Raymond, *Introduction to the Philosophy of History,* trans. by George J. Irwin. Boston, Beacon Press, 1961 (French revised ed. 1948).

BESSON, Waldemar, ed., *Geschichte.* Frankfort-am-Main, Fischer Bucherei, 1961.

FLINT, Robert, *History of the Philosophy of History . . . France and French Belgium and Switzerland.* New York, Scribner, 1891.

* References listed here are in addition to those mentioned in the text.

GARDINER, Patrick, ed., *Theories of History: Readings from Classical and Contemporary Sources.* Glencoe, Ill., Free Press, 1954.

GOTTSCHALK, Louis, ed., *Generalization in the Writing of History,* Chicago, University of Chicago Press, 1963.

MANUEL, Frank E., *Shapes of Philosophical History.* Stanford, Stanford University Press, 1965.

MARCUS, John T., *Heaven, Hell and History from Antiquity to the Present.* New York, Macmillan, 1967.

MAZLICH, Bruce, *The Riddle of History: The Great Speculators from Vico to Freud.* New York, Harper and Row, 1966.

MEYERHOFF, Hans, ed., *The Philosophy of History in Our Time.* Garden City, N. Y., Doubleday (Anchor Books), 1959.

SAMARAN, Charles, ed., *L'Histoire et ses méthodes.* Paris, Gallimard, 1962.

SCHIEDER, Theodore, *Begegnungen mit der Geschichte.* Gottingen, Vandenhoeck and Ruprecht, 1962.

TOYNBEE, Arnold, *A Study of History,* vol. 12. London, Oxford University Press, 1961.

WIDGERY, Alban G., *Interpretations of History: Confucius to Toynbee.* London, Allen and Unwin, 1961.

Current thinking may be sampled in the journal *History and Theory* and in the standard historical reviews, particularly the *Revue historique.*

II. History of history

A. In the West

ANTONI, Carlo, *From History to Sociology: The Transition in German Historical Thought,* trans. by Hayden V. White. London, Merlin Press, 1962.

BLACK, John B., *The Art of History: A Study of Four Great Historians of the Eighteenth Century.* London, Methuen, 1926.

BURY, J. B., *The Ancient Greek Historians.* New York, Macmillan, 1909.

BUTTERFIELD, Herbert, *Man on His Past: The Study of the History of Historical Scholarship.* London, Cambridge University Press, 1955.

FUETER, Eduard, *Geschichte der neuren Historiographie.* Munich, R. Oldenbourg, 1925.

GILBERT, Felix, *Machiavelli and Guicciardini, Politics and History in Sixteenth Century Florence.* Princeton, N. J., Princeton University Press, 1965.

GOOCH, G. P., *History and Historians in the Nineteenth Century.* London, Longmans, 1959.

GUILDAY, Peter, ed., *Church Historians.* New York, Kenedy, 1926.

GUILLAND, Antoine, *Modern Germany and Her Historians*, London, Jarrolds, 1915.

GUSDORF, Georges, *Introduction aux sciences humaines: Essai critique sur leurs origines et leur développement*. Paris, Les Belles Lettres, 1960.

Histoire et historiens depuis cinquante ans, 2 vols., Paris, F. Alcan, 1927.

Hundred Jahre Historische Zeitschrift, 1859–1959, Schieder and Kienast, eds., *Historische Zeitschrift*, vol. 89, Munich, R. Oldenbourg, 1959.

KNOWLES, M. D., Rev., "Great Historical Enterprises," in Royal Historical Society, *Transactions*, 1957–1961.

KRAUS, Michael, *The Writing of American History*. Norman, Okla., University of Oklahoma Press, 1953.

MEINECKE, Friedrich, *Die Enstehung des Historismus*. Munich, R. Oldenbourg, 1959.

MOMIGLANO, Arnaldo, *Studies in Historiography*. London, Weidenfeld and Nicolson, 1966.

RITTER, Moritz, *Die Entwicklung der Geschichtswissenschaft*. Munich, R. Oldenbourg, 1919.

SHOTWELL, James, *An Introduction to the History of History*. New York, Columbia University Press, 1922.

THOMPSON, James Westfall, and HOLM, Bernard J., *The History of Historical Writing*, 2 vols., New York, Macmillan, 1942.

B. Middle and Far East

BEASLEY, W. G., and PULLEYBLANK, E. G., eds., *Historians of China and Japan*. London, Oxford University Press, 1961.

HALL, D. G. E., ed., *Historians of Southeast Asia*. London, Oxford University Press, 1961.

LEWIS, Bernard, and HOLT, P. M., eds., *Historians of the Middle East*. London, Oxford University Press, 1962.

MESKILL, John, ed., *The Pattern of Chinese History*. Boston, Heath, 1965.

PHILLIPS, C. H., ed., *Historians of India, Pakistan, and Ceylon*. London, Oxford University Press, 1961.

WATSON, Burton, *Ssu-ma Chien, Grand Historian in China*. New York, Columbia University Press, 1958.

Part Two

Historical Study
in
France

MICHEL FRANÇOIS,
with the assistance of Boyd C. Shafer

I. The Training of Historians

A. Secondary education

Instruction in history in France takes place within an educational system that had its origins during the era of the French Revolution and Napoleon. Considerably modified during the Third Republic, this system has undergone rapid reform since World War II. In France, as in other countries, school enrollments have grown swiftly since the war. This increase brought not only pressure to enlarge the schools and universities but it has also accentuated demands for fundamental changes in instruction.

In general, education is universal, compulsory to age 16, free, and, to a large extent, lay. Further, education in France is subjected to more centralized control by the national state than it is in other western nations. This centralization, however, does not permit easy generalization. In higher and professional education there is both change and variation in the nature and duration of education. This is true not only in the work offered for the different professional fields and academic disciplines, but also in the kinds and qualities of work being done at the several kinds of educational institutions. While all the universities offer work in the basic fields of history, their specialties differ. Again, while a student must take nationally prescribed, rigorous examinations at stated intervals during the various stages of his education, an advanced student chooses the university he will attend, the specialty he will pursue, and is himself responsible for his own preparation.

Historical study in France begins in the primary and secondary schools, but the purpose of these schools is not to train historians.

The basic text of Professor François has, with his approval, been amplified by Boyd C. Shafer in order to provide information not readily available to students outside France.

The *lycées* and *collèges* for the young were created during the Revolution to provide a general education in which all disciplines were equitably represented. The award of the *baccalauréat* then and now marked the completion of this education. From the sixth class[1] to the terminal classes (in philosophy, elementary mathematics, or natural sciences), that is, during seven years, students in all lycées and collèges, whether state run, independent *(libre)*, or religious, are introduced to all history, from ancient Egyptian through Oriental, Greek, Roman, to contemporary history. They, however, encounter ancient and medieval history but once and only during the earliest classes. In contrast, emphasis is put on modern and contemporary history to 1960, the only period covered from the second class upward.

The instruction, of two hours a week, is given by teachers who are licensed or certified (in principle those in the collèges) or certified or *agrégés*[2] (in principle those in the lycées). They use different texts. These generally are both well-illustrated and constantly revised. More important, they are also usually well done although they sometimes ignore the needs of children and sacrifice basic facts and chronology for generalities and interpretations which exceed the normal capacity of young minds.

Because of the obvious overloading of the secondary curriculum, suggestions have been made in recent years to reduce the number of hours devoted to history and geography. These suggestions have not been followed. Quite to the contrary. To combat some of the student disaffection with history and geography, it was decided in 1960 to include questions at random on history or geography in a written examination for the *baccalauréat*—the previous testing in the two subjects having been oral.

B. *Higher education—the universities*

Historical training as such takes place only at the level of higher education, though a student's desire to become an historian may be, and likely is, aroused during his studies in secondary school. In re-

[1] The designation of classes in France differs from that in the United States. In secondary schools the lowest class has the highest number, the lowest class in the lycée being the sixth while the highest classes are first and terminal.

[2] For a definition see below, p. 40.

cent years considerable student interest may also have been stimulated by student visits, organized by French archivists, to departmental archives, where the students hold documents, evocative of the history of France or of their region, in their hands while a professor judiciously comments.

Training in history as a discipline begins in the universities. For purposes of university education France is divided into twenty-three districts. Sixteen universities,[3] each of which offers instruction in history, are fully functioning and others are being organized or planned. French universities, unlike those in some other countries, do not have faculties in history. Instruction in history is given in the faculties of letters and human sciences (psychology, sociology, etc.). Student admission to the faculties is not, of course, unrestricted—even the possession of the baccalauréat is no longer enough.

The offerings in history of each of the various faculties of letters is different. In 1964 Paris, with its large number of historians and wide range of courses, gave instruction in the following fields:[4]

Histoire Ancienne

Egyptologie
Langue et civilisation des anciens Sémites
Histoire grecque
Epigraphie grecque
Papyrologie
Histoire ancienne
Histoire romaine
Epigraphie latine
Histoire du Christianisme
Archéologie classique
Archéologie romaine
Civilisation de l'Inde et du Sud-Est asiatique

[3] Aix, Besançon, Bordeaux, Caen, Clermont-Ferrand, Dijon, Grenoble, Lille, Lyon, Montpellier, Nancy, Paris (Sorbonne and Nanterre), Poitiers, Rennes, Strasbourg, and Toulouse. The seven other university districts are Amiens, Limoges, Nantes, Nice, Orléans, Reims, and Rouen to which will be added in a few years Brest and Pau.

[4] From *Vingt-cinq ans de recherche historique en France (1940–1965)*, vol. I, p. 7. The information which follows can indicate only the general nature of historical instruction because of the continuous changes resulting from educational reforms in 1966 and 1967.

Histoire du Moyen Age

Histoire du Moyen Age
Histoire économique du Moyen Age
Histoire et civilisation byzantine
Histoire de l'Art du Moyen Age

Histoire Moderne et Contemporaine

Histoire moderne
Histoire moderne et contemporaine
Histoire de la Révolution française
Histoire contemporaine
Histoire économique
Histoire de l'Art moderne
Histoire de la Musique
Histoire de l'Art contemporain
Histoire de la Colonisation
Histoire de la Civilisation de l'Afrique Noire
Histoire contemporaine de l'Afrique Noire
Histoire et civilisation des Slaves
Archivistique
Ethnologie
Ethnologie sociale et religieuse
Ethnologie de l'Afrique Noire
Histoire de l'Orient musulman

Until 1966 entrance into a faculty took place after a year of *propédeutique* (preparation). During this year the student, who held the baccalauréat, followed courses of general instruction accompanied by practical exercises, both of which were required. There were three options, literature, philosophy, and history. The reform of higher education of June 23, 1966, however, abolished the propédeutique year. Higher education is now divided into three cycles of two years each.

The first cycle, in effect, replaces the propédeutique, but the instruction is now spread over two years. Moreover, the work is subdivided into nine sections and a student must complete the work of the section he enters. Of the nine sections, one is in history. In this section during the first year the student has fifteen hours of instruction a week in four theoretical and in two practical exercise courses;

both types are required. The work covers modern history from the fifteenth through the eighteenth century, contemporary history from the nineteenth century to the present, general physical and human geography, and either (depending on the student's choice) an ancient or modern language. During the second year the student has the same number of hours of instruction each week but these are now devoted to ancient Greek and Roman history, to medieval history, to the auxiliary sciences of history, to regional geography, and again with a choice, to ancient or modern languages.

At the conclusion of these two years the student takes an examination to obtain a newly created diploma, the *Diplôme universitaire d'études littéraires*—the DUEL (University Diploma of Literary Studies). Acquisition of this diploma permits admittance to the second cycle of studies.

The reform of higher education took place at two different times. During the academic year 1966–1967, only the first year of the first cycle was put into effect. The second year of the first cycle and the complete second cycle were instituted in October, 1967.

The second cycle, like the first, takes two years, and, of course, there is a section for history. The instruction prepares students for the Certificates of Higher Studies. Two certificates are necessary to obtain the designation of *Licencié en histoire,* a title which may be obtained at the end of the first year. The acquisition of the license permits the holder to teach in the collèges.[5] The second year of the second cycle prepares for the newly created rank of *Maîtrise* (Master).To obtain this rank the student must acquire a third Certificate of Higher Studies. Under the personal supervision of a professor he is to write a paper in the form of a lecture based on research. The rank of Maîtrise will be required for teaching in the lycées. It will also be required for entry into the third cycle which will be devoted to research in the form of either a thesis of the third cycle or a thesis for the doctorate (see below).

Before the full application of the reform of 1966, the acquisition of the license in history required four certificates, in ancient, medieval, modern and contemporary history, and in geography. Candidates who wished to specialize in geography had an option in geography, likewise with four certificates, general geography, regional geography,

---

[5] The *collège* in France is a preparatory school and should not be confused with the college in the United States or Great Britain.

ancient and medieval history, and modern and contemporary history —the last being identical with the certificate under the history option. Each certificate required the study of a certain number of questions (five or six) and these were covered in the courses given during the academic year. The same question remained in the syllabus for three years to permit the professor to cover it in all its aspects.

Each professor offers three hours of instruction each week.[6] These consist of a major course of two hours and a practical exercise or demonstration session which is essentially a commentary on the texts relating to the question being studied. The major course is given in large lecture halls to considerable crowds of listeners. The commentaries on the texts are done in groups of about forty students, each of which is supervised by a "master-assistant" or assistant. A corps of assistants and masters was created about ten years ago to assist the professors in tasks that had become too heavy because of increased enrollments. This corps has been created by recruitment of young professors, the *agrégés* of lycées, who are preparing theses and hope to teach in institutions of higher learning.

For the written examination required to obtain the certificate of *licence* the candidates must do a dissertation relating to one of the questions of the syllabus and a commentary on a text; they must, in addition, take practical tests in epigraphy, archaeology, or papyrology, in paleography, diplomatics, archaeology, or other "auxiliary sciences" of history. For the oral examination they must pass two tests, one relating to one of the questions of the syllabus, the other to the general history of the historical period of the certificate.

A candidate for the license in history who hopes to teach does not satisfy all his obligations when he has the diploma of license in his hands, successfully obtained the four certificates, and proven, as he must also do, his ability in a foreign language by reading and translating a page in a volume of modern history. He must also present a written treatise (*travail d'étude et de recherche*) to obtain the *Maîtrise*. This must be his own original work, on a topic suggested in conference by the professor or chosen by the student himself. Here for the first time in the cycle of studies the professor takes a personal part—as director of research (a role to be discussed later).

The two certificates mentioned above constitute what is called the license in teaching. But faculties of letters also offer other certifi-

[6] See section V on "working conditions" of French professors.

cates of higher study as well. These are certificates of specialized study which, added to those for the license in teaching or combined to the total of four, give the candidate a *Maîtrise à quatre certificats*. The number and nature of these certificates in specialties varies with each faculty and they are, of course, more numerous at the Sorbonne than in the provincial faculties. By way of illustration, the specialties in history may be the history and philosophy of science, aesthetics and science of art, history of music, history of religion, history of ancient art, history of the art of the Middle Ages, history of modern art, institutional and social history, economic history, history of colonization, demography, and Byzantine history and civilization. The following table lists the principal specialties offered at the various universities for the certificates of higher studies in medieval, modern and contemporary history.[7]

> Méthodologie des sciences historiques: Nancy
> Histoire du Moyen Age: all faculties
> Etudes médiévales françaises: Grenoble, Clermont
> Civilisation du Moyen Age: Nancy
> Etudes supérieures médiévales: Rennes
> Etudes médiévales: Montpellier
> Etudes sur la Renaissance française: Poitiers
> Histoire moderne et contemporaine: all faculties
> Histoire des temps modernes: Strasbourg
> Histoire contemporaine: Strasbourg
> Histoire économique: Paris
> Histoire économique et sociale: Aix, Strasbourg, Lille, Nice, Paris
> Histoire économique et constitutionnelle: Rennes
> Histoire économique du Moyen Age et des temps modernes: Toulouse
> Histoire économique moderne et contemporaine: Lyon
> Histoire du christianisme: Aix, Bordeaux, Montpellier, Lyon, Strasbourg, Nice
> Histoire des religions: Lille, Paris, Rennes, Strasbourg
> Histoire et géographie coloniales: Lyon
> Histoire de la colonisation française et étrangère: Aix, Bordeaux, Lille, Montpellier, Paris, Toulouse
> Histoire et philosophie des Sciences: Paris
> Histoire militaire moderne et contemporaine: Rennes

[7] *Vingt-cinq ans* . . . , p. 11.

Including the two years of the first cycle, at least three years are as yet required to obtain the license, and four the diploma of *Maîtrise*. Those with the license in history and with the diploma of higher studies in history now comprise the total corps of professors of history in the lycées and collèges, both the general and the technical. The scarcity of professors in universities makes it necessary to find some in the lycées. But as a general rule, the professors of history and geography of the lycées are professors *agrégés*—and these usually give instruction only from the second class up.

The *agrégation* is a separate competition by examination for those young men and women who already have the teaching license, though the number of those who obtain this title depends not only on the examination but on the number of openings in teaching to be filled. To provide preparation for it, special courses are given in the faculties. These cover the questions contained in the announcement of the competition. Only those with the license who have had at least three weeks of (practice) teaching in a lycée can enter the competition, and there is a common competition for history and geography. The competition is severe. Most university professors of history are agrégés, but the competition is especially designed to obtain teachers for the lycées and success in it is not necessary for teaching in a faculty. Another competition to recruit professors for lycées and collèges was instituted in 1949, the CAPES—or Certificate of Aptitude for the Professorat of Secondary Education. It also requires a period of teaching as well as written and oral tests, all of which must be completed during a two-year period. It supplies a body of teachers similar to that of the professors agrégés—the "certified" teachers.

The highest academic degree in history in France is the *Doctorat ès Lettres* (the Doctorate of the State). It and it only gives access to the chairs of the faculties. And much of the true historical research in France is done in the preparation of the doctoral theses. The doctoral theses, in fact, have a much greater role in French historical scholarship than they do in other countries. They often set the course of much future research, as did, for example, the theses of Ernst Labrousse and Fernand Braudel in the 1940's in economic history and "géohistoire."[8]

---

[8] Labrousse published his *Esquisse du mouvement des prix et des revenus en France au XVIIIe siècle* in 1933 but only his doctoral dissertation, *La crise de*

To work for the Doctorat ès lettres a candidate must possess the minimum qualification of the license. Usually also he has the Certificate of Higher Studies (and thus served an apprenticeship in research), and through competition has won the title of *Agrégé*. The earliest possible age for beginning work is 21 but most students are 25 or older. The candidate begins when he registers the topic of his theses (two) with the secretary of the faculty. These topics he has chosen in agreement with the professor who will supervise his work.

The work for the doctorate is personal and the candidate must prepare himself as he sees fit—with the knowledge that he must ultimately satisfy the desires of his major professor and the examining committee. No courses of study are prescribed, though the student customarily (if he has not already done so) takes courses in the general fields of the topics of his theses and special courses given by the professor under whom he works. The chief requirements for the doctorate are two: successful preparation of the theses, one principal and one complementary; and public defense of these theses before a committee of professors (usually five). It is in the preparation of the theses that true historical research is done and it can be said that the best works of history appearing in France are the doctoral dissertations.

The major thesis demonstrates the candidate's abilities in critical research. In the words of one of the best-known French historians, Pierre Renouvin, "it must give proof of a major individual effort in critical, interpretative documentary research and be an original work based on as exhaustive research as possible." The subject must be sufficiently large either for "its value to general history" or "for the perspectives it opens on new methods of research," and the candidate, as well, must reveal his "aptitude for synthesis and learning." The complementary and lesser thesis, by preference, makes a learned contribution to the study of history in the form, for example, of a critical catalogue or a scholarly edition of a text. It may be, and usually is, related to the principal thesis, though this is not a requirement.

---

l'économie française à la fin de l'Ancien Régime et au début de la Révolution (1943) enabled him to direct the work of students. Braudel's great work, *La Méditerranée et le monde méditerranéen à l'époque de Philippe II* (1949), led to studies on "empires, oceans, and the Iberian world in the sixteenth and seventeenth centuries."

Often 600 printed pages and sometimes more than 1,000 pages in length, the principal thesis is a sustained (*longue haleine*) work. Customarily, its preparation takes eight to ten or even more years and the candidate is 38 years old or older before he completes it. Many candidates teach in a lycée or collège while they do the research and writing. In recent years some of them have received aid from the Centre national de la Recherche scientifique (CNRS) and they may be "attached" to this center for as many as three or four years while they do their research.

Because the major theses play such an important role in French historical scholarship and reveal its trends, the authors and titles of the thirty—one for the Doctorat ès lettres at the Sorbonne from February, 1964, to June, 1966, are of interest.

Ancient History (7)

Mme Danielle Bonneau, *La crue du Nil—Ses descriptions, ses explications, son culte d'après les auteurs grecs et latins et les documents des époques ptolémaïques, romaine et byzantine*

Paul Courbin, *La céramique géométrique de Argolide*

Louis Foucher, *Hadrumetum*

Marcel Leglay, *Saturne africain*

Georges Le Rider, *Suse sous les Séleucides et les Parthes; les trouvailles monétaires et l'histoire de la ville*

Claude Nicolet, *L'ordre équestre à l'époque républicaine (312–343 av. J. C.)*

Jean Rougé, *Recherches sur l'organisation du commerce maritime en Méditerranée sous l'Empire romain*

Middle Ages (5)

Hélène Ahrweiler, *Byzance et la mer. La marine de guerre, la politique et les institutions maritimes de Byzance aux VIIe–XVe s.*

Jean Favier, *Les finances pontificales à l'époque du Grand Schisme d'Occident*

René Fedou, *Les hommes de loi lyonnaise à la fin du Moyen-âge—Etude sur les origines de la classe de robe*

Maurice Rey, *Les finances royales sous Charles VI; les causes du déficit, le domaine du roi (1388–1413)*

Christine Thouzellier, *Catharisme et valdéisme en Languedoc à la fin du XIIe et au début du XIIIe s.; politique pontificale et controverses*

Modern and Contemporary History (19)

Paul Bisson, *L'activité d'un procureur général au parlement de Paris à la fin de l'Ancien régime: les Joly de Fleury*

André Corvisier, *L'armée française de la fin du XVIIème siècle au ministère de Choiseul: le Soldat*

Louis Dermigny, *La Chine et l'Occident; le commerce à Canton au XVIIIe s. (1719–1833)*

Mlle Jeanne Ferté, *La vie religieuse dans les campagnes parisiennes 1622–1695*

Paul Gerbod, *La condition universitaire en France au XIXe s., étude d'un groupe socio-professionel: professeurs et administrateurs de l'enseignement secondaire public de 1842 à 1880*

Paul Huot-Pleuroux, *Le recrutement sacerdotal dans le diocèse de Besançon de 1808 à 1960*

Mme Annie Kriegel, *Histoire du mouvement ouvrier français (1914–1920) —Aux origines du communisme français*

Emmanuel Le Roy Ladurie, *Les paysans de Languedoc*

Maurice Levy-Leboyer, *Les banques européenes et l'industrialisation internationale dans la première moitié du XIXe s.*

Jacques Lombard, *Structures de type "féodal" en Afrique noire; étude des dynamismes internes et des relations sociales chez les Bariba du Dahomey*

Jean-Etienne Martin-Allanic, *Bougainville navigateur et les découvertes de son temps*

Andre Martel, *Les confins saharo-tripolitains de la Tunisie (1881–1911)*

Georges Mercier, *La tendance non-figurative dans l'art sacré chrétien contemporain*

Xavier de Montclos, *Lavigerie, le Saint-Siège et l'Église, de l'avènement de Pie IX à l'avènement de Léon XIII, 1846–1878*

Abel Poitrineaux, *La vie rurale en Basse-Auvergne au XVIIIe s. (1726–1789)*

Albert Silbert, *Le Portugal méditerranéen à la fin de l'ancien régime (XVIIIe–début XIXe s.)*

Jean René Suratteau, *Le département du Mont-Terrible sous le régime du Directoire (1795–1800). Étude des contacts humains, économiques et sociaux dans un pays annexé et frontalier*

Jean Tudesq, *Les grands notables en France (1840–1849); étude historique d'une psychologie sociale*

Claude Willard, *Le mouvement socialiste en France (1893–1905); les Guesdistes*

The principal theses must be printed before their defense, though the complementary theses need only be typed.[9] Both of them must, of course, be approved by the supervising professor and have often undergone much revision before approval is forthcoming. At the public defense, which lasts five or more hours, the candidate introduces his work with a statement of about a half hour. In this introduction he "summarizes his work," emphasizes the difficulties he has encountered, the methods he has used, and his conclusions. His discourse enables judgment of his ability to teach.

The candidate whose theses have been approved for defense is almost certain to obtain his degree. Whether his name will be inscribed on the list of those eligible for teaching in higher education depends upon the qualifying phrase of the examining committee. Only if the theses are deemed "très honorable" can the author hope for a teaching position and even the qualification "honorable" has a pejorative meaning. After the defense the president of the examining board makes a report to the Minister of Education in which he discusses the candidate's qualities and this report becomes an important part of the new doctor's dossier.

French historians have raised questions about the nature of the doctoral theses. Does their preparation take too long? And does not their length detract from other profitable work? Because of the restricted audience the theses will reach, is it not too difficult to find publishers for them? Are not the printing costs prohibitive, at least in some cases, and does not this unreasonably delay publication of the theses and hence the award of the doctorate? In recent years the Minister of Education has given subsidies of forty-five to fifty percent toward printing costs, but a young teacher may be forced to himself pay a sum equivalent to a year's salary.

Even so, there seems to be general agreement that the doctoral theses "constitute a contribution of first importance to historical research in France."

Another question of different nature is also raised. For several reasons, among them the high prestige of degrees from Paris, about twice as many Doctorats ès lettres are granted at the Sorbonne as at all the other universities in France combined. In recent years there have been an increasing number awarded at Toulouse, Lyon, and

9 This discussion of the *Doctorat ès lettres* follows in part that of Pierre Renouvin in *Vingt-cinq ans* . . . , pp. 146–162.

Aix. But still the load at Paris is heavy indeed. In 1964 one professor was supervising sixty theses and two others had thirty each. Up to the present no effective steps have been taken to change this situation.

Besides the Doctorat ès lettres, since the beginning of the century, there has been another Doctorate, that of the University. This was instituted in the main for foreign students who wished to obtain the title of doctor from a French university without having to satisfy the requirements of the Doctorat ès lettres. The candidate must write and defend a thesis and prepare and discuss in public examination three questions chosen by himself in agreement with the professor who supervises the work.[10] The defense may be presented in typed copies and the thesis must be written in French. Among the theses presented recently at the Sorbonne were: Myriam Yardeni, *La conscience nationale en France pendant les guerres de religion (1559–1598);* John Bradley, *La légion tchécoslovaque en Russie (1914–1920);* Yousef Youakim, *Staline et Trotsky—L'opposition de gauche 1923–1927;* Joan Wheeler, *L'action missionnaire de la congrégation du Saint-Esprit au Cameroun entre 1919–1939;* and Alfonz Lengyel, *Les sculpteurs français du XIXe siècle dans les collections des États-Unis.*

The special fields offered for the Doctorate of the University vary with the university as the following table reveals:[11]

> Archéologie: Clermont
> Archéologie et histoire de l'art: Toulouse
> Archéologie et histoire des milieux méditerranéens:
>   Montpellier
> Archéologie et histoire de l'art: Bordeaux
> Egyptologie: Lyon
> Art de l'Antiquité classique: Caen
> Civilisation et histoire de l'Orient ancien: Paris
> Histoire de l'art antique, médiéval, moderne: Lyon
> Histoire de l'art médiéval: Caen
> Histoire de l'art de Bourgogne, de Franche-Comté et de
>   Suisse: Besançon
> Préhistoire: Montpellier

[10] No firm basis for comparison exists but the Doctorate of the University in France has been compared to a high level master's degree in the United States.

[11] From *Vingt-cinq ans . . . ,* p. 15.

Histoire: Nancy, Toulouse, Rennes
Histoire de l'Antiquité: Lyon
Histoire romaine: Caen
Histoire médiévale: Grenoble
Histoire du Moyen Age: Lyon
Histoire et civilisation de l'Occident médiéval: Paris
Histoire byzantine: Paris
Histoire du Moyen Age, d'Italie, Renaissance: Poitiers
Histoire moderne et contemporaine: Caen, Lyon, Paris,
    Poitiers
Histoire moderne. Histoire régionale: Grenoble
Histoire du Christianisme: Paris
Histoire de Provence: Aix
Histoire religieuse et contemporaine: Besançon
Histoire de l'humanisme: Caen
Etudes méridionales: Toulouse
Ethnologie: Paris
Musicologie: Paris

A decree of 1951 created still another doctorate in the faculties of letters and social sciences, that of the *troisième cycle* (third cycle). This doctorate was created not only in the hope of involving the research faculties more fully in deepening students' knowledge and in training them in methods of research but also in the desire to obtain additional qualified teaching assistants in the universities. In order to be admitted to the program of the "troisième cycle," the student must have the *licence-ès-lettres* (in this case the license in history) or give evidence of special aptitudes in research. Students allowed to register must engage in the activities of a working group supervised by a director of research. The time of the cycle is two years, during which the candidates must defend a "doctoral thesis of the third cycle," which they present in typed copies. The defense takes place in public before an examining board of three professors. Foreigners may become candidates, take the training, and present a thesis—which must be written in French. Instruction in the "troisième cycle" began slowly but at present is taking place on a large scale, both at the Sorbonne and at provincial universities. Among the thirty-four theses defended at the Sorbonne in 1963–1964 were the following in varied periods of history: Rémi Gossez, *Les ouvriers de Paris (1848–1851)*; Jean-Michel Desbordes, *Les limites de la Civi-*

tas Suessionum: Etude de géographie humaine; Diana Pachlewska-Gasparini, *L'opinion publique à Paris et la Russie d'après la correspondance diplomatique et la presse (1865–1870);* Anne-Marie La Bonnardière, *Recherches de chronologie augustinienne;* Andre Bianconi, *Le syndicat national des Instituteurs de 1920 à 1939;* and Robert Favreau, *Une famille bourgeoise de Poitiers: Les Claveurier XVe siècle–début XVIe siècle.*

To this review of the historical work done within the faculties something more must be added. Because the faculties are always concerned with research as well as teaching, they have created their own institutes and centers of research. Directed by a professor, these constitute centers of research with their own specialized libraries and they sometimes hold seminars. Candidates both for the *Maîtrise* and for the doctorate participate in the work of the institutes and assist the professors in their own research. At the Sorbonne there are, for example, institutes for art and archaeology, the history of the French Revolution, modern and contemporary history and civilization, economic and social history, the history of contemporary international relations, the history of religion, the history of science and technology, as well as centers of research for modern European civilization, and Byzantine, Slavic, and Latin American history and civilization. Some of the institutes in Paris and in the provinces are well organized, but their organization and the work they do varies widely. At each of the provincial faculties there is also a chair for regional history. The holder of the chair supervises student work in his field. Finally, there are additional institutes or centers of research outside the universities.

C. Higher education—other institutions

The above account makes it clear that the faculties of letters and social sciences almost exclusively provide for the training of future professional historians. But there are also other institutions of learning outside the universities and not under their control.[12] These come directly under the General Director of Higher Education in the Ministry of Education. Existing only at Paris these institutions are the Collège de France, the Ecole nationale des Chartes, and the Ecole pratique des Hautes-Etudes.

[12] A list of the extra-university institutions in Paris is given in the *Livret de l'étudiant de l'Université de Paris, 1963–1964,* pp. 357–361 and 463–499.

The Collège de France, founded by Francis I in 1530, employs its professors without consideration of rank. The work it offers does not prepare for any specific examination. Its instruction, then, is not required to follow any definite plan, its professorial chairs are not in principle permanent, its professors have no teaching duties other than to give a certain number of lectures (about thirty-five) a year on topics they choose, anyone can attend these, and no degrees are given. From the beginning the function of the Collège has been to offer opportunity for the freest form of independent research. In it history is represented by chairs of Indo-European civilization, Assyriology, Egyptian archaeology, Hebrew and Aramaic languages, Western Asian and Far Eastern civilization, Greek antiquity, early Christian and Byzantine archaeology, Roman civilization, the historical geography of France, the history of modern civilization, contemporary Islamic social history, and the history of North American civilization.

The Ecole nationale des Chartes, founded in 1821, is the great national school for instruction in the auxiliary sciences of history and for the training of future archivists, librarians, museum curators, etc. Only former students teach in it. Instruction is spread over three years. If students wish to obtain the diploma of paleographic archivist, they prepare a thesis during this period which they must defend publicly in the year following their enrollment. The purpose of the training is to give students thorough knowledge of the basic disciplines of scholarly research, especially but not exclusively in those related to the history of France, that is, in paleography, Roman philology, archival techniques, bibliography, medieval Latin, the sources for the history of France, institutional history, the history of civil and canon law, and archaeology. In addition, complementary lectures are also given in numismatics, heraldry, historical cartography, etc. Three classes of twenty-five students each, admitted after competition, take the courses. These courses are also open to foreign students who have the credentials.

The Ecole pratique des Hautes-Etudes was founded in 1868 to permit students to complete their theoretical education by practical work on texts. There is no examination or competition for entrance. Access to the lectures can be obtained simply by registering at the Secretary's office. Of the five sections in the school only the fourth, Historical and Philological Studies, and the Sixth, Economic and

Social Sciences, need be mentioned here, though history is also represented in the fifth section, Religious Studies, which includes the history of religion in China and India as well as medieval and early modern theology. The teaching is usually done by professors who hold chairs in the Collège de France, the Ecole nationale des Chartes, or in a university faculty. All fields of history are represented, from the standard—as Renaissance history—to the most recent, as modern social and intellectual history. The sixth section, Economic and Social Sciences, is the only place in France, in addition to the Sorbonne, where there is instruction on ancient and modern China, in African research, and in the study of industrial civilizations and the sociology of work and leisure.

One other school which gives instruction of interest to historians must be mentioned, the Ecole du Louvre, which is under the Minister of State charged with cultural affairs. This school trains students for the national museums and learned inquiries *(missions)*. The course includes the history of the arts—sculpture, painting, design, and applied arts. It takes two years at the end of which those students who successfully defend a thesis obtain the degree of students agrégés of the Ecole du Louvre. A course on the history of music is given in the Conservatoire national supérieur de Musique.

Outside and distinct from the universities there are other institutions of higher learning which are, in some degree, subject to control by the state. In France, as elsewhere, independent, Catholic, and Protestant institutions award their own diplomas and give their own work in which history has an important part. There are, for example, the five Catholic Institutes, those of Paris, Lille, Angers, Lyon, and Toulouse. Each of these Institutes has a faculty of letters in all respects like those of the state. But the Institutes have also faculties of theology—with chairs that relate to history: Christian Origins and Patristic Theology, of Law and the History of Canon Law, and Medieval, Modern, and Contemporary Ecclesiastical History. And they also have faculties of philosophy with chairs in the history of ancient and medieval philosophy. At the faculty of letters of the Institute of Paris there is also a Center of Research in Religious History. This is charged with two functions: to assemble the sources for and to define the religious structures of modern and contemporary France.

Finally, it is necessary to mention one other famous school, the

Ecole normale supérieure of the Rue d'Ulm, created by the Convention during the French Revolution. It no longer gives independent instruction or awards its own diplomas. Its students take the courses and examinations of the Sorbonne. But the exceptional scholarships and the communal life they enjoy creates the well-known "esprit normalien." Fifty students enter the Ecole Normale each year after a severe competition. Of these fifty, about ten will engage in the study of history.

II. Aids for Historical Study

The universities, the *grandes écoles,* the higher institutions of learning are both teaching and research institutions. In France it is undisputed dogma that it is impossible to separate teaching from research—at least in the historical disciplines. For a professor, teaching is a stimulus as well as an instrument to guide and test his own research. It is not surprising, therefore, that professors constitute the majority of the members of the historical commissions of the Centre national de la Recherche scientifique (CNRS), which has become an institution of major importance to scholarship in France. This body in France, like somewhat similar bodies in other countries, is the modern incarnation of Maecenas, the Maecenas of the state.

The present functions and structure of CNRS date from the end of the Second World War. It stimulates scientific research in all the exact and human sciences through commissions or sections composed of sixteen members elected by their colleagues and six named by the government. Of the thirteen sections in the fields of the human sciences, five are in or related to history: anthropology, prehistory and ethnology, ancient languages and civilizations, national monuments and medieval history, and modern and contemporary history. The sections, meeting twice a year, award subsidies to those doing research either in or outside the universities. These are actually grants, limited usually to three or four years. In 1964 those receiving grants from the modern and contemporary history section totalled 53. Further, the CNRS supplies technical collaborators for the Institutes and research centers and subsidies for individual publications and for scholarly periodicals.

Those doing research are classified in an ascending hierarchy from beginner to director of research, with the stages in between of *attaché, chargé,* and *maître.* Some who have proven their research ability are able to skip the various grades of the hierarchy and through CNRS make an actual career of research without the burden of teaching. But it must be noted that, while this may be the rule in the exact sciences, it is quite exceptional in the human sciences, hence in history.

The CNRS also organizes conferences in which foreign historians take part and which are devoted to a well-defined subject, such as "Charles V and His Times," or the "Cities of Latin America." It creates working teams for special research tasks—on African civilization and on the "lost [*disparus*] villages" of France, for example. Finally, a specialized institute, the Institute for Research on and the History of Original Texts, has been created within the CNRS. Divided into several sections, Latin, Greek, Arab, French, diplomatics, etc., this institute centralizes all information on literary and historical manuscript texts, has an important film library, and since 1953 has undertaken publication of a series of medieval texts. This last, designed for university students, includes not only critical editions of the texts themselves but their translation into French. Parenthetically, it must be noted, texts of sources in languages other than French are never published in translation only because the user should always be able to check the translation with the original. The first volume of a new series of texts, *Vie de Robert le Pieux,* was published in 1965. This series, with the general title of *"Sources d'histoire médiévale,"* will take the place of the old, well-known *Collection de textes pour servir à l'étude et à l'enseignement de l'histoire.*

This grouping of historians within CNRS represents the most recent and active way of organizing historical research in the different fields of history; in any case, it is the best endowed. But French historians did not wait until the twentieth century to begin cooperative work, both in their academies and in their learned societies. Before describing the latter, the work of the Comité des Travaux historiques et scientifiques should be described. Though the Committee was created more than a hundred years ago it is still vigorous. Established by Guizot in 1834 under the aegis of the Ministry of Public Education and reorganized in 1881, it is an official body in which the study of history has an important place. History is represented in the Section of History and Philology (which comes down to 1610), in the Historical Section (to 1789), in the Archaeology Section, and in the Commission for Research in and Publication of the Documents on the Economic Life of the French Revolution. The Committee has an impressive number of publications under way. Among these are the *Collection de documents inédits sur l'histoire de France* of which over 400 quarto volumes have been published, the *Dictionnaire topographique de la France* which has appeared for 37 Departments, and the *Bibliographie générale des travaux historiques et archéologiques publiés par les Sociétés savantes de France.* A new collection, just begun, will publish the cartularies and municipal accounts of medieval cities.

The major mission of the Committee, however, has been (and still is) to organize a Congress of Learned Societies every year, usually in a university city. This Congress affords opportunity for local historians to present the results of their current research. The research is conducted according to a planned list of themes proposed by resident members of the Committee who meet every month in Paris. In recent years a general subject has been defined for each Congress. In 1962 for the 87th Congress at Poitiers the subject was "Urban History," for the 88th in 1963 at Clermont-Ferrand, "The Forest," for the 89th in 1964 at Lyon, "France and the Empire," for the 90th in 1965 at Nice, "The Medieval Village," and for the 91st in 1966 in Rennes, "Maritime History." The papers given at the Congress are published in the annual *Bulletin* of the Committee in two volumes, one for the period before 1610, the other for the period since.

One other committee plays an important role in French historical scholarship, the Comité français des sciences historiques. Representing the learned bodies, the universities and local societies, its purposes are to provide for French representation at the international congresses organized by the International Committee of Historical Sciences, to promote bilateral international conferences with foreign historians, and to coordinate the action of local historical groups. Since 1955 the French Committee, in cooperation with CNRS, has undertaken the publication of the *Bibliographie annuelle de l'histoire de France* which lists all works appearing each year in France and abroad on French history from the fifth century to 1939.

The history of France, as of all countries, is based on documents preserved for the most part in archival establishments and in some great libraries. It is also true, of course, that a considerable number of documents are still privately owned by churches, businesses, and families.

This brief survey cannot completely describe the archives and libraries of France, even less what they contain. Many volumes are devoted to these topics. Here only that information useful for understanding the part these institutions play in historical work will be covered.

The Administration of the Archives of France is now under the Minister of State charged with cultural affairs. Under its authority are (1) the National Archives at Paris, (2) the Departmental Archives (a depot in each department), and (3) the Communal and Charitable (*hospitalières*) Archives. The professional staff of the National and Departmental Archives is composed entirely of archivists and paleographers—that is to say, of former students of the Ecole nationale des Chartes.

The inventories, both printed and manuscript, created for each series of archival documents are now complemented by "Research Guides." These are compiled by categories of research: genealogy, history of art, literary history, legal archives, economic archives, etc. These systematic guides, a new form of instrument for research, have proved to be very useful. Tried first in the National Archives, they are now becoming widely utilized in the Departmental Archives.

Since 1930 a major effort has been made to collect notarial as well as business and family records in the National and Departmental Archives. These are deposited in the Archives according to a contract, always revocable, between the Archival Administration and the depositor.

At the National Archives a Bureau of Information receives research requests for documents on various subjects and the archivists give information without charge. About two thousand requests are received annually. The Bureau of Information also collects all information on theses in preparation as well as on all scholarly historical work being done in France. This it has published since 1952 in the biannual *Bulletin du Centre d'information de la recherche d'histoire en France.*

By their training and through their professional work, the archivists, or most of them, are directly associated with historical research. It is they, naturally, who help students when the inventories are incomplete or faulty. More than anyone else they possess thorough knowledge of the materials in their charge. Often the introductions they write for their inventories are original studies of high quality.

Much the same situation exists in the major libraries, that is, those called *"classées,"* which are under the Minister of National Education. As is well known, the Bibliothèque nationale, formerly the King's library, contains not only several million printed volumes but also an important manuscript division. It also possesses valuable historical documents, particularly for the sixteenth to eighteenth centuries. Its departments of medals, prints, and geography (or cartography) are likewise very rich. The scholarly personnel of all these departments give daily attention to both French and foreign readers.

In Paris, too, both the Bibliothèque Mazarine and the Bibliothèque Arsenal are well known for the important research materials they contain, the first for its Jansenist documents, the second for its collections of the Archives of the Bastille as well as those concerning the history of the theater. The major libraries of the provinces all have manuscript collections and, in addition, contain books from the religious establishments abolished during the Revolution of 1789.

University libraries in France, both old and new, are developing rapidly. Planned basically for the professors and students of the whole university, they are also being extended to provide special libraries for each institute or research center.

III. *Learned Societies and Historical Reviews*

French historians have been individualistic by nature, but they have long formed learned societies and historical associations. Essentially, the learned societies are academies founded by the state. At the Institut de France created in 1795, history is included in the Académie des inscriptions et belles lettres and in the Académie des sciences morales et politiques. The first Académie goes back to the reign of Louis XIV, while the second dates from 1832. Their members are chosen by cooptation and some are also members of the Académie française. At each of their weekly meetings a member presents a paper, a resume of which appears in the *Comptes rendus des séances de l'Académie des Inscriptions et belles lettres* or in the *Revue des travaux de l'Académie des sciences morales et politiques.* Each of the Academies, in addition, has other publications. The Académie des Inscriptions, with a long tradition of research, publishes, for example, the *Journal des Savants* (founded in 1665), the *Notices et extraits des manuscrits* (on French literary history), the *Diplômes des rois mérovingiens et carolingiens,* the *Pouillés des diocèses de France,* the *Comptes royaux* (of the Middle Ages), the *Historiens des croisades,* the *Corpus inscriptionum semiticarum,* and the *Corpus philosophorum medii aevi.* The Académie des sciences morales et politiques has charge of publishing the *Ordonnances des rois de France*—those of the reign of Francis I are now being published.

In the departments there are other academies which, though less famed than the Institut de France, are scarcely less important for their scholarly work. The Académie des Jeux Floraux à Toulouse is the oldest literary society in Europe. The Académie de Stanislas at Nancy, created by the Duc de Lorraine Stanislas, King of Poland, goes back to 1750. Among other well-known academies are those of Angers, Grenoble, and Nîmes. There is some question whether the local Academies are as important as they once were. It is not possible to say because, in earlier times, local "notables" and independent scholars had wealth and leisure which their successors lack. The "sociétés des antiquaires" deserve special mention. The Académie celtique, established in 1803, has become the present Société nationale des antiquaires de France—the word antiquarian here being understood in the historical, not the commercial, sense. It publishes an annual *Bulletin* and *Memoirs* as do similar societies at Poitiers, Caen and Rouen, Amiens, and St. Omer.

As a good many local historical societies no longer have the members or means they formerly possessed, there have been attempts recently to combine, or, at least, federate them. This grouping has often taken place around the universities or with the help of the CNRS. The latter has intervened not by subsidizing the many societies which have few activities but rather by supporting the important local reviews of the highest scholarly quality. Among these are the *Revue du Nord, Annales de l'Est, Revue d'Alsace, Annales de*

Bourgogne, Provence historique, Annales du Midi, Annales de Bretagne, Annales de Normandie, and the *Cahiers d'histoire* published by the three universities of Clermont-Ferrand, Lyon, and Grenoble.

It is not necessary to supply an exhaustive list of French historical periodicals here. In any case, they are listed at the beginning of each volume of the *Bibliographie annuelle de l'histoire de France*[13] of which the last volume, that for 1966, has recently appeared. At the present time the number of French historical periodicals covered has reached the impressive number of 350.

With the exception of the publications of the Institute of France, only the periodicals of local learned societies have thus far been mentioned. The learned societies of Paris which are devoted to particular aspects of the entire history of France deserve special mention.

The earliest to be founded is the Société de l'histoire de France. It is also the most important, not because of the size of its membership which has never exceeded 500, but because of the volume of its publications. Founded by Guizot in 1834, it began its work during the great nineteenth-century revival of history. With its membership composed both of professional historians and members of historically important French families, it has never ceased to hold a major place in French historiography, particularly because of its editing and publication of historical source materials.

Four hundred and seventy volumes have appeared in its collections and in addition it has, since 1925, continued the earlier publications of the Société d'histoire contemporaine. Among the published narrative sources are the master historical works of France, as the *Historia Francorum* of Gregory of Tours, the *Chroniques d'Anjou,* the *Grandes chroniques de France,* the *Chronique des quatre premiers Valois,* the *Livre des fais et bonnes moeurs du sage roy Charles V* of Christine de Pisan, the *Chroniques de Louis XII* of Jean d'Auton, and the *Mémoires* of Martin and Guillaume du Bellay. The other varied publications of the Société can only be sampled here: the accounts of the kings of the fourteenth and fifteenth centuries, the letters of Louis XI, Charles VIII, and of Henry

---

[13] The *Bibliographie générale des travaux historiques et archéologiques publiés par les sociétés savantes de France* should also be noted. It lists the articles by learned societies in each department. The last period covered is from 1910 to 1940, in four volumes.

III (in progress), the *Correspondance secrète du comte de Broglie* with Louis XV, the reports to the Committee of General Security under the title of *Paris pendant la Terreur,* and the *Régime de l'industrie en France de 1814 à 1830.* The Société has several additional collections of sources under way, the *Procès de condamnation et de réhabilitation de Jeanne d'Arc,* for instance, and the *Chroniques* of Froissart. In addition, it issues an *Annuaire-Bulletin* which includes a list of members, the minutes of the annual meeting, and an original study or the text of a document.

The 700–800 members of the Société d'histoire moderne, unlike those of the French Historical Society, are nearly all professors of history. As its name indicates, the Société moderne is concerned only with the period beginning with the sixteenth century. But if it stresses French history it does not, for this reason, neglect the histories of other countries. Numerous foreign historians are among its members and it organizes meetings with historians of other countries, as those of Belgium and the United States. The Société publishes the quarterly *Revue d'histoire moderne et contemporaine* and an annual *Bulletin.* With its monthly meetings (held on the first Sunday) it is one of the most active societies of France.

Besides these two major societies are two which specialize in religious history: (1) the Société d'histoire de l'Eglise de France which has, since 1926, published the biannual *Revue d'histoire de l'Église de France* and, since 1952, a series of works relating to the history of the church in France; and (2) the Société de l'histoire du Protestantisme français, founded in 1822, which possesses an important library of books and documents and publishes a quarterly *Bulletin.*

Other Parisian societies (this list is not all-inclusive) devote themselves to limited periods of history and the problems related to these. The Société d'études du XVIIᵉ siècle publishes the quarterly journal entitled *XVIIᵉ siècle* which on occasion is devoted to a particular question, as "How Frenchmen viewed France during the seventeenth century." Two other similar societies are the Société d'histoire de la Révolution de 1848 and the Société d'histoire de la IIIᵉ République. Somewhat different is the Comité d'histoire de la deuxième guerre mondiale, an official body attached to the Prime Minister. It has been publishing, since 1950, a quarterly, the *Revue d'histoire de la deuxième guerre mondiale,* devoted as the title indicates, to the period 1939–1945 and it maintains not only a special library but also a documentary center which increasingly covers the history of the Resistance in France. Neither of the two French reviews known all over the world, the *Revue historique* and the *Annales,* are published by societies. The first, the scholarly quarterly founded in 1876 by the outstanding scholar, Gabriel Monod, under the auspices of a commercial publisher, covers all fields of history. It is famed not only for its substantial articles but also for its bibliographic essays[14] and its book reviews. The *Annales* (with the subtitles of *Économies, Sociétés, Civilisations*) is the continuation of the well-known *Annales d'histoire économique et sociale* founded in 1929 by Marc Bloch and Lucien Febvre, two of the most imaginative and influential historians of the last generation. It is now a publication of the Sixth section of the Ecole pratique des Hautes-Etudes. Its orientation and its effect on French historical thought will be discussed later.

IV. Present Trends in French Historiography

France is a very old country. This means that French historical study is not only deeply rooted in tradition but also has rich and diverse materials to apply to the weighty and difficult subject of the national history. But the history being done in France is not exclusively related to the national past; French historians have always turned their attention to other countries and civilizations. Hence the work of French historians must be viewed in the light of their two interests as we attempt to describe their conception of history. Here our observations are confined to the period since the First World War. France, as much of the rest of the world, took leave of the nineteenth century in 1914. The present tendencies of historical study in France arose during the period between the two wars.

A preliminary observation cannot be avoided. Though some foreign observers may believe otherwise, French historians are profoundly individualistic. They continue to be even when they are convinced that the immense tasks of research can only be successfully accomplished by teams. Their attitudes illustrate their concern,

---

14 These have been of considerable use in the preparation of this essay.

their almost primordial concern, to protect their freedom. This is so true that even when they hold strong philosophical and political convictions they wish to retain their individual judgment. Indeed, their sense of relativism remains so strong that they generally refuse to commit themselves to a cause. Whether they conceive of history as a science or an art, whether they think of it only as a personal experience, believe it to have practical application, or conceive of it as purely speculative, they do not modify their fundamental faith in individual freedom.

Their thought remains that of free men for whom conclusions depend upon the particular issues, or for whom description and an attempt to understand and clarify must precede judgment. There are scarcely any French historians who could not make their motto the old Roman, *Historia, testis, posteros monet.* They do not, then, think that history is useless or with Paul Valéry that it is not only vain but dangerous speculation. For them it continues to be a useful way of thinking, and at its best, a way of understanding man.

We will return shortly to this fundamental characteristic of French historical work. There is a second preliminary observation equally revealing. French historians have little taste for grand philosophic schemes.[15] They believe these schemes have little or no meaning and speculation about them ought to be left up to the philosophers. They are even reluctant to enter into discussions of a subject that they deem to be without useful purpose. At the Stockholm Congress of the International Committee of Historical Sciences in 1960 all the papers on philosophic themes except one were given by historians of other countries.

During the last forty years, the French school of historians has revealed its dynamic qualities and its capacities for renewal. Hence it has merited and still merits a major place in contemporary historical work. It owes its new views to men who broke with orthodox views of history, men who, sure of their ground, dared escape from the sclerosis which was about to envelop and immobilize the study of history. The men were: (1) Henri Berr and the group around his *Revue de Synthèse historique;* (2) François Simiand, who

---

[15] But one of the ablest contemporary students of problems of historical methodology and meaning is the French sociologist and publicist, Raymond Aron. See his *Introduction to the Philosophy of History,* translated by George J. Irwin, Boston, 1961, first published in France in 1938.

borrowed from Paul Lacombe the qualifying word *événementiel* (event history) which the latter created to define and stigmatize the old and outworn forms of history; (3) Lucien Febvre and Marc Bloch, who broadened the scope and depth of history both through their own work and their editing of the *Annales;* and finally, (4) Georges Lefebvre, who stressed social and economic forces in his research on the last years of the Old Regime and on the Revolution.

The historical work being done in France today is still strongly influenced by the great efforts to revivify the study in the aftermath of the First World War. But is it completely so determined? This would be to assert too much, for reactions to a movement that itself threatened to become too exclusive have not failed to arise.

Without doubt the greatest advances have been in the fields of economic and social history, the economic being dominant at first over the social to which, at present, most attention is being given. Studies on the history of prices, incomes, economic cycles and crises, and economic enterprise are still the "order of the day." About half the doctoral theses in preparation at the Sorbonne are now devoted to these subjects—generally accompanied with the phrase that has won favor, "les problèmes de conjoncture." But historical study now wishes to be first of all a "science of the social," of "man living in society, that is, to conceive of history as a study of the human condition."

In order to understand what this means it is necessary to define certain key words, *événementiel, conjoncture,* and *structure,* used by contemporary historians, and to discuss the values attached to them. It cannot be doubted that these historians use *événementiel* in a pejorative sense. Of what good is historical study, they argue, if it is satisfied to set forth events and facts only in their chronological succession as this has been done in diplomatic, military, political, and religious history and especially in the classical "history by monarchical reigns"—in other words, when it is content to be descriptive or to be research only for the picturesque?

That the irritating question arises—what is the purpose of history?—is natural, and historians, as I will show later, do raise this question. They now think, in any case, that history is something more than the description of events. The view is not, of course, so new. Fustel de Coulanges raised it in the late nineteenth century and expressed it in a remark to his students at the Sorbonne. "Suppose a hundred specialists divided up the history of France by lot. Do you believe that they would be able to write the history of France? I doubt it. There would be lacking the relationships among the facts. Now these relationships also constitute historical truths." And he added, "History is not an easy science, the object it studies is infinitely complex." Fustel was right. And he had thus outlined the way and the contemporary French school of history has not refused to follow it. The relationships between the facts are in themselves elements of historical explanation. Now this is what the historian must attempt and this means he must not only describe but interpret and evaluate, and to accomplish these ends he must take account of all the elements which compose the particular past he is studying and which by their interaction condition its nature.

It is all this that French historians put into the expression, "the problems of *conjoncture*." Pierre Chaunu well defined "conjoncture" in a recent article in the *Revue historique* (vol. 229, 1963) on the problems of Spanish colonization. "*Conjoncture* has nothing in it of *deus ex machina,* of stupid fatalism in a purely mechanical world which physically impresses itself on men reduced to mechanized animals. Composed of free acts, it conditions but does not determine other free acts. It is one of the elements of the flowing structure on which the acts of history inscribe themselves." More simply, *conjoncture* is the totality of conditions, basically material but also political, moral, and other, in which men have acted, whatever the sphere of action.

In the attempt to give substance to history the word "structure" takes on first importance. This is a complex term belonging more to the terminology of economics than to the language of history. But historians cannot avoid using it, particularly when they are concerned with economic and social history, as so many French historians are. By "structure" is meant the permanent elements, the lasting components of a given reality, for example, the classes or orders of a society, the financial burdens imposed upon a group, the conditions of existence in a given place and time. And all of these seen in the perspective of long duration. To render an account of these structures and to comprehend their interplay, one must, of course, study them in themselves.

This means that the historian must not only have new conceptions but new methods as well. These involve the use of long-neglected archival categories, fiscal rolls, electoral lists, notarial records, and mortgage and legal records. It also involves new ways of using these documents, for archivists had established their categories for purposes other than those now sought. Among the new favored subjects is "social mobility"—the study of the movement of individuals and families from one social group or class to another. There have been several recent and important works on the "notables" of modern and contemporary France centered on this theme.

It would be wrong to believe that only modern historians have been affected by the confrontation of the historian with his calling. There are, naturally, differences among historians based in part on differences in documentary sources, but all the traditional fields of research have been influenced and enriched by the new emphases, including diplomatic, political, and religious history. Religious history, for example, has experienced a remarkable revival during the last twenty years through the stimulating work of Gabriel Le Bras.

Because they illustrate the new outlook of French historians, three major series of works should be mentioned: the *Histoire des Civilisations,* published by the Presses Universitaires and now completed in seven large volumes, the *Grandes Civilisations,* now being published by Editions Arthaud, and *Civilisations, Peuples et Mondes* by Editions Lidis. The volumes in these series, though the work of proven scholars, are written in the hope of reaching a large public. In this last respect they differ from the excellent and well-known volumes of the *Evolution de l'humanité* (started many years ago by Henri Berr) which are designed for informed readers.

To be precise on specific trends one should first stress present French efforts in the history of technological and economic ("matériel") aspects of civilization.[16] Compared to the work in this field being done in other and particularly the eastern European countries, it is true that the work being done in France lags behind, but it is still substantial. Naturally, the research under way is chiefly in the periods of the latter Middle Ages and the Old Regime. In these periods historians give equal attention to problems concerning the means of production, to technology as well as agrarian structure, to the provision and costs of food supplies, and to the mechanisms of economic growth—particularly in the nineteenth century. At the

---

16 The expression *"culture matérielle,"* unhappily so often used, does not belong to the genius of the French language.

same time, demographic inquiries are multiplying—inquiries that employ new methods of using the registers of parishes, the predecessors of modern state registers of vital statistics, and that concern subjects such as the effect of the diminishing death rates in the eighteenth and nineteenth centuries. Finally, stimulated by informed specialists, the history of science is experiencing remarkable activity.

In the field of the cartographic history France on the other hand, must make up for a long delay. An attempt is being made at present by the Commission nationale de géographie historique and the Laboratoire de cartographie of the sixth section of the Ecole pratique des Hautes-Etudes.

In brief, French history is now concerned with everything—as much with lost villages, the minting of money, the volume of economic trade, the cemeteries of the barbarians, the definition of frontiers, and linguistic and ethnic areas, as with currents of thought. On this last subject, historians are devoting much attention to the study of the phenomena of group psychology and to the definition of "mentalités" [collective psychology]. Their work should culminate in the creation of a *"dictionnaire des notions"*—that is to say, the definition of the different meanings men have given the same word in different eras, or even in the same era by different groups of men.

This last field of research, so rich in potentialities as are all those just mentioned, brings up a need common to all historians. Successful completion of research cannot be accomplished through individual efforts alone and the individual researcher must somehow be part of a team. But even this is not enough. This historian can no longer work in an ivory tower. He must turn to the related disciplines of ethnography, sociology, philosophy, linguistics, and aesthetics while at the same time these disciplines might very well benefit from history—which too often they have thought they could ignore. It is the whole phenomenon of man that must be studied, it is "man living in society" and not man segmented into the sterile categories of the nineteenth-century historian—not economic man, not political man, not religious man.

All this, is it so new? Not so much, perhaps, in the purpose as in the means of arriving at it. More than one nineteenth-century historian had this purpose: Augustin Thierry, for example, published his *Essai sur l'histoire de la formation et des progrès du Tiers État* in 1850 and even earlier, in 1840, his *Considérations sur l'histoire de*

France; Leopold Delisle as early as 1851 published his *Études sur la condition de la classe agricole et l'état de l'agriculture en Normandie au moyen âge;* and Levasseur's *Histoire des classes ouvrières et de l'industrie en France de 1789 à 1870* appeared in 1904. Behind the "cloak of the court"—the history of kings and of wars—Augustin Thierry sought the "whole body of the nation." But these early efforts were not immediately followed by productive results. Contemporary French historical study has again undertaken the interrupted task and with some success.

The danger of abandoning documentary inquiries too quickly in efforts like these is easy to see—just as is the danger of leaving them incomplete and subject to hasty and unfounded interpretations and syntheses. But in France there are enough well-trained historians to avoid this danger. The effort that must be made is being made.

These are the major currents of thought that now animate French historical research. Their directions have been the subject of an excellent study, that of the French Committee of Historical Sciences published for the Twelfth International Congress at Vienna in 1965, *Vingt-cinq ans de recherche historique en France (1940 à 1965),* with its important though incomplete (about 6,500 items) bibliography which serves as an illustration.

The perhaps too broad generalities offered above can be substantiated by noting those works, which, either because of the influence of their authors or because of their conceptual framework, may be considered representative of present ways of understanding and writing history in France.

A recent book that marks a milestone in French historiography is *L'Histoire et ses méthodes,* published under the editorship of Ch. Samaran in 1961. Perhaps the most informed French authority on the nature of historical study, Professor H. I. Marrou, wrote the beginning and concluding chapters. Asking the question, "What is history?" he answers that it is a science with its own methods, methods that it amplifies and perfects constantly. He then shows that historical study is unable to escape philosophical, even ideological coloration and that it cannot do so because it always reflects the interests of its time. Hence he agrees with Marc Bloch, who in his well-known essay, *Apologie pour l'histoire ou métier d'historien* (published posthumously), entitles one of his chapters, "To Comprehend the Past by the Present." I myself would add, yes, but on condition that the present not be projected into the past, which is the worst way to write history.

Marrou, along with A. Latreille, opposes the view of R. Sedillot and others who maintain that history makes no sense. Discussing ideas on "how to understand history," first developed in his important book, *De la connaissance historique* (1960), Marrou once again maintains that facts and events have intrinsic value, but he particularly stresses the interpretive effort the historian must make if he is to comprehend the multiplicity of so-called facts in all their complex reality—facts so numerous that a selection must always be made. This necessity of interpretation, he declares, means that historical explanation always has a subjective character.

History thus reconstructed may be of Marxist inspiration and historians of Marxist views are certainly not lacking in contemporary France. The Marxist views they profess, however, are not instruments of propaganda or of conversion unless, as is the case of F. Châtelet in his essay, "Non l'histoire n'est pas insaississable" (in *La Nouvelle critique*, 1955), they deny relativism in history. Among the most important recent works of the Marxist school are: J. Bouvier, *Le Crédit Lyonnais de 1863 à 1882* (1961); J. Chesnaux, *Recherches sur l'histoire du mouvement ouvrier chinois de 1919 à 1927* (1962); A. Kriegel, *Aux origines du communisme français 1914–1920* (1962); A. Soboul, *La Révolution française* (1948), and the collective work on the Commune of 1871 published in 1960 under the editorship of J. Bruhat, J. Dautry, and E. Tersen.

The high place of Georges Lefebvre in historical work during the period between the two wars has already been mentioned. For him, the history of economic facts was indispensable for understanding social conditions. On this point he followed the road laid out by Marc Bloch and Lucien Febvre. And this is always the main route of contemporary historical research in France.

At this point one should note several of the works developed in the Sixth Section of the Ecole des Hautes-Etudes under the supervision of Fernand Braudel and Ernst Labrousse, both the books and the articles published in the *Annales*. Some of these studies were done as doctoral theses, for example, P. Goubert, *Beauvais et le Beauvaisis, 1600–1730* (1960), H. and P. Chaunu, *Séville et l'Atlan-*

tique, 1504 à 1650 (1960); and R. Baehrel, *Une croissance: la Basse-Provence rurale, fin XVIe s.–1789* (1961). Others have taken a place in already existing series, the work of R. Mandrou, *Introduction à la France moderne 1500–1640* (1961) in the "Bibl. de synthèse historique," for example, and that of J. Le Goff, *La civilisation de l'Occident médiéval* (1964) in the series, "Les Grandes Civilisations."

Economic and social history are, then, at the very center of present-day French historical interests. So much is this true that they no longer appear to be a subordinate aspect of history, as was true in the past, but the essential core of historical work. Thus in ancient history, the volume of F. Villard, *La céramique grecque de Marseille* (1964) has the little-expected subtitle of *essai d'histoire économique.* Again, the recent book of J. Rouge is entitled, *Recherches sur l'organisation du commerce maritime en Méditerranée sous l'Empire romain* (1966). And once more, in medieval history, B. Guillemain studying *La Cour pontificale d'Avignon* (1962) added the subtitle, *étude d'une société.* And so it is in other fields. Economic and social considerations loom large in institutional history, in the theses, for example, of B. Guenée, *Tribunaux et gens de justice dans le bailliage de Senlis à la fin du Moyen Age* (1963), and R. Fedou, *Les hommes de loi lyonnais à la fin du Moyen Age; étude sur les origines de la classe de robe* (1964). In the history of the sixteenth century, two theses particularly emphasize these central themes: R. Mousnier, *La vénalité des offices sous Henri IV et Louis XIII* (1946) and J. Delumeau, *Vie économique et sociale de Rome dans la seconde moitié du XVIe s.* (1959). In the fields of modern and contemporary history it would be necessary to note nearly all of the recently published works; the recent thesis of J. Tudesq, *Les grands notables en France, 1840–1849,* with its subtitle, *étude historique d'une psychologie sociale,* is especially characteristic.

With this being the dominant interest, it is natural that agrarian history gets much attention. To it there is now devoted a specialized review, *Etudes rurales* (founded in 1962) as well as the series, "Les hommes et la terre" of the Sixth Section of the Ecole des Hautes-Etudes. In the latter there has appeared the work of L. Merle, *La métairie et l'évolution agraire de la Gâtine poitevine de la fin du Moyen Age à la Révolution* (1958). It is also the subject of other first-class works, among them the book of G. Duby, *L'économie rurale et la vie des campagnes de l'Occident médiéval* (1962), that of

P. de Saint-Jacob, *Les paysans de la Bourgogne du Nord au dernier siècle de l'Ancien régime* (1960), and three recent theses, those of G. Fourquin, *Les campagnes de la région parisienne à la fin du Moyen Age* (1964), A Poitrineau, *La vie rurale en Basse Auvergne au XVIIIᵉ s.* (1966), and E. Leroy-Ladurie, *Les paysans de Langue-doc* (1966). The classic work in this field, Marc Bloch's *Les Caractères originaux de la campagne française,* was revised and brought up to date in 1956 by R. Dauvergne.

Social history depends in large part upon the results of research in an allied field that was long neglected but now is in great favor, demography. A review, *Population,* inspired largely by Professor M. Reinhard of the Sorbonne, is devoted to it and Reinhard's own books are illustrative, *Histoire de la population mondiale de 1700 à 1948* (1949) and *Etudes de la population pendant la Révolution et l'Empire.* In this field several other works should be mentioned as well: G. Fournier, *Le peuplement rural en Basse Auvergne durant le Haut Moyen Age* (1961); A. Armengaud, *Les populations de l'Est aquitain au début de l'époque contemporaine, 1845–1871* (1961). Likewise worthy of mention is the establishment of a method of using the parish registers in M. Fleury and L. Henry, *Des registres paroissiaux à l'histoire de la population . . .* (1956) and the article, "Inventaire par sondage des registres paroissiaux de France" (*Population,* vol. XV, 1960).

In the same general field special notice must be given to the work of L. Chevalier who goes beyond the dry statistics of the censuses to formulate a sociological synthesis in his book, *Classes laborieuses et classes dangereuses à Paris pendant la première moitié du XIXᵉ s.* (1958) as well as to the research of R. Mousnier on Paris in the seventeenth century, of Mlle Daumard and F. Furet, *Structures et relations sociales à Paris au milieu du XVIIIᵉ s.,* and to the thesis of A. Corvisier, *L'armée française de la fin du XVIIᵉ s. au ministère de Choiseul; le soldat.* The last has revived military history in establishing a census of recruits and showing how they fit in the population of the country.

I turn now to technological history and in a more general way to the history of science. Since the work of Pierre Duhem, these varieties of history have been given little attention in France. But they are being studied by a whole group of students. Ironmaking has been given particular attention with the establishment of a

Revue d'histoire de la sidérurgie and a museum at Nancy. But agricultural techniques (B. Gille, G. Duby), the navy (A. Bernard, M. Mollat), and banking (B. Gille) have also been studied. The four historians just mentioned have collaborated on a large *Histoire générale des techniques* (published in four volumes since 1962), while the history of science has been the subject of another collaborative study, *Histoire générale des sciences* (four volumes published, 1957–1964) under the editorship of R. Taton. Taton also directs the Centre de recherche d'histoire des sciences et des techniques, founded in 1958 and supported by the Sixth Section of the Ecole des Hautes-Etudes and the Centre international de synthèse.

It would be wrong to think, however, that quantitative and statistical history is the only form of historiography in France today. Major currents of research and new interpretations are fed always by traditional sources. In a sense these reestablish the necessary equilibrium. Thus B. Guenée (see above), who has been part of the new school of French historians, has published an article *(Revue historique,* vol. 232, 1964) which is not as retrospective as the title would indicate. In his "L'histoire de l'Etat en France à la fin du Moyen Age vue par ses historiens français," he stresses the necessity of reestablishing political history and the history of institutions—not fleshless, abstract, static political history, but political history resulting from the action of individuals. The course on the history of institutions that I myself give at the Ecole nationale des Chartes is completely oriented in this direction. And in considering political and diplomatic history, the master of these subjects, Pierre Renouvin, has never ceased to emphasize the leading part taken by individuals in the unfolding of history and he has recently reiterated this view in a speech before the Société de l'Histoire de France (published in the *Annuaire–Bulletin* of the Society, 1966–1967). Though some French historians reject biography it should not be forgotten either that the individual may be considered not only as a personality influencing his contemporaries but as a thinking being who symbolizes the things he shares with his contemporaries and which he expresses in words. It is owing to this point of view that research on the history of "collective psychology" or states of mind has received so much favor. This last is especially stressed by A. Dupront in his course at the Sorbonne and by V. Tapié and R. Mousnier at the Centre de recherche sur les civilisations de l'Europe moderne. Related to this trend of study are two recent studies on books as "instruments of culture," those by F. Furet, *Littérature et société en France au XVIIIe s.*—a report at the International Congress of 1965 in Vienna, and R. Mandrou, *De la culture populaire aux XVIIe et XVIIIe s.* which largely depends, for its evidence, on the production of a printing workshop at Troyes which specialized in popular books (livres de colportage). Special attention should also be drawn to the research being done by Michel Mollat of the Sorbonne on "Les Pauvres et la Pauvreté" during the Middle Ages and to that of Philippe Wolff of Toulouse on the "Histoire du travail."

Even religious history is influenced by the major interests of French historiography. G. Le Bras has pointed the way with his works on religious sociology, notably his *Introduction à l'histoire de la pratique religieuse en France* (1942). This was followed by J. B. Duroselle's *Les débuts du catholicisme social en France, 1822–1870* (1951) and in the theses of Abbé Molette on the *Association catholique de la jeunesse française* and of Abbé Marchasson on *Sillon*. Most typical of the theses recently defended in this field, however, is Madame C. Marcilhacy, *Le diocèse d'Orléans sous l'épiscopat de Msgr. Dupanloup (1849–1878); sociologie religieuse et mentalités collectives* (1962).

That this sketch of recent French historical interest may not be too incomplete, the present interest of French historians in the press, both as a source of information and as an object of study, must be mentioned. The spokesman here is the Institut français de presse which J. Godechot now directs. This Institute has just published an original research aid, the tables of the newspaper *Le Temps* for the period 1861–1870. This has had so much success that it will be continued. And the series "Kiosque" continues to publish, as it has for ten years, original works devoted to the press.

Finally, it is desirable to draw attention to the various "historical series." Launched by commercial houses, they inevitably have their commercial side—which justifies the distrust that arises concerning them. But at present an encouraging tendency manifests itself among professional historians who no longer leave the writing of popular works to quacks. They believe, on the other hand with good reason, that it is one of their duties to write popular works aimed at a wide public just as they are now willing to participate in radio and television broadcasts which reach even larger audiences. I note here, by way of example, the series entitled "Trente journées qui ont fait la France." Among its volumes are four which are truly authoritative: G. Tessier, *Le baptême de Clovis;* R. Folz, *Le couronnement de Charlemagne;* R. Mousnier, *L'assassinat d'Henri IV;* and E. Faure, *La disgrâce de Turgot.* Moreover, half way between works of learning and of popularization is another series that reflects the major interests of French historical study, that named "Economies, Sociétés, Civilisations" in which there has appeared Y. Renouard, *Les hommes d'affaires italiens du Moyen Age;* L. Febvre, *Combats pour l'histoire;* and G. Duby and R. Mandrou, *Histoire de la civilisation française.*

Another generation will judge what has been accomplished by this generation in learned and popular history. At the least, it will have a documentary basis for its judgment.

V. Note on "Working Conditions" of French Professors

There is no special legislation for French professors. As state functionaries they are part of the "Fonction publique" and are remunerated in accordance with that statute.

The salary of professors of history varies with their qualifications and length of service. A professor *agrégé* of a lycée, unmarried and at the beginning receives, with all benefits included, about 1,300 francs ($260) a month. A professor in higher education at the end of his career receives a salary of about 4,500 francs ($900) a month.

A professor in a lycée teaches about fifteen hours a week, a professor on the Faculty of a university three hours a week. Most professors hold additional appointments, in a Research Institute (as the Ecole pratique des Hautes-Etudes), or in a semi-public institution (as the Ecole des sciences politiques).

Other perquisites of university professors are usually uncertain. Except for the deans or directors of groups, no history professor has his own office in his university, but the situation is changing.

Professors of the Collège de France have a special statute. They are required to give only thirty-five lectures a year and do not need to give examinations because entrance to the institution is completely free. A number of them have other duties, for example, the direction of studies at the Ecole pratique des Hautes-Etudes, and all of them, on occasion, participate in the examinations for the defense of theses at the Sorbonne.

Professors at the Ecole nationale des Chartes and directors of studies at the Ecole pratique des Hautes-Etudes give two lectures of two hours each week.

Bibliographical Note

There is no need for an extended bibliography here not only because of the recent two volumes of the Comité français des sciences historiques, *Vingt-cinq ans de recherche historique en France (1940–1965)*, but also because most of the relevant studies have been mentioned in the text and because the *Revue historique* periodically publishes analyses of historical work in France, such as the important article by H. I. Marrou, "Théorie et pratique de l'histoire," vol. CCXXXIII, 1965, pages 139–170. Nevertheless, a student may find the following additional items of interest.

ARON, Raymond, *Dimensions de la conscience historique.* Paris, Plon, 1961.

GUSDORF, Georges, *Introduction aux sciences humaines: Essai critique sur leurs origines et leur développement.* Paris, Société d'Edition, 1960.

HYSLOP, Beatrice, *France, A Study of French Education* . . . , n.p., American Association of Collegiate Registrars and Admission Officers, 1964.

MALE, George A., *Education in France.* Washington, Government Printing Office, 1963.

RENOUVIN, Pierre, "Research in Modern and Contemporary History: Present Trends in France," *Journal of Modern History,* vol. 38, 1966, pages 1–12.

SCHNEIDER, J. and VIGIER, P., "L'orientation des travaux universitaires en France," *Revue historique,* Vol. CCXXV, 1961, pages 397–405.

Part Three

Historical Study
in
Western Germany

WOLFGANG J. MOMMSEN

I. The Development of Scholarly Historical Study
   in Western Germany

The particular nature of contemporary historical study in Germany is best understood through knowledge of its development, for only in this way can the peculiarities of this study be made clear to students who are not reared in the German idealistic tradition. American students often and sometimes automatically accept history as one of the social sciences. With their empirical-pragmatic assumptions they see the tasks of history to be (1) to shed light on the consciousness of a society that is autonomous in its political and economic decisions, and (2) to describe the evolutionary forces to which this society finds itself subject. In general, the German study of history is no longer far from this view, but it is intellectually rooted in a different philosophical soil. The nature of this soil deeply influenced not only the ideological structure but also the organizational form of historical studies.

The road to the recognition of history as an independent discipline within the framework of the general development of knowledge was, of course, long and difficult. In the medieval educational system, history, as a part of the *studia humanitatis,* had a completely subordinate position; attached to rhetoric it actually served as a source of illustrative material for moral instruction. Not until the beginning of the sixteenth century was an independent chair of history founded, and even this establishment was but division of labor and did not change the fact that history supplied material for the moral and humanistic education of those students who are now commonly termed undergraduates.

It is true that history began to assert itself in the course of the seventeenth and eighteenth centuries, but only insofar as it was able to free itself, in piecemeal fashion, from its role as a preparatory discipline, valuable exclusively as a preparation for the study of the truly scholarly *(wissenschaftlichen)* disciplines of theology, medicine, and jurisprudence. Even after this incomplete emancipation it remained a servant, an auxiliary discipline serving higher studies. As church history established itself as an important field within theological studies, historiography served theology. This was true particularly during the time of the Reformation and the Counter-Reformation. The main task of the numerous chairs for universal history in the German Protestant as well as Catholic universities was to show the divine plan of salvation in the events of the historical world.

Much more important for the development of history as a scholarly discipline was its role as an auxiliary to jurisprudence. The relationship of the study of law to history is demonstrable, for example, in the work of Samuel von Pufendorf, who, through his book, *De jure naturae et jus gentium,* became one of the founders of modern international law. Pufendorf was also the author of major historical works and his theory of natural law was based in no small way on the foundation of thorough historical study. For a number of reasons, favorable conditions existed for the emancipation of history as a branch of knowledge *sui generis* within the framework of jurisprudence. The development of the modern territorial state in Germany as well as the closely related advance of Roman law led to a constantly increasing demand for legally trained administrative officials. This increased the significance and academic importance of jurisprudence. Following the expansion of state functions and needs during the eighteenth century, a group of special disciplines, administrative theory, public finance, political science, and others, developed out of jurisprudence. These new fields, at the time, were subsumed under the common title of cameralism. Within this framework, history found an important though still subordinate function. The pre-revolutionary society of the eighteenth century was deeply connected with a past which reached back for centuries. Everywhere, in daily life and especially in the realm of law, one encountered the legal remains of old social structures based on privileges and inherited exceptional rights. Even the political and constitutional structure of the Holy Roman Empire could be properly understood only by recourse to its long historical development. Numerous historical auxiliary disciplines were, therefore, indispensable for the jurist: diplomatics, for example, which developed historical methods to examine the validity of ancient documents, heraldry, genealogy, legal and constitutional history, and territorial history. It was precisely here, in the area of auxiliary science, that critical methods were first used in historical writing. These, however, were as yet without lasting influence for history. The much acclaimed Göttingen school, developing in the second half of the eighteenth century with Johann Stephan Pütter (1725–1807) as its most distinguished representative, was no exception, though its influence in the first half of the nineteenth century was to be by no means small.

The writing of history continued, of course, outside the universities, while the universities themselves degenerated into training institutions for state officials. But during the eighteenth century this writing was more a literary pursuit than a scholarly study of the past. An important role was played by court historiography. By the seventeenth century it had become good style at the European princely courts to maintain official historians both as *laudatores temporibus acti* and as literary representatives of the several state-political interests. Such significant thinkers as Pufendorf and Leibniz spent long years as court historians in various European courts. This kind of historiography was usually limited to the history of diplomatic actions and intrigues or to description of the deeds of great monarchs or statesmen. As it restricted itself strictly to the classic cabinet politics of the century, it was little aware of the people and even less of the great forces of historical development. In the narrow meaning of the word it was pragmatic. It looked for instructive examples of clever diplomatic operations in history and had as its goal, to paraphrase Jacob Burckhardt's famous dictum, to make people "clever on occasion," not "wise for always." It is clear that genuine historical understanding as well as methodological criticism of sources was rarely to be found in this genre of historiography.

This was even truer of the new secularized form of universal history developing under the influence of the thought of the Enlightenment. As is well known, this form had its most prominent spokesmen in Voltaire, Hume, Robertson, and Schlözer. Their theme was the progress of civilized humanity since the dark days of the Middle Ages. Full of optimism about the future, they passed sentence on the past in order to show the advantages of the new era of rationalism and civilization and they frequently arrived at schematic judg-

ments about all history. It was against one of these works, Iselin's
History of Humanity, which arranged world history on the basis of
a naive scheme of progress, that Johann Gottfried Herder argued in
his pamphlet *Auch eine Philosophie der Geschichte der Menschheit*
in 1774. This essay can be considered the *Pronunciamento* of the
new, of the modern writing of history, if one overlooks Giambattista
Vico's battle for a "New Science" of a century before, which then
went unnoticed. Herder for the first time formulated what became
one of the most basic principles of German historical writing,
namely that every historic structure has its own intrinsic value and
must be regarded as unique. Herder's charge to future historians
was, "Do not rely on the mere word, but go into the whole age, the
heavenly sphere, all history, feel yourself in everything." Every historical phenomenon should be understood in terms of its own presuppositions and one should not dare impose upon it an abstract,
entirely contemporaneous, rationalistic, or moralistic pattern of
progress. To be sure, even Herder did not deny progress in history,
but nevertheless he argued for the equal right for every historical
phenomenon, particularly for every nation, whatever its stage of
historical development. "Every nation has in itself the central point
of its happiness, just as every sphere has its center of gravity." Of
course, his thinking was embedded in a specific Protestant *Weltanschauung.* All peoples, so taught Herder, had come equally out of
the hand of God and every historical formation had its own worth in
the divine order of salvation.

This new idea, expressed by the romantic counter-movement
to the rationalism of the Enlightenment in myriad variations, was
of decisive significance in the rise of a new attitude toward the past
and a new form of historical writing. The fanciful adoration of the
past inspired by romanticism, the rediscovery of the Middle Ages in
all their splendor and their richness, the enthusiastic search for the
original literary forms of expression of the various *Volksgeister,*
served as an accompaniment. There came now a third element, the
philosophical onset of German idealism which wiped out the meta-
physical theories of the Enlightenment's philosophy and demanded
a place for the idea of the autonomy of the ethically responsible
individual. In the completely ahistorical system of Kant the significance of this new beginning for historical thinking was not yet clear,
but with Fichte the implications of the new idea of "causality

through freedom" became clearly evident. The historical world appears here precisely as the *"Materiale der Pflichterfüllung"* of the ethically responsible human being, his personal destiny being decided in historical action. Georg Friedrich Wilhelm Hegel then succeeded in linking this idea, that individuality can be realized only in the historical reality, with the prodigious structure of his philosophy of history, thus uniting the principle of creative individuality with the traditional idea of history as a universal process obeying an inherent law of sublime reason and directed toward *one* definite goal.

The importance of these new intellectual impulses on the development of historical thought in Germany can scarcely be overestimated. The new teaching, that the human being becomes aware of himself as an individual as he acts creatively out of a free choice, left a deep impression on the leading minds of that generation. In addition there came the discovery of the immense wealth and unending variety of the diverse national histories which stimulated the romantic *Lebensgefühl* (sense of life) much as the national feeling of the time was inflamed by the Napoleonic wars. But this was not enough to bring history to the rank of an independent, scholarly discipline. For this a new, thorough, and scholarly (scientific) methodology was required.

For this achievement we must first thank the historiographical accomplishment of the two great teachers of modern historical study, Barthold Georg Niebuhr and Leopold von Ranke, and their predecessors in the field of Greek and Roman philology, August Böckh and Friedrich August Wolf, who first developed the so-called philological methods of interpretation of sources. In the preface to his *Geschichte der romanisch-germanischen Völker* of 1824, Ranke professed the principle of writing history, "wie es eigentlich gewesen," and in his treatise *Zur Kritik neuerer Geschichtsschreiber* he harshly judged previous methods of historical writing. These, he said, had resulted in uncritical collections of the narratives of other authors whose works had been quoted again and again without ever being seriously questioned. Strict methodological standards were established, first of all the most extensive utilization of primary sources possible and in particular the documents of the European archives.

Today the methodological principles, which Niebuhr for the first time applied consistently to the field of Roman history and

Ranke to the field of modern European history, have become the common property of the discipline of history, though indeed, through constant refinement, the methods of history now go far beyond those of Ranke. History, of course, has long since forged far beyond into new fields of research, as economic and social history, in which the classic principles of philological criticism have only a secondary significance. In their day, however, joined with the revival of the historical sense through romanticism and German idealistic philosophy, these principles constituted a veritable revolution. Because of them history, at least in essence, became an autonomous scientific discipline.

All of the above factors suddenly combined to give history, previously only an auxiliary discipline, the status of a basic field of knowledge. The process of the reversal of the relationship of history to theology and jurisprudence was partly the result of the general intellectual development from the late eighteenth century, which gave history a privileged position within the intellectual world, and partly the result of a basic reorganization of the German university system in the first decades of the nineteenth century. The first step was taken by Wilhelm von Humboldt, the Prussian Minister of Education, with the reform of the University of Berlin. As is well known, this was undertaken in the years of the military breakdown after 1806 in order to gather the intellectual energies of the German nation to the Prussian state.

Following the proposals of such men as Fichte, Schelling, Schleiermacher, and von Humboldt, the philosophical faculty from this time on would play the leading role in the universities. All of these reformers were firmly convinced that all sciences drew their power from the thought of the autonomous individual who consciously determined his actions on the basis of ideal principles. This brought the final emancipation of history. As one of the basic fields of the philosophical faculty, it could from then on assert a priority, even in relation to theology and jurisprudence. This was possible, it is true, because in the wake of these reforms a new ideal of education prevailed in the German universities. From this time on the universities were committed exclusively to the idea of a pure scholarly method. Accordingly, any divergence of teaching from the strictly scientific search for truth appeared dangerous to idealistic reformers. The university, Humboldt believed, could have a future only if it functioned simultaneously both as a research and as an educational institution. "When one ceases to aim at true scholarship or one imagines it does not have to be brought forth from the depths of the mind but can be attained through simple collection and neat filing, then everything is irretrievably and eternally lost. . . . Only scholarship, which is born within and can be planted within, transforms character. . . ."[1] The idea of the unity of research and teaching gradually found its realization in all of the German universities, as far as they survived the revolutionary times, and finally, in some degree, it conquered the world.

The birth of academic history in the spirit of idealistic philosophy had a lasting effect on the inner development of historical study as well as on its organizational forms. Humboldt's idea of the unity of research and teaching was fulfilled particularly in the form of the seminar—after the traditional lecture course, still the most important form of historical instruction at German universities. The seminar was, as Josef Engel recently said, the precise expression of the new scholarly attitude.[2] The seminar as a unique form of instruction, as a free community of teachers and students combining for scholarly discussion, was by no means reserved to history alone. Originally developed in ancient philology, it became commonly used in the entire philosophical and even in the theological faculties. At the beginning, the seminar was a very esoteric affair. It was open primarily to interested scholars, only secondarily to those who were students. Neither Ranke in Berlin nor Niebuhr in Bonn had a seminar in the proper sense of the word. The first historical seminar possessing an institutional basis was founded in Königsberg in 1832. Yet Ranke's regular disputations, usually held in his home with his own students, became the model for coming generations of academic historians. Today the seminar constitutes the most important form of academic instruction in history. But in view of the quite different relationship in numbers between the teachers and the students, it has lost its original purpose as a purely scholarly community for discussion. It now serves primarily pedagogical purposes, though its discussions still motivate scholarly efforts more than do factual lectures.

The long-range effect of the idealistic scholarly revolution

[1] *"Über die innere und äussere Organization der Höheren Wissenschaftlichen Anstalten in Berlin," Werke,* Akademieausgabe, vol. 10, pp. 280 ff.

[2] *"Die deutschen Universitäten und die Geschichtswissenschaft," Historische Zeitschrift,* vol. 180, 1959. I wish to thank Engel for a large number of ideas in the above account.

can, up to the present, be seen not only in the institution of the seminar but also in the way academic instruction in the discipline had been organized within German universities. The old ties of history with political science *(Staatswissenschaften)* were dissolved, especially those with the older cameralist studies, although in specific cases they would survive institutionally into the 1860's. History thus established itself as an autonomous discipline, separated sharply from the "purpose-directed" utilitarian sciences, such as cameralism or economics, through its own ethos closely related to philosophy. The idealistic goal toward which history then strove—to coordinate all events into one dominant principle—long delayed the division of history into numerous specialized disciplines. This development took place more recently. The traditional division into ancient history, medieval history (from the *Völkerwanderung* until the end of the fifteenth century) and modern history (from the beginning of the Reformation) still determines the organization of history as a discipline at German universities, though recently numerous special chairs, as those for Contemporary History or the History of Eastern Europe and the like, have been established.

The nineteenth century, as has been said, was undeniably the century of history. The *Zeitgeist* regarded history with fascination, as the creation and the destiny of mankind. This fascination, reinforced by the rising nationalism, strongly encouraged the expansion of historical thinking. Historiography hence grew by leaps and bounds in the nineteenth century. The opening up of the medieval world, through the research of such men as Waitz, Böhmer, Pertz and Ficker, and the publication of the medieval sources of German history in the great undertaking of the *Monumenta Germaniae Historica* created milestones on the road of development, just as did the research of Johann Gustav Droysen on the history of Hellenism and somewhat later that of Theodor Mommsen on Roman history. In the field of modern history not only a genuine historical interest but also an awakened national consciousness and a passionate liberal conviction—at least with the north German historians—stimulated historical study. Men such as Dahlmann, Sybel, Gervinus, and Baumgarten belonged to the great generation who laid the foundation of modern history in Germany although they did not always follow Ranke but often criticized him for his conservative views. The founding of the *Historische Zeitschrift* in 1859 as a national forum for scholarly discussion marked an important step in the consolidation of history as a discipline. The public prestige of the *Historische Zeitschrift* was never greater than in the decades just before and just after the founding of the Empire.

Related to this was the new position which history now assumed vis-à-vis its sister disciplines. The old subordinate relationship reversed itself as history invaded the fortresses of jurisprudence, national economy, and theology. The historical study of law, rejuvenated by Savigny, the historical school of national economics of Roscher and Schmoller, the theological works of Semmler, David Friedrich Strauss and Harnack, were all examples of the transfer of historical methods and patterns of thought to neighboring disciplines. On the other hand, the methodological demands on history based on models derived from the natural sciences were vigorously rejected. With the proud self-consciousness of an historian rooted in idealistic philosophy, Droysen rejected the proposals of Comte and Buckle that history be studied with "natural-scientific" or at least with statistical methods. The field of research that gave historiography its particular importance among the other scholarly disciplines was precisely that of the creative action of the individual in history who felt himself committed to ideal values, or as Droysen said, "moral forces." This could never be explained through the detection of historical laws however subtle. The duty of the historian was rather to arrive at understanding through research ("forschend zu verstehen").

German historical study remained loyal to this view well into the twentieth century. For this reason, from the beginning of the 1880's it developed in isolation from the developing social sciences which were committed to the concepts of natural science. The dividing wall between the methods of the natural sciences and those of the humanistic disciplines was cemented by the neo-Kantian philosophy of Windelband and Rickert, who described these basically different methods as ideographic and nomothetic. The ideographic method was to give individualizing descriptions of unique phenomena and developments, while the nomothetic was to generalize and establish general laws. It is also in part ascribable to the influence of the idealistic philosophy that in the nineteenth century, political history, particularly governmental history, occupied a dominant position within the discipline as a whole. For Ranke the states were "realgeistige Ideen," the basic elements of the historical world; and for those historians who followed Fichte and Hegel, the state was the highest form of the ethical configuration of human culture. The nationalism of the time pointed in the same direction, particularly after it had been imbued with Bismarck's principle of "Realpolitik." It is not surprising, therefore, that the conflict which chiefly occurred during the early years of the twentieth century between the dominant group in German history and the Leipzig historian Karl Lamprecht over the application of social scientific and especially social psychological methods in history, was fought under the misleading alternatives of "Kulturgeschichte" or "politische Geschichte." Lamprecht's no doubt methodologically vulnerable attempts to set up a theory of the historical development of the German people as a sequence of typical socio-psychological states of mind involving the national consciousness had no noticeable effect on historical study in the universities. There was only an occasional bridging of the gap to the social sciences, in Ernst Troeltsch's *Soziallehren der christlichen Kirchen,* for example, or Otto Hintze's comparative typology of a European constitutional history, which was strongly influenced by the sociological work of Max Weber.

While German history in the nineteenth century can point to great achievements in the field of economic history (Alphons Dopsch on early medieval history), political history (with its emphasis on the role of leading statesmen) and the history of ideas together comprised the mainstream of German historical thought until recently. The history of the German national state attracted the first interest, of, for example, Georg von Below in medieval history, and, more emphatically, Heinrich von Treitschke and Wilhelm Oncken in modern history. In the writings of Max Lenz and Erich Marcks, Rankean teachings about the "great powers" as the determining factor in historical life experienced a renaissance, and these teachings were transferred to the wider field of world politics. Through the work of Troeltsch about the social teachings of the Christian churches and the famous study of Max Weber, *The Protestant Ethic and the Spirit of Capitalism,* the field of the history of ideas likewise received a new impulse. Troeltsch and Weber showed that religious ideas influenced social developments even more than the prevailing ideas of nationalism and liberalism and at times exerted even more

power on the great historical processes. It was not, they thought, social and economic developments that conditioned ideas; rather, it
was the other way around. Still the main emphasis in the field of
the history of ideas remained on national politics. The history of
the German Reformation, for instance, was interpreted almost without exception by the north German Protestant historians as the first
step in the process of national emancipation. Yet historical writing
oriented toward universal history continued, as the work of Wilhelm
Dilthey shows.

In the course of the second half of the nineteenth century, historiography experienced strong institutional expansion. This expansion was evidenced not only by an enormous increase in the number
of professorships but also by the numerous publications of primary
sources, for example, the Reichstag records of the fourteenth to the
sixteenth centuries, the *Nuntiaturberichte,* the *Jahrbücher für
deutsche Geschichte,* and the *Corpus inscriptorium latinarum.* The
scholarly large-scale enterprises, which began to replace the works of
the great pioneers of the first generation, achieved much but they frequently became choked in routine. Favored by the positivistic currents of the later nineteenth century, German historiography sometimes lost itself in technically perfect, detailed research and fell short
of the idealistic goals of a Ranke or a Droysen, although German historians continued to invoke the name of Ranke, who had written so
many works of general nature in a literary form that was rarely
equalled. Hence some uneasiness arose among far-sighted men over
the apparent relativeness of historical truth, a relativism arising from
a consistent and pervasive application of historical method. Specifically, this was illustrated by Ernst Troeltsch who first spoke of a crisis
in historicism that had to be overcome.

In fact the victorious advance of historicism had aroused critical
opposition much earlier. Among the first to speak was Nietzsche, in
his wordy polemic against the repudiation of contemporary life
through history, the famous "Untimely Observations" concerning the
"Uses and Disadvantages of History for Life." At the time this criticism remained insignificant. Until the First World War, historical
scholarship retained its conviction that it could continue, undis-
turbed, to build on methodological foundations created by Ranke,
Niebuhr, Waitz, Mommsen, and others. Lamprecht's call for new

ways and new methods remained, as already noted, without response and Otto Hintze's researches in comparative constitutional history found few followers.

The defeat of Germany in the First World War and the consequent revolutionary changes in political life plunged German historical study into deep crisis. The assured political and ideological *(weltanschaulich)* values, which had formed the basis for the approaches to historical problems and judgments, were suddenly questioned. In the light of the German and Russian revolutions, the concept of continuity, which had become one of the assumptions of historical thought during the nineteenth century, suddenly seemed unreliable. The public reputation of scholarly history of the universities was undermined by outsiders like Spengler. This, of course, applied especially to modern history.

Monographical research is still lacking on the development of the historiography of the Weimar period, but something can be stated on the basis of present knowledge. As with the educated classes in general, a majority of the German university historians never came to terms with the realities of the new republican era. For the conservative and national liberal historians, that is most of the German professors, the glory of the Bismarckian Reich remained the point of departure for historical judgment, and not the concrete reality of the weak Weimar party state, chained as it was from outside to the Treaty of Versailles. They preferred to interpret this state of things merely as a transitory phase in the evolution of the German nation. Illustrative of this fact was the great increase in Bismarckian research in the 1920's inspired by the feeling of adoration for the great national statesman. The concept of a unique German way, a particularly German organization of the state and society which accepted neither the western principle of democratic parliamentarism nor the eastern principle of the authoritarian state, strongly affected even historians who otherwise held moderate views. Many a historian sought outlet in German national feeling in which emphasis was laid on culture as opposed to politics. This tendency found expression in Gerhard Ritter's biography of Luther in 1925. The leading school of German historical writing in those years, that led by Friedrich Meinecke, tried to rise above the problematical dilemmas of a political historiography determined by contemporary events by turning to a high, "sublime" form of the history of political ideas.

Meinecke's *Idee der Staatsraison* pursued the problem of the power state on a level of greatest abstraction. A few, mostly younger historians such as Veit Valentin, Johannes Ziekursch, or the outsider Erich Eyck, tried to view German history from a democratic standpoint but they had comparatively little influence in the academic world.

The seizure of power by the National Socialists found German historiography, with few exceptions, in a state of relative helplessness.[3] None of the leading German historians of that time was in any way a partisan of National Socialism; definite opponents were far in the majority. But as a consequence of their intellectual traditions the great majority had a strong national and anti-democratic bias. Much like the German middle-class intelligentsia, German historians in general did not have the strength to resist the assault of the new ideology of the "nationale Volksgemeinschaft." In addition there came the "blood-letting" of emigration; a large number of the important historians not only of the old but also of the middle generation left the country to find new chairs of history in foreign countries. Walter Franck, the leader of the newly founded "Reichsinstituts für die Geschichte des neuen Deutschland," did not find it too difficult to force those remaining into passivity and, in increasing measure, into making concessions to the regime. And yet principles of rigorous scholarship were retained even through this epoch of unreason (*Ungeist*) by many, in particular by Friedrich Meinecke and Walter Goetz.

The period after 1945 meant a new beginning. The radical break with the recent past which the catastrophe of 1945 produced in the German historical consciousness proved itself a great opportunity. Comparatively, it allowed unprejudiced, critical stock taking. The monstrousness of the recent past forced an absolutely honest examination of the traditions and opinions of German historiography. Above and beyond that, Germany opened itself in an enlarged measure to outside influences, in particular to west European democratic ideas. The methods and results of the historical research of France, England, and the United States were given more attention than ever before. It is, of course, a tragic chapter in the book of the German national destiny (though one brought about by Germany's guilt) that German history which had just been freed from the pressures of National Socialism almost immediately found itself ex-

[3] See below, pp. 122–123.

posed in "Mitteldeutschland," that part of Germany occupied by the Soviet Union, to a new political *Gleichschaltung.*

In West Germany since the beginning of the 1950's, historical study has made a rapid surge upward, as is shown by the increase in the number of students, by the exceptional though still not large enough increase in the number of professorships, and finally by the annual increase in the number of historical publications. Originally with the aid of the occupational powers and later with that of the political authorities of the revived German state, much was done to achieve critical confrontation with problems of the recent German past. This has been chiefly effective on the institutional level. For predominantly political considerations many special professorships and institutes were established at universities in the field of contemporary history. The same is true of the field of political science; after having led a shadowy existence for a century in German universities, it began a rapid ascent. This is significant for history because the great majority of professorships of political science are at present occupied by historians who are, of course, mainly concerned with contemporary history. The greater measure of cosmopolitanism of German historical research reveals itself in the founding of a series of professorships for American studies. As a result of the world political situation there has also taken place a major development in east European research. At all West German universities today there are special professorships for Eastern European history, most of them in connection with independent research institutes. Research in the history of the Afro-Asian world, however, is still in its primary stages, unless the traditional research fields of Sinology, Japanology, Oriental studies, and Byzantine studies are considered.

The question of how far German historiography has met the challenge posed after 1945 and given a critical accounting to the German people of its most recent past must still, even after twenty years, be considered premature. But it can be said that the emigration of leading historians in the 1930's is still making itself felt and all the more so because those who were forced to leave the country were those who were predominantly progressive and liberal. In few cases has it been possible to persuade them to return. They and their students in the United States or in England have, it is true, entered into the discussion of issues of recent German history with many outstanding works. But in Germany the number of those belonging to the middle generation and who survived the years of the national socialist power without damage to their scholarly reputations is not large. Dominant in that group are the historians who were conservative or moderately conservative. Those who belonged to the large group of "national-liberal" historians, insofar as they did not take the difficult decision to emigrate, found it more difficult to resist the pressures of national-socialist ideology. Those who stood on the political left were always few in the ranks of German historians and, because most of them emigrated, they are thinly represented in Germany today. It is not surprising, therefore, that postwar discussion and revaluation of German history has begun to gather momentum only in the last few years and only after the publication of a great number of detailed monographs and documents established the essential preconditions. It may be said, nevertheless, that the connection of German historical research with the great traditions of the nineteenth century has been, after the nadir of national socialism, again achieved.

II. Professional Training of Historians[4]

A. Preliminary education of history students

To understand the peculiarities of the study of history at German universities, some knowledge of the whole German educational system is necessary. In Germany there is a much closer connection between the high school system and university training than there is, for example, in the United States and Britain. The high schools have long abandoned their exclusive role as preparatory schools for the universities, as was true of the humanistic *Gymnasium* until the twentieth century. Their curricula remain, however, primarily organized to meet the demands of university study. In addition, instruction at universities is based in large measure on what is taught in the high schools. Thus, the universities waive their own entrance examination, demanding from entering students only that they have passed their final examination, traditionally termed the *Abitur*. It is usually a matter of indifference which of the various types of high

4 See below, pp. 95–99.

schools the future student has attended, be it the humanistic Gymnasium which puts an emphasis on ancient languages, the modern language Gymnasium, or the *Realgymnasium* which devotes more attention to the natural sciences. Only in exceptional cases is a supplementary examination necessary, when, for instance, the student cannot show a competence in Latin comparable to the so-called *"Groszes Latinum."*

Attendance at a four-year *Volkschule* (grade school) and, depending on the legal variations in the German states, eight- or nine-year attendance at a high school form the basis for academic study in Germany. In addition, the *Abitur* can be achieved by an adult in night school if he so wishes, but this step is taken by few because of its difficulties. All the above is perhaps well known but it is important to note that the German high schools, unlike those in the United States, subject students to a strict process of selection. Two-thirds of the students fail at some level of this process or leave high school for other reasons. Only about a third of those originally accepted into high school after an entrance examination pass the final examination. Thus, the high school undertakes selection of talent for the university.

Further, the German university requires substantially more from entering students than is true elsewhere. They require, for example, a satisfactory knowledge of at least three foreign languages, Latin, English, and French, with the possibility that Greek or Russian may in individual cases be substituted for one of the two modern languages. Thus, once more, German high schools are still strongly aligned with the requirements of the universities both in curriculum and in basic educational goals.

The rigorously constructed curriculum, nevertheless, offers the student a relatively broad acquaintance with all areas of knowledge. Compared with practices in the United States, the possibility for specialization and for the election of particular areas of work is extraordinarily limited. The student is permitted to choose among the previously mentioned types of schools, the ancient language, the modern language, and the Realgymnasium, but other than that, only very limited specialization is possible and that during the last two years. A long series of attempts have been made under the influence of the North American models to make the traditional rigid educational program provided by German high schools more flexible.

Nevertheless, a future university student usually receives a rather well-rounded education before he is nineteen or twenty years old and enters the university.

In Germany there is not the North American institution of the "college," which exclusively provides undergraduate education and thus forges a link between "school" and graduate education. German universities do not recognize those differences between undergraduates and graduates which are obvious in the United States. Though it is difficult to draw direct comparisons between two systems of education which proceed from such different assumptions, it is likely that the last two years of the German high school have educational objectives similar to the first two undergraduate years at most American universities. There is no formal equivalent in the German university for the last undergraduate years. From the time he enters the university, a German student of history is treated like a first-year graduate student in America, although he has usually not attained the same level of knowledge and on the average is a year younger than the American.

Without the rigorous foundation of knowledge that the average German student brings, or should bring, with him from high school, it would not be possible to give him the freedom of study he is given from the beginning. Compared with the American undergraduate the German student receives a minimum of guidance. He can almost completely organize his study according to his own judgment. No one forces him to listen to a lecture or to attend a certain seminar, to read specified books or regularly write papers. There is at present in Germany, a strong movement under way to effect reform and to demand a rigorous plan of study for the beginning work, but little has been accomplished. It is difficult for German students to plan their courses of studies in the presence of myriads of lecture offerings and classes, and it is even more difficult for foreign students in German universities.

It is important not to judge the German university system on false assumptions. Since Wilhelm von Humboldt, the German university has held fast to the central idea that it is a community of those teaching and those learning, built on the double principle of the freedom of teaching and of learning. For that reason it has energetically resisted an organization of studies comparable to that of high schools. Because of this a student of history will not find a definite program of study telling him exactly what he should study and how he should plan his university years. This has certain disadvantages, but also great advantages, for the student can freely follow his own interests, though he must always face the prospect of the stiff final examination. During his student years he has almost unlimited opportunity to act on his own initiative. If he understands how to best use his freedom, he can work to his greatest advantage. But it is obvious that the German system is aimed at the specialized students, at those students who have decided on a special field of study —in this case, history.

B. *Courses of study for historians and formal requirements for the study of history*[5]

The German student of history may conclude his study in two ways. He may take the so-called "State Examination for Teaching at High Schools" or he may obtain the degree of Doctor of Philosophy. He may, of course, do both. The majority of students who take the "State Examination" take it first and then some go on to take the doctoral examination. This sequence may be reversed since the two examinations are unrelated. To be exact, the "State Examination" is only an examination for admission to preparatory training for a career as a teacher in the high school. It is not, in the strict sense, an academic examination although it is given by professors who test and judge the candidate. Only the Doctor of Philosophy is achieved through an academic examination in the proper sense of these words. The title of Doctor is granted by the faculty on the basis of a scholarly work, completed under the supervision of a professor, and an additional oral examination. Contrary to widely held opinion, the "State Examination" is not a prerequisite.

Recently most universities, as Freiburg, Cologne, and the Free University of Berlin, have introduced the degree of *Magister* which may be taken instead of that of Dr. Phil. The *Magister artium* was a

---

5 This survey is limited to the Federal Republic of Germany. The quite different situation in East Germany is not considered. Those interested should consult Albrecht Grimm, *Das Fach Geschichte in Forschung und Lehre in der Sowjetisch besetzten Zone Deutschland seit 1945*, Bonn and Berlin, 1965, as well as W. Riese, *Geschichtswissenschaft und Parteiauftrag. Zur Situation der Geschichtswissenschaft der Sowjetisch besetzten Zone seit dem 11. Internationalen Historikerkongress in Stockholm*, Bremen, 1966.

familiar figure in the medieval university. The title has survived in England in the form of the Master of Science, or M.S. In Germany, the title of *Magister* has been introduced to counteract the "inflationary" decline in value of the doctorate. It affords an opportunity to complete study with an academic degree much easier to acquire than the doctorate. The required thesis can be done in a much shorter time and it is not to be judged according to the high standards of the doctoral dissertation. The title of *Magister* has not yet won much public esteem and it cannot be known whether it will become popular among students or find a permanent place in the academic world.

As the goal of their studies, a large majority of all students of history wish to achieve the "Qualification for the Teaching Profession," (*"Befähigung für das Lehramt an höheren Schulen,"* as it is called in good bureaucratic German). Educational authorities demand that future *Studienräten* (those with the rank of high school teacher) be qualified to teach in several fields and in specific combinations. Consequently, German history students always study one or more additional fields, for example, history and *Germanistik,* or history, philosophy, and geography, or *Romanistik* (romance languages) and history, or whatever combination can be utilized in high school instruction. The details are of no interest. The fact is important, however, that the German student, unlike the French or English student, can devote only a part, often only a small part, of his work to the study of history.

A German history student's study generally culminates in the passing of the *Staatsexamen,* covering his fields of study. This can be done after eight semesters (the equivalent of four years). As a rule, however, most students now study for ten, eleven, or even more semesters before they venture to take this examination. Only recently have new regulations been introduced which set a limit to such prolongation of study. It is doubtful, however, whether full success can be attained as long as the conditions of study remain more or less the same.

The formal requirement of a rather comprehensive examination does give a certain general framework to the student's studies which are otherwise very loosely regulated. For the field of history, attendance at a series of seminars is required. They are generally the introductory seminars (proseminars) in ancient, medieval, and modern history as well as two seminars in two of these fields. Yet these formal stipulations for the course of the historical study usually have limited meaning. In the course of his four- to five-year study the student takes more seminars than the five specified. It is also important to note that the *Staatsexamen* forces study of some breadth; a satisfactory knowledge of ancient, medieval, and modern history is essential for the passing of this examination. The student is thus not allowed to specialize early in a certain area or on a certain period of time, although specialization is recommended for the concluding work.

Thus the course of studies of the German student of history is determined in great degree by the requirements of the *Staatsexamen*. While an American student gradually earns the number of credits for graduation, a German student must prepare himself for this one examination which will ultimately determine his success or failure. In principle, it is of no importance what he did during his years of study, whether he attended lectures regularly or whether he "cut" them constantly: he must achieve a high level on the test.

This system of study has long been attacked in many quarters. It allows incapable students to begin and carry on university study without restriction, for students never have to pass a serious test during the course of their studies. That some of them ought never to have pursued this kind of study is revealed only by the State Examination taken at the end of many years. At present, German universities are overcrowded. It appears to be all the more reasonable that these students be dropped at an earlier stage of the educational process. For this reason many philosophical faculties have recently decided to introduce a formal *"Zwischenprüfung"* which must be passed at the end of the third or, at any rate, fourth semester. Further study, in particular the admittance to the seminar courses, is to be made dependent on success in this intermediate examination. These new regulations were put into force for the first time for those students who entered universities in 1966, though in some cases for those who entered in 1965. It is not yet certain that this new intermediate examination, a step toward a greater rigidity of university study in the humanities, will work, that is, that it will really sort out the unqualified students. At this time very little can be said about the nature of this new intermediate examination. As far as history is concerned, the examination is to cover the subject matter taught in the preparatory seminars in ancient, medieval, and modern history.

In principle, foreign students must undergo this test just as German students, but certain exceptions will be granted on special request.

At any rate, it is not to be expected that success in this examination will be a necessary prerequisite for doctoral work, the other and advanced form of finishing study in the humanities. The German Dr. Phil. may be said to be roughly equivalent to a doctorate in the humanities at an American university, though American standards may at times be higher. The difficulty of acquiring a German doctorate and its prestige vary considerably, depending upon the university as well as upon the major professor with whom the work is done. The formal requirements for admission to the doctoral examination are minimal. It is expected that the candidate has had a proper academic study of at least eight semesters, the last two of which should be done at the place of the award (*"Promotion"*). As regards the other six semesters, study at foreign universities is counted depending on the circumstances. The decision in all these matters rests with the *Dekan* of the respective faculty, and hence the *Dekanat* (his office) ought to be consulted before study is undertaken. This is true also with regard to the only other formal requirement which may sometimes cause difficulties for Americans: The candidate must show a "satisfactory knowledge" of Latin corresponding to the *"Groszes Latinum."* If ancient history is selected as the doctoral field, a "satisfactory knowledge" of Greek is required also. Otherwise there are no formal barriers for a foreigner who wishes to acquire a German doctoral degree.

To obtain the doctorate, there are, of course, certain other scholarly requirements. The student must find a professor who is willing to supervise his dissertation and finally he must present this dissertation to the faculty. The dissertation is expected to deal with a specific and hitherto unexplored research problem and to constitute an independent scholarly achievement. In addition to the *"Doktorvater,"* two other professors who are chosen by the faculty must judge its qualities. If it is accepted by the faculty, on the basis of their expert judgment, the candidate must pass an oral examination. This consists of a one-hour examination in the field in which he has written the doctoral dissertation and two half-hour examinations in two minor fields. At least one of these two minor fields should have no direct connection with history. This regulation is meant to prevent narrow specialization. The requirements for minor fields are not, however, as rigid as it might seem. At most German universities (with some local differences) the fields which can be taken as minors in a doctoral examination are defined rather liberally. Thus "Prehistory," "Ancient History," "Medieval and Modern History," "East European History," "Historical Auxiliary Sciences," and in other cases "Anglo-American History," "Ibero-American History," and "Contemporary History" are considered independent disciplines which may be chosen either as a major or a minor field in a doctoral examination. Hence a candidate who is going to earn his doctorate in "Medieval and Modern History" (for traditional reasons still a single discipline, although a great degree of specialization is in fact the rule) may choose "Anglo-American History" or "Contemporary History" as a minor. But nevertheless, the rules forbid the election of all fields from history. Thus a historian must always be examined in one non-historical field, in *Germanistik* or *Anglistik,* for instance, or perhaps even in sociology. If a doctorate in "Ancient History" is sought, a minor in *Altphilologie* is obligatory. A combination of two closely related fields is natural in most cases. To be sure, the requirements in the half-hour examination in each of the two minor fields are not nearly as high as those in the major. The requirement of a minor in a non-historical field should not, then, deter anyone from working for the doctorate at a German university.

Publication of the doctoral dissertation is obligatory. The title of Doctor can be assumed only after the dissertation has been printed and a certain number of copies have been deposited with the faculty.

For students beginning study at a German university other facts are important. For history at German universities there is no *numerus clausus,* i.e., there are no limitations regarding registration as a student. Anyone who has a German *Abitur* or has passed an equivalent foreign final examination can matriculate at a German university of his choice without a special examination. Likewise it is possible, without difficulty, to change universities from semester to semester as long as one formally withdraws from the university in time to matriculate in the new place of study. This freedom of movement constitutes one of the great advantages of the German university system, even though the opportunity is used less frequently now than in the past. It affords a student, especially a foreigner, the possibility of hearing different professors and personally becoming acquainted with different historical schools. On the other hand, too frequent transferring is certainly not advisable; a semester is needed to become adjusted to the peculiar conditions of each university and only in the second semester can a student carry on a fruitful course of study.

When a student enters a German university, confusion, if not despair, may be inevitable. In the catalog of lectures (*Vorlesungsverzeichnis*) and on large blackboards he will find a profusion of historical lectures and seminars on widely differing historical subjects but no information on which of these he should attend. If he is lucky he will succeed in finding the Department of History (*Historische Seminar*). Here he also will find notices. In some cases he must buy a seminar card entitling him to the use of the facilities of the seminar, and only then will he find himself in a historical library with work rooms for students. If he is unusually lucky he will be able to latch onto an assistant or sub-assistant who may explain to him a few of the peculiarities of the system and give him a few hints about what he should do, which lectures and proseminars and seminars he would perhaps profit most. This is often not the case as no one is assigned or obligated to concern himself with new arrivals, whether German or foreign, old or new students. With certain exceptions, which will be covered later, there are no rules covering the lectures and seminars a student should attend. The choice is exclusively his own. He may select the lectures and seminars in which he would like to participate according to his own interests and inclinations. Attendance at lectures, other than the formal obligation of the evidence of a *Studienbuch,* is subject to no rules. The student is not even expected to be regularly present. Moreover, he cannot be questioned by the lecturer (*Dozent*), who usually is not sure who is sitting in front of him. On the other hand, the German student cannot ask the *Dozent* questions about the lecture. Traditionally, the lecture should acquaint the student with a special field of study or set of problems and this in the most complete way and in accordance with the newest research. Copious bibliographies give him the chance to explore the problems discussed in the lecture, but there is no requirement that he do so in any particular way. Didactic purposes occupy a subordinate role in the lecture system at the German universities. Whether the student understands how to benefit from the lectures or whether he reacts to the given stimulus for his independent reading is completely up to him.

The situation is different in regard to the seminars (sometimes simply called *Übung*). These are the working groups under the guidance of a professor. Their work is at the very center of history study. Every term a great variety of these is offered, each of them devoted to a special theme, say, "The Outbreak of World War I" or "Machiavelli's *Prince,* Book II." German seminars are comparable to but not exactly like those at the graduate schools of American universities. Students are expected to participate actively. They are usually asked to prepare special papers on specific topics and to present these orally. The other students have a chance to ask questions and raise problems. Sometimes they rather harshly criticize their fellow students' papers. The seminars meet once a week for two hours. While student attendance at lectures is not compulsory, it is required in the seminars and a student who must miss a session is expected to explain his absence.

It is in the seminar, in competition with his fellow students, that a student must prove himself. Here also the student may attract the special attention of a professor who may, later, decide to offer to supervise his doctoral work. It is in the seminar, too, that the student is most likely to meet fellow students with similar scholarly interests. The achievement of the student is usually evaluated at the end of a semester in the form of a seminar certificate; occasionally it is measured by a final examination on the material dealt with in the seminar.

There are different types of seminars. Special introductory courses are called *proseminars.* These provide a general introduction to the discipline, be it ancient, medieval, or modern history. In these proseminars much attention is given to the transmission of the techniques of the historian and to knowledge of the most important sources and bibliographical reference materials. The evidence of successful participation in the proseminar constitutes the prerequisite for admission to a regular seminar in the same field. The seminars are sometimes divided into *Mittelseminare* and *Oberseminare;* in the *Oberseminare,* the requirements are higher. As a rule a student who has passed a proseminar and has an adequate knowledge of the relevant foreign language has free access to all seminars of the same field. In seminars on ancient history, a satisfactory command of Latin and often Greek is expected. Latin is also necessary for most seminars in medieval history, while most professors of modern history expect their students to have an adequate command of French and English. In some cases the student who wishes to take part in a particular seminar must pass a special qualifying test. Beyond the regular seminars, special *Arbeitsgemeinschaften* or colloquia for advanced students are sometimes offered. These are, as a rule, reserved to those students working on their doctoral dissertations or students who have especially qualified themselves in a seminar of a professor, and admittance to them depends on the decision of the respective professors.

Actual practice, of course, always lags somewhat behind formal requirement. A lack of language competence should not frighten anyone away from a seminar, for only in a seminar does learning really go on. Furthermore, if the student aspires to the doctorate, the only way to a dissertation is through the seminar exercises of the professor whom the student would like to have as *Doktorvater*. On the other hand, even the most glittering references would not prevent the German university teacher from asking a student who would like to be a doctoral candidate with him to give a report in his seminar first.

For the German student of history, then, there is a minimum of regulations. Seminar participation alone follows a hierarchical principle, at the beginning the proseminar, at the end the *Oberseminar,* and on occasion the colloquium or the *Arbeitsgemeinschaft* for the advanced student. The student himself must choose suitable lectures and seminars out of the profusion of historical courses, ranging from Prehistory, Ancient History, Byzantine History, Medieval History, Auxiliary Sciences, Modern History, Economic History, Constitutional History to Contemporary History. A student usually does best when he picks the lecture courses and seminars of those professors he finds most interesting, without, of course, neglecting other possibilities.

C. Careers of historians

After their studies, the vast majority of German students plan to become teachers in the public high schools. For acceptance into the two-year preparatory service as *Referendar,* the *Staatsexamen* is sufficient, but the doctorate as a further scholarly qualification is often desired and affords somewhat better chances for advancement. Only a fraction of the teachers who teach history in high schools, of course, have majored in history. Frequently they have studied history only as a minor. But inasmuch as history is obligatory in all classes of high school (although in some states in the upper classes it has been combined with *Gemeinschaftskunde* or social studies, or other forms of political instruction), the teacher of history occupies a position of some importance.

Recently a new opportunity for history students has been opened. After a shorter study of only six semesters they may take the test to become a *Realschule* teacher. The *Realschulen* are a new type of school between the *Volkschule* (first four years) and the high school. The student terminates with the *"Mittleren Reife,"* at about the age of 16. At the moment, the *Realschulen* are rapidly developing in Germany, especially in the rural areas. Many students now prefer to use this opportunity for quick entry to a well-paid official position. Strictly considered, however, the *Realschule* teacher is not regarded as a member of an academic profession. This is also true of the *Volkschule* teacher, whose training is taken at special pedagogical colleges (*Hochschulen*). Although the pedagogical colleges in some states, as in Hamburg, Hesse, and Bavaria, are attached to the universities, they differ considerably from the universities in instructional goals and methods. While the pedagogical colleges also have history departments and history professorships, special study of history is rarely possible. This is true for several reasons, among them the fact that the *Volkschule* teacher is, unfortunately, not trained as specialist. Instead, at least theoretically, he is asked to know all subjects taught in the several grades. Occasionally a *Volkschule* teacher may be a scholarly historian but this is due entirely to his personal effort. In principle there remains the old sharp differentiation between the *Volkschule* teacher, who has to be "jack of all trades," and the teachers in high schools, who are proud of their scholarly training.

There are, in addition, other careers open to historians though, unfortunately, no statistical information is available about them. There is, for example, opportunity for historians to become scholarly archivists in one of the many archival establishments of the country.[6] For this the prerequisite is a grade of "good" on the *Staatsexamen*

6 See below, pp. 116–120.

and a doctoral examination with *cum laude*.[7] After a two-year attendance at the Archival school in Marburg an der Lahn, which has thorough, specialized training, the historian may obtain a well-paid position as *Staatarchivrat*. The chances of advancement, however, are very limited. Another career often followed by historians is that of scholarly librarian at one of the many university or public libraries. For this, also, there is the general requirement of the *Staatsexamen* and the doctorate. This position, achieved after a two-year *Referendar* training, is not uninteresting. Not infrequently the librarian (*Bibliothekrat*), as an official expert in history, decides on the acquisition of historical literature for a large library. For this a broad and bibliographic knowledge of history is indispensable. A further opportunity for the historian is to enter the full academic career, although this is naturally reserved for an elite group.

Unlike the case in England or the United States, the doctorate in Germany as such does not open the way for a university career, although it is a necessary prerequisite for it. In order to become a member of the teaching staff a historian must submit an "habilitation" thesis to a philosophic faculty. This is expected to be an original scholarly work of a comprehensive nature. The faculty may then, if it considers the candidate to be sufficiently qualified, accept him as a new member. He must, however, also give a lecture before the whole faculty. This, a remnant of the ancient "disputation," has deteriorated into a rather formal affair. But then, and only then, is the candidate entitled to give lectures and seminars. Traditionally he is called a *Privatdozent,* roughly the position of an American assistant or associate professor. If he succeeds in becoming known in his field through his publications, another faculty of another university may then decide to offer him a chair, either as *"Ordinarius,"* which is on top of the scale and is equivalent to a full professorship at American universities, or as *"Extraordinarius,"* which may be compared to an associate professorship in the United States. In both cases he is now entitled to be called professor. The road from the doctorate through the "habilitation" or "inauguration" to a *Dozentur* and finally to a professorship is still long and difficult, although the eventual success now depends less on chance than it did at the time of Max Weber (see his famous essay *"Wissenschaft als Beruf"*).

---

[7] Requirements have been somewhat relaxed. In some cases the doctorate is no longer required, in others it is.

There are, however, lower academic positions whose importance within the framework of the German universities is growing. With the ever-increasing stream of students to the universities, the teaching staff has been enlarged especially in the lower ranks, and the responsibilities of the latter have been increased. The research assistants should be mentioned first. They still are, as a rule, affiliated with a particular professor and assist him in teaching as well as in research. But while traditionally they were free from actual teaching, nowadays in increasing degree they teach introductory classes, proseminars, and the like. An assistantship nonetheless remains the usual transitory position on the road to the habilitation. In addition, the urgent need for instruction on the lower levels had led in the last years to the creation of wholly new teaching positions within the so-called Mittelbau, the position of "Studienrat im Hochschuldienst" and the position of "Akademischer Rat." The former are high school teachers employed at the universities for academic instruction on the lower levels, the latter are actually lecturers who need not have passed the habilitation barrier, and who concentrate on teaching only. Both these positions are of a permanent nature, but neither the "Studienräte im Hochschuldienst" nor the "Akademischen Räte" are expected to write an habilitation thesis and become full professors, although they may do so in special cases.

The fifty-two pedagogical colleges (*Hochschulen*) of the Federal Republic also employ trained historians for their professorships in history. And other historians may become research workers in one of the numerous historical research institutes.

Finally, there are the careers outside of the public educational system for which historians are frequently preferred, particularly those trained in modern history. Among the journalists of the daily and weekly newspapers, the magazines and the mass media, one often encounters historians with specialized academic training. This is true also of the editors of the publishing houses or in the leading positions of community schools of adult education. Numerous institutions dedicated to political education and public relations require the cooperation of historians. The list could be expanded, but it is clear that professionally trained historians find varied career opportunities even in positions which are not specifically of an historical nature. As in every other highly developed social system, so in Germany, professionally trained historians have numerous special tasks.

In spite of competition from sociologists and political scientists, historians still constitute an important element of the political, social, and cultural life of the German Federal Republic.

III. Resources of the Historian

A. Bibliographic sources for German history

This is not an exhaustive survey. Rather it is but a brief introduction to those important bibliographical tools which might be helpful to non-German students of German history. Those bibliographies, works, and other aids mentioned below are generally available in seminar libraries. The great bibliography of Dahlmann and Waitz (*Quellenkunde zur deutschen Geschichte,* 9th ed., 1931) dates from the pioneering period of German historiography. Up to 1931 it was constantly reedited and despite many deficiencies it remains a standard reference. It includes all the sources and literature on the history of Germany and Austria-Hungary from the early Middle Ages to 1919. Though it is now considerably out of date it will remain indispensable until the revised edition, now being prepared by the *Max-Planck Institut für Geschichte* in Göttingen, is completed. Dahlman-Waitz may be supplemented by the slender selected bibliography of Günther Franz, *Bücherkunde zur deutschen Geschichte,* Munich, 1951, which lists works to 1933, as well as by von Werner Trillmich, *Kleine Bücherkunde zur Geschichtswissenschaft,* Heidelberg, 1949. In addition there are the comprehensive bibliographies in the *Jahresberichte zur deutschen Geschichte* which go back to 1878 and have appeared annually in a new series since 1952. These list all sources and writings as well as the bibliographical and reference literature. The listings always lag behind eight or nine years, and now reach volume 9/10, 1957/58.

Recent German history, happily, is better provided for. Here there is the exemplary *Bibliographie zur Zeitgeschichte,* published since 1953 by the *Institut für Zeitgeschichte* in Munich as a supplement to the *Vierteljahreshefte für Zeitgeschichte.* In addition, there is the *Jahresbibliographie der Bibliothek für Zeitgeschichte,* appearing since 1960 through the *Weltkriegs-Bücherei* in Stuttgart. Of great value to historians interested in contemporary history, though prepared for political scientists, is the *Literaturverzeichnis der Politi-*

schen Wissenschaften, published yearly since 1952 by the *Hochschule für Politische Wissenschaften* in Munich.

For early and late medieval German history there is the exemplary survey of all preserved written sources in Wilhelm Wattenbach's work, *Deutschlands Geschichtsquellen im Mittelalter bis zur Mitte des 13. Jahrhunderts.* For this bibliography there are new editions of large sections: *Vorzeit und Karolinger,* revised by W. Levison and H. Löwe, 1952–1957, *Die Rechtsquellen,* revised by R. Buchner, 1953, as well as the *Deutsche Kaiserzeit, 900–1215* of R. Holtzmann, 2nd edition, 1948. Although these critical surveys have considerable gaps, they have exceptional value for students of medieval history. The attempt to create a similar work for more recent German history has unfortunately bogged down. We still have only the extraordinary survey prepared by Franz Schnabel on the period of the Reformation: *Deutschlands geschichtliche Quellen und Darstellungen in der Neuzeit,* Part 1, *Das Zeitalter der Reformation 1500–1550,* Leipzig and Berlin, 1931. For later periods there is nothing comparable. There is, unfortunately, no survey of the immense and ever-increasing number of publications of official files or documents of modern and recent German history, such as the important and well-known *Die grosse Politik der europäischen Kabinette, 1871–1914* (40 volumes). An international group of editors is now working on the publication of the German foreign policy documents of the Weimar and National Socialist periods. The Bundesarchiv in Koblenz is working on a publication of the Cabinet minutes and the most important documents on internal policy of the Weimar period. For research students there are, in addition, a constantly increasing number of special bibliographies, directed to special themes, to important historical figures, or to certain areas. These can be easily located in the above bibliographies.

The general handbooks for German and European history afford ample information on recent work. They almost always contain bibliographies essential for an introduction to basic research problems. There are not, however, too many of them. Bruno Gebhardt's *Handbuch der deutschen Geschichte,* 4 volumes, 8th edition, 1954–1960, is indispensable because of its references to literature. Furthermore, there are *Deutsche Geschichte im Überblick,* published by Peter Rassow, 1953; *Handbuch der deutschen Geschichte,* published by Brandt, Meyer, and Just, 4 volumes, 1955 ff.; and for the entire

European development the four-volume work edited by Gerhard Ritter, *Geschichte der Neuzeit* (Erich Hassinger on 1300–1600, Walter Hubatsch on 1600–1789, and Hans Herzfeld on 1789–1914 and 1914–1945), as well as the *Handbuch der Europäischen Geschichte,* Stuttgart, 1967 ff., of which vol. 6, ed. by Th. Schieder, has been published.

A student may also wish to refer to Hermann Bengtson, *Einführung in die alte Geschichte,* 3rd edition, Munich, 1959; Heinz Quirin, *Einführung in das Studium der mitteralterlichen Geschichte,* 2nd edition, Braunschweig, 1961; A. von Brandt, *Werkzeug des Historikers, Eine Einführung in die historischen Hilfswissenschaften,* Urban-Bücher, Volume 33, 2nd edition, Stuttgart, 1958; Paul Kirn, *Einführung in die Geschichtswissenschaft,* Sammlung Göschen, Volume 270, Berlin, 1963; and the quite practical volume, *Geschichte* of the Fischer-Lexikon, edited by Waldemar Besson, 3rd edition, Frankfurt, 1965.

Beyond the well-known *Konversationslexika* of Brockhaus, Meyer and Herder are two special lexicons which, for historians, have only limited usefulness: Roessler-Franz, *Sachwörterbuch zur deutschen Geschichte,* 1958; and Bayer, *Wörterbuch zur Geschichte. Begriffe und Fachausdrücke,* Kröner-Ausgabe, Stuttgart, 1960. But there are numerous biographical lexicons, particularly the monumental lexicon of 56 volumes, *Allgemeine Deutsche Biographie,* which contains several hundred short biographies of famous Germans from 1875 to 1912. This has been supplemented for more recent years by the five-volume work, *Die Grossen Deutschen: Deutsche Biographie,* 1956–1957. A revision of the *Allgemeine Deutsche Biographie* has been in progress since 1953, and only six volumes have appeared so far. Finally, there should be mentioned the four volumes of *Geschichte in Gestalten,* Fischer-Lexikon, Frankfurt, 1963, which contains short but handy biographies of important statesmen and other personalities in world history.

Of importance to the historian are also the several series of special lexicons which usually consider recent research. For the ancient historian there is the *Realenzyklopädie der klassischen Altertumswissenschaft* published by A. Pauly and G. Wissowa; begun in 1893, it is still a rich source of information. There is also the *Reallexicon für Antike und Christentum;* in progress since 1950, it now has five volumes. The medieval historian can draw with profit upon the *Lexikon für Theologie und Kirche,* which has appeared since 1957 in two editions, and the reference work *Religion in Geschichte und Gegenwart,* of which a second edition has recently appeared. Even the modern historian can find useful information in these lexicons since they deal with the entire domain of social life and do not limit themselves to theological or religious questions. The historian of modern times may also consult with great profit the *Staatslexikon,* which has a Catholic-Universalist orientation, the *Handwörterbuch der Sozialwissenschaften,* appearing since 1956, and Strupp-Schlochauer, *Wörterbuch des Volkerrechts,* 3 volumes, and index, 1960–1962.

B. German historical journals

The historical journals constitute the forum of discussion of the study of history. The student who attentively follows the historical journals can keep up with the changing views and research in the discipline. From the dialectical confrontations of opinions emerge the possible new interpretations and new theses. The value of the journals in the search for truth can scarcely be exaggerated. They provide information on the newest literature and the newest research in certain fields of history. The book reviews and bibliographic reports not only provide valuable knowledge of new works, they also guide the student through the mazes of new literature.

Specialization in historical study has brought both considerable multiplication of and strong specialization in historical journals. The American volume of 1961, *Historical Periodicals: An Annotated World List of Historical and Related Serial Publications,* lists not less than 383 German-language historical journals. In the following survey, only those journals of decisive importance for the course of historical research are mentioned; because of space limitations, little attention is given to the large number of journals dealing with regional and local history, though their value for research, particularly in European medieval history, can hardly be overestimated.

The leading journal of German history is, of course, the *Historische Zeitschrift,* founded by Heinrich v. Sybel in 1859. This has remained, in large degree, the official spokesman for German historical writing. In line with its universalist orientation, an inheritance of the great epoch of the German historical thought of the late nineteenth century, it publishes articles of leading researchers in all historical fields. Foreign scholars increasingly publish in it. Its large book review section provides a periodic survey of new historical literature on general as well as German history. Recently the editors began to publish book reviews of new literature in non-German history in a special supplement in order to decrease the pressure on the already large book review section. The *Historische Zeitschrift* dedicates itself primarily to political history, but it does give attention to intellectual history and historical methodology. In recent years the *Historische Zeitschrift* has published trail-blazing articles, as those from Fritz Fischer, Gerhard Ritter, Egmond Zechlin, and Hans Herzfeld on the history of the First World War, and recently that of Gerhard Lipgens on Bismarck and the question of Alsace-Lorraine.

The journal *Saeculum: Jahrbuch für Universalgeschichte,* first published in 1950, has a completely different goal. It is primarily concerned with intellectual and cultural history and aspires to serve as a forum for a comparative universal history. The journal *Geschichte in Wissenschaft und Unterricht,* published since 1950, is directed, as its title indicates, to the teaching of history. It devotes most of its space to the pedagogical aspects of instruction, but it also attempts to give high school teachers information about recent developments in research and it contains highly informative articles on historical literature.

Other journals specialize in certain periods. For ancient history, there is *Klio: Beiträge zur alten Geschichte,* published since 1903, and the more recent journal, *Historia: Zeitschrift für alte Geschichte,* founded in 1950. The leading journal of German medieval history is the *Deutsches Archiv für Erforschung des Mittelalters,* the successor to the *Neues Archiv der Gesellschaft für ältere deutsche Geschichtskunde,* founded in 1876. This was published by the *Monumenta Germaniae Historica* and at its beginning served exclusively as an organ of discussion for the critical methodological problems that arose out of the editorial work of the *Monumenta.* Today it presents German medieval research in general. For medieval history, there is also the *Mitteilungen des österreichischen Instituts für Geschichtsforschung,* which began in 1880, though they are not, of course, devoted solely to German history. Special questions of research on medieval charters are the concern of the *Archiv für Diplomatik,* founded in 1955, as the successor to the *Archiv für Urkundenforschung.* Legal historical studies appear in the famous *Zeitschrift der Savigny-Stiftung für Rechtsgeschichte* which appears in three sections, a German, a Roman, and a canonical. The *Historische Jahrbuch der Goerres-Gesellschaft,* in existence since 1890, provides an outlet primarily for historians with a catholic-universalist orientation. Finally, there should be mentioned the *Blätter für deutsche Landesgeschichte,* published since 1936. The journal has particular importance for medieval research as it publishes regular surveys of studies in regional and local history, studies which otherwise would be almost buried in the profusion of regional and local historical journals. The center of gravity of modern research of the Middle Ages is indeed in local history, for detailed regional studies frequently supply information which challenges traditional assumptions about medieval history in general.

Social and economic history, though of a constantly increasing importance, is served by only one journal in Federal Germany, the *Vierteljahrschrift für Wirtschaft und Sozialgeschichte,* published since 1903. An important role for recent history is played by the *Vierteljahrshefte für Zeitgeschichte,* which devotes itself particularly to the background and history of National Socialism but which also, since 1958, considers non-German subjects such as Italian fascism or the *Action Française.* The *Vierteljahrshefte für Zeitgeschichte* also contains documents on contemporary history and thus makes available scattered source material. It also includes a comprehensive, continuing bibliography on contemporary history.

This summary may end with the mention of two historical journals limited exclusively to reviews of historical publications, *Das Historisch-Politische Buch,* published since 1953 by the Ranke-Gesellschaft in Göttingen, and the journal *Neue Politische Literatur,* published since 1956. The critical surveys of new historical books appearing in the latter give reliable information on new developments in historical research. Both journals, however, are restricted to modern and contemporary history.

IV. Teaching and Research Institutions

A. History seminars and institutes at universities and technical colleges

In the Federal Republic, full academic study of history is now offered at twenty-one universities. These are the Free University of

Berlin, the Universities of Bonn, Erlangen, Frankfurt, Freiburg, Giessen, Göttingen, Hamburg, Heidelberg, Kiel, Cologne, Mainz, Mannheim, Marburg, Munich, Münster, Regensburg, Saarbrücken, Würzburg, as well as the newly founded University of Bochum, whose philosophical faculty began instruction in the summer of 1965. To these is now added the University of Constance and there will be the Universities of Düsseldorf, Bielefeld, and Bremen which are now in the planning stage. History can also be studied at the technical colleges (*Technische Hochschule*), although lectures and seminars at these institutions are meager. At the Technical College at Aachen, however, there has been recently established a philosophical faculty which provides for full study. At the Technical University of Berlin, the Technical Colleges of Braunschweig, Darmstadt, Hanover, Karlsruhe, and Stuttgart there are also professorships of history.

A foreign student might ask about differences of quality in German universities. Beyond a doubt, great differences do exist in historical study, but it is impossible to establish definite rankings. In history, the Universities of Berlin, Göttingen, Freiburg, Heidelberg, Tübingen, Bonn, and Munich traditionally enjoy particular prestige, but prestige does not always accord with fact. There are not in Germany, as is the case in England, France, and the United States, great differences in quality among the various universities, for all German universities are public, and, in addition, qualitative differences in the faculties are constantly changing. Lively competition among the German universities and the frequent shifting of professors keep the situation fluid. In Germany one asks first not about the university at which one has studied but about the professor with whom one has studied. The student does not call himself a graduate, for example, of the University of Heidelberg in the sense that in the United States he calls himself a graduate of Harvard, but instead describes himself, if at all, as a student of the famous Professor X. A foreign student should, therefore, be guided in his selection of place of study by consideration of where the best history department exists and where the best specialists teach in the particular fields in which he is interested. The lecture catalogues of the German universities, which can be obtained from the universities' secretariats three months before the beginning of a new semester, generally provide reliable information.

In all universities and in the majority of technical colleges, there are special departments of history and other institutes for every major field of history. These constitute the actual centers of history instruction. Conditions differ, naturally, at the various universities and there is no uniform plan for the various specialties. At all institutions, however, there is a general trend toward specialization both in teaching and in research. It should be noted that the field of prehistory always has its own department and that ancient history is usually combined not with other history but with classical philology. In Berlin, Bonn, Kiel, Cologne, and Münster, for instance, the student will find only institutes for Ancient Studies, which have a special section devoted to Ancient History. In contrast, the fields of Medieval and Modern History are usually united in a common historical department or seminar. Yet even in these fields of history specialization has made inroads. In some cases the history departments have added special sections, e.g., "Contemporary History," "Economic and Social History," "Regional and Local History," "Latin-American History," and "Anglo-American History." In other cases these special disciplines have independent departments or institutes outside of "General History." Eastern European History at almost all German universities has its independent departments which keep little contact with the discipline as a whole. But boundaries often change and in individual cases it is not so much the organizational form as the person of the leader of the institute and his specialized interests that determine the degree of cooperation with the other historical groups.

Historical departments had their origin in the desire to create institutional support for the principle of unity in research and teaching. Today the historical seminars and institutes are always both teaching and research institutions. They have their own libraries which serve both teaching and research purposes. In almost all cases these are open to the student for his unrestricted use. As in many libraries in the United States, a student can go to the bookshelves and select the books he wants. As seminar libraries are always arranged according to subject matter, they permit a quick survey of the available literature on a specific subject. The user has also an author catalogue available, although rarely a subject catalogue. A student accustomed to American university libraries may be disappointed, for libraries are not as easy to use in Germany as they are in the United States. Cataloguing is based on the principles of the Prussian library regulations. Series and periodicals, in so far as there is no separate catalogue, are to be sought in the general catalogue on the following principles: First noun, first adjective, second noun, second adjective. *Deutsches Archiv zur Erforschung des Mittelalters* will be found under the heading: *"Archiv, deutsches, Mittelalter,"* while the *Zeitschrift für die gesamte Staatswissenschaft* is to be sought under *"Zeitschrift, Staatswissenschaft, gesamte."*

In the seminars and institutes there are work areas available to students. The pertinent handbooks, bibliographical guides, references, and journals are usually found there. Beyond these the student can usually obtain advice and information from assistants. Historical seminars serve, as has been noted, not only teaching but research as well. The progressive development of historical studies on the one hand and the sharp increase of students on the other have often led, as in the United States, to tensions between the two basic aims of the seminars. In general, therefore, the tendency is to attach seminars to history departments or institutes of research, or to establish such institutes independent of the seminars and to provide them with their own research libraries, on the model of the English institutes for advanced studies. But this development is still in its infancy.

B. Historical research institutes

The oldest and most honored historical research institute in Germany is the *Monumenta Germaniae Historica, Deutsches Institut für die Erforschung des Mittelalters,* in Munich. It emerged out of the *Gesellschaft für Deutschlands ältere Geschichtskunde,* founded by the Baron vom Stein, and assumes the responsibility for the great editing program of the German medieval source materials bearing the same title. It continues to be one of the most significant centers for German medieval research. The *Max-Planck Institut für Geschichte* in Göttingen dedicates itself to supra-regional research. Among other works it is preparing, as mentioned above, a new edition of the Dahlmann-Waitz, *Quellenkunde zur deutschen Geschichte.* It is also concerned with the publication of the *Monumenta Sacra,* the great collection of medieval church and monastic charters. Furthermore, it engages in comparative studies in general European history, as, for example, the class structure *(Ständewesen)* in the time of Absolutism.

Of major significance is the *Institut für Zeitgeschichte* in Munich.

It devotes itself to research on National Socialism and, for its comprehensive archive created by Thilo Vogelsang, it gathers sources and literature on contemporary history. For contemporary history it issues the *Vierteljahresheft für Zeitgeschichte* as well as the *Schriftenreihe zur Zeitgeschichte.* While students, as a rule, cannot work in the *Institut für Zeitgeschichte,* they can obtain information from it. The *Forschungsinstitut für Sozialgeschichte* in Heidelberg devotes itself to the great subject of modern German and European social history in which there are many unexplored subjects. Through regular symposia on theses of German social history it endeavors to acquaint wider circles of German historical science with social historical questions. The research department of the historical seminar of the University of Cologne has assumed the special task of research on the history of European national states and endeavors for this purpose to develop a comparative, typological, analytical method.

Of special significance for questions of modern German party history and the history of German parliamentarism is the *Kommission für Geschichte des Parlamentarismus und der politischen Parteien* in Bonn. In addition to numerous carefully annotated publications of sources, particularly the model *Edition of the Minutes of the Interparty Committee of 1917–1918,* it is preparing an election atlas for Germany. The *Johann-Gottfried-Herder Institut* in Marburg specializes in regional studies (*Geschichtliche Landeskunde*) and the social and economic developments of East Central Europe. It publishes among other works the *Zeitschrift für Ostforschung.* The *Osteuropa-Institut* in Munich devotes itself especially to questions of modern Russian history. The *Institut für Osteuropaische Geschichte* at the University of Tübingen, which functions as a research institute, also publishes the *Handbücher zur Geschichte Osteuropas.* These handbooks, organized along national lines, must be considered as standard textbooks on East European history. The *Bundesinstitut zur Erforschung des Marxismus-Leninismus* in Cologne concerns itself particularly with the development of the communist system and communist ideology. It is supported by the Federal Ministry of Interior.

The objective of the *Institut für Europäische Geschichte* in Mainz, with its departments for *Universalgeschichte* and *Abendlandischen Religionsgeschichte,* is less specific. It provides opportunity for independent research for not only a large number of scholars from the various Western countries but also from the Eastern. In addition, it has its own series of publications.

Large themes of war and military history are the specialty of the *Forschungsstelle für Militärgeschichte* in Freiburg. Under the Federal Ministry of Defense, this research agency primarily serves military needs, but it also constitutes an important center for research in the military history of the First and Second World Wars.

The list of institutes devoted to special research could be expanded almost indefinitely. Worth mention in this short listing are the *Franz-Dölger-Institut zur Erforschung des Spätantike* in Bonn and the *Thomas-Institut* in Cologne, which concerns itself primarily with medieval scholasticism. A significant foreign base for German history is the *Deutsches Historische Institut* in Rome. It has emphasized research on German-Italian relations, particularly in the medieval period. A similar function for French history is performed by the *Institut Historique Allemand* in Paris. This list, however, cannot be exhaustive.

C. *Historical commissions, societies, and associations*

A nearly infinite number of historic commissions and associations support historical research, partly with private and partly with public funds. A large number of local and regional historical societies assist historical research and not infrequently publish their own journals. Germany is covered by a network of such historical societies which usually are concerned with a formerly independent territory or Prussian province. They have divided up the German territories carefully among themselves and consider themselves responsible for historical research in the history of their limited realms. Usually these historical societies were created at the time of the awakening historical consciousness in the early nineteenth century. Although they frequently receive some support from city, county, or state authorities, they still depend largely upon the unremunerated service of private individuals. In many cases they actively cooperate with the state historical institutes or with departments for regional and local history at the universities and related archival institutions. Among these societies there is an extraordinary measure of interwoven personal relationships and inevitably their spheres of interest overlap numerous local and state institutes. This fact makes it impossible to draw a precise picture of their work. Among the most important are the *Hansische Geschichtsverein,* devoted to the history of the Hansa towns of Hamburg, Bremen, and Lübeck, the *Gesellschaft für Rheinische Geschichtskunde* in Bonn, the *Historische Verein für den Niederrhein, besonders für das Erzbistum Köln* in Düsseldorf, the *Gesellschaft für Schleswig-Holsteinische Geschichte* in Kiel, the *Württembergischen Geschichts-und Altertumsverein* in Stuttgart, and the *Historischen Verein der Pfalz* in Ludwigsburg. German historical societies united in 1852 to form the *Gesamtverband deutscher Geschichts-und Altertumsvereine.* With its headquarters in Wiesbaden, it publishes the *Blätter für deutsche Landesgeschichte.* Every two years they report on the research of regional historical societies and institutes supported by state authorities.

Originally, local feeling and patriotism motivated the founding of local societies. Since the 1940's the significance of local and regional historical investigation, not only in the area of medieval but also in modern history, has constantly increased. In spite of the useful work of these societies, public institutions with their greater financial support now do a larger share of the work.

The historical commissions supported by the various federal states for the study of regional history also play an important role, the *Historische Kommission für Hessen und Waldeck* or the *Kommission für geschichtliche Landeskunde* in Baden-Württemberg, for example. They chiefly devote themselves to the editing of local historical sources for the medieval and modern history of their territories and engage in many regional historical research projects. In addition, there are public research institutes for historical area studies, for instance, the *Institut für westfalische Landes- und Volkskunde* in Münster or the *Landesamt für geschichtliche Landeskunde* in Marburg. All of these have united in an organization providing for the coordination and the definition of research plans, the *Arbeitsgemeinschaft der Historischen Kommissionen und landesgeschichtlichen Institute* in Wiesbaden.

A few of the many commissions and societies tower above others because of their supra-regional importance. Most important is the *Historische Kommission zu Berlin* at the Friedrich Meinecke Institute of the Free University of Berlin. It publishes its own series of papers, the *Veröffentlichungen der Historischen Kommission zu Berlin beim Friedrich-Meinecke-Institut der Freien Universitat Ber-*

lin (19 volumes published). These publications are concerned with questions of general history, and in particular with the history of the German study of history. The *Johann-Gottfried-Herder-Forschungsrat* in Marburg is engaged in research on the history of East Central Europe.

Special mention must be made of the historical commissions of the four scientific academies surviving in the Federal Republic, the *Akademie der Wissenschaften zu Göttingen,* the *Bayrische Akademie der Wissenschaften* in Munich, the *Heidelberger Akademie der Wissenschaften* in Heidelberg, and the *Akademie der Wissenschaften und der Literatur* in Mainz. Each of these academies has created a number of commissions to support and finance research projects in history. By far the most important and most honored of these commissions is the *Historische Kommission,* founded in 1858 by Leopold von Ranke at the *Bayrische Akademie der Wissenschaften.* It can look back on great editorial achievements, for example, the publication of the German *Reichtagsakten* of the fifteenth and sixteenth centuries and the *Jahrbücher für deutsche Geschichte,* the *Allgemeine Deutsche Biographie* and its successor the *Neue Deutsche Biographie,* as well as the 43 volumes of *Deutsche Geschichtsquellen des 19. und des 20. Jahrhunderts.* At the *Bayrische Akademie der Wissenschaften,* other commissions are concerned with various areas of historical research. Among those worth mention are the *Kommission für Sozial- und Wirtschaftsgeschichte* (the only one of its kind in Germany) as well as the *Kommission für bayrische Landesgeschichte.*

Each of the other scientific academies have commissions for specialized historical editing: at Göttingen, for example, the collection of the inscriptions of the German Middle Ages and the publication of the older papal documents, and at Heidelberg, the publication of the collected writings of Nicolas of Cusa. A cooperative commission of the four academies is working on a scholarly edition of the writings of the Church Fathers. The *Akademie der Wissenschaften und der Literatur* in Mainz has a commission for Ancient History and for Medieval and Modern History which has in recent years published many important historical sources.

Since 1945 in the Federal Republic of Germany historical study has experienced strong institutional support and many research institutes have been founded. At the present there may be too many research institutes and commissions and too few scholars. Further development of historical study in Germany will depend primarily on the new generation of historians.

V. German Archival Establishments and Scholarly Libraries

The present disastrous condition of German archives mirrors the unhappy historical evolution of Germany since 1933. Perhaps the only happy note is that German archival materials, up to 1945, are in principle open to any user, while in England, France, and Italy they remain closed after much earlier dates. Nowhere, on the other hand, did the war tear such disastrous gaps in archival holdings as in Germany and the post-war division of Germany has been calamitous for those who wish to use official documents.

The files of the central government of the former German Reich and of Prussia are in the hands of the East German government. The holdings of the former state archives are, with a few exceptions, in the *Deutsches Zentralarchiv I* in Potsdam. This is also true of the papers of the economic policy and the press departments of the Foreign Office. The holdings of the Prussian *Geheimes Staatarchiv* are in the *Deutsches Zentralarchiv II* in Merseburg; these contain not only the papers of the Prussian central authorities, but numerous residua of prominent personalities. All of these are open to the western user only with difficulty. The scholar must have a special user's permit from the state administration of the archives of the Ministry of Interior of the German Democratic Republic. The chances of receiving such a permit change with the political situation. The same is true of the regional and public archives of the territories of the GDR. The files concerning the territories on the other side of the Oder-Neisse have been partly handed over to the Polish authorities, even though they once belonged to the central German archives. They are being prepared for scholarly use but little is known about the terms for their use.

By far the larger and at the same time the least explored part of the papers of the central Prussian authorities and the former German Reich are, hence, open to West German historians with great difficulty and at times not at all. This is especially true for papers of particular political importance; some of these are preserved at the *Institut für die Geschichte des Marxismus-Leninismus* and are thus not open to general usage. Only the holdings of the Foreign Office, with exceptions noted above, are in the Federal Republic. After they had been confiscated by the victors in 1945, brought to Whaddon Hall in England, and there for the most part filmed, they have been returned to the *Politisches Archiv des Auswärtigen Amtes* of the Federal Republic in Bonn with the stipulation that every one have free access to them. Microfilms of these documents are to be found in the Public Record office in London and in the National Archives of the United States in Alexandria, Virginia. Copies of these films, of course, can be purchased.

Of the files of the political authorities of the German Reich and Prussia relatively few were destroyed in the war or burned on orders from the National Socialists during the last days of the war. Even so, there are serious gaps for the National Socialist period and the greatest part of the former *Heeresarchiv* in Berlin was burned. The same is true of a great number of private papers which were in the possession of the *Reichsarchiv* or in private hands. In the Federal Republic the *Bundesarchiv* in Coblenz, the authorized federal archive, has taken over the functions of the former *Reichsarchiv*. That portion of the papers of the former *Reichsarchiv* or the papers which in 1945 were still in the record offices of the central authorities of the German Reich and which have survived in the Federal Republic have been assembled in Coblenz, for example, the papers of the Weimar period (with the exception of those of the Foreign Office in Bonn) and the *Reichspräsidialamt* which is in Potsdam. Some holdings of the former Prussian *Geheimes Staatsarchiv* came into the possession of the *Bundesarchiv,* e.g., the papers of the Prussian Ministry of Justice until 1934. The small remnant of the Prussian *Geheimes Staatsarchiv,* which were not safeguarded in salt mines during the war and were preserved in Berlin, are now in the *Geheimes Staatsarchiv* of the *Stiftung Preussischer Kulturbesitz* in West Berlin-Dahlem. Very important materials about the National Socialist period are collected at the American "Documentation Center" in West Berlin. Unfortunately, however, these papers have been organized about the main personalities mentioned in them and have thus been taken out of context with the result that the work of the historian has been made difficult.

For the inventory of holdings in the central authorities' archives of both parts of Germany, there are printed catalogues which together provide a good survey. These include *Das Bundesarchiv und seine Bestände. Übersicht. Schriften des Bundesarchivs* (volume 10, Boppard, 1961), the *Übersicht über die Bestände des Deutschen Zentralarchivs Potsdam,* Berlin, 1957, and the catalogues of the *Politisches Archiv des Auswärtigen Amtes: A Catalogue of Files and Microfilms of the German Foreign Ministry Archives* (volume 1, 1867–1920, Stanford, 1962; volume 2, 1920–1945, Stanford, 1964).[8]

Beyond the central archives, German archival holdings present a confusing picture for anyone who is beginning study. They reflect rather exactly the territorial splintering of Germany and the federative constitution of the Bismarckian Empire. The archives of the former German federal states and their historical predecessors in general have remained intact, although the administrative agencies in charge usually have adjusted their sphere of coverage to the contemporary administrative boundaries. Even for Reich politics they are of great importance, for in the *Hauptarchive,* which administer the holdings of the former German federal states, much historically important material can be found which is lost in the central archives or not easily available there.

For German regional holdings there are printed inventories only in exceptional cases.[9] The historian is largely dependent on his abilities as a detective. Knowledge of German constitutional development and the complicated history of the German territories is indispensable. But it is not too difficult to track down archival holdings on the basis of their source. In general, the various regional archives have continued since the middle of the nineteenth century to maintain the state archives of their territories. The archives of Sigmaringian province, for instance, are now in the *Staatsarchiv Sigmaringen* and the papers of the former Kurhessen territories in the *Staatsarchiv Marburg.* Only in rare cases have the archival holdings originating from the archives of a former territory or territorial state been divided into various archives; usually they have been preserved

8 See also, *A Catalogue of Files and Microfilms of the German Foreign Ministry Archives,* published by the American Historical Association in 1959.

9 Of special importance is *Das Staatsarchiv Düsseldorf und seine Bestände,* Siegburg, 1957–, of which volumes 1 and 4 are available, as well as Haase/Deters, *Übersicht über die Bestande des Niedersächsischen Staatsarchiv in Hanover,* vol. I, Göttingen, 1965.

as a unit and they are organized on the basis of the old state records. The *Landesarchive* of the present federal states (*Bundesländer*) in general continue the tradition of the central archives of the former German federal (*Bundesstaaten*) states. They are basically as follows:

Bavaria	*Hauptstaatsarchiv*, Munich
Baden-Württemberg	*Hauptstaatsarchiv*, Stuttgart
Berlin	*Landesarchiv*, Berlin
Bremen	*Staatsarchiv*, Bremen
Nordhein-Westfalen	*Hauptstaatsarchiv*, Düsseldorf
Hamburg	*Staatsarchiv*, Hamburg
Niedersachsen	*Staatsarchiv*, Hanover
Rheinland-Pfalz	*Staatsarchiv*, Coblenz
the Saarland	*Landesarchiv*, Saarbrücken
Schleswig-Holstein	*Schleswig-Holsteinische Landes-archiv*, Schleswig
Hessen	*Hauptstaatsarchiv*, Wiesbaden

For the former Land Baden, united in 1951 with Württemberg into the Land Württemberg-Baden, the *Generallandesarchiv*, Karlsruhe.[10]

To these central archives of the federal states (*Landesarchive*) the *Staatsarchive* are subordinated. These usually collect and preserve the numerous archival materials from specified regional administrative units which often correspond to older historical boundaries. At the same time, they continue archives of earlier origin. An interested historian may use the comprehensive survey of the German archives in *Archivum: Revue internationale des archives* (volume 5, 1955, 46 ff). The numerous city archives are contained in this survey as well. The situation is much worse in regard to archives from private (non-public) sources, e.g., institutions, party organizations, corporations, and individuals of some distinction. There are, of course, a large number of private archives of very differing quality. Only the Freiherr-vom-Stein Archiv in Cappenberg and the Theodor-Heuss Archiv in Stuttgart need to be mentioned here. For private archives, few catalogues exist. In modern history, the organizing process is just beginning. Recently, however, the *Bundesarchiv* and other public archives have energetically begun to collect and pre-

---

[10] A survey of the present *Landesarchive* in the territories of the GDR has been omitted.

serve the private papers of significant personalities, but the confusion of the years before and after 1945 has made it difficult to trace archival materials still in private hands. Published inventories exist only for sources on medieval history in certain private and ecclesiastical archives. A preliminary inventory of these efforts is contained in the survey of *Die schriftlichen Nachlässe in den zentralen und preussischen Archiven* by Wolfgang Mommsen, *Schriften des Bundesarchivs Koblenz* (volume 1, Koblenz, 1955). The private papers found in the *Bundesarchiv* as well as in the *Geheimes Staatsarchiv* in Berlin and in both departments of the *Deutsches Zentralarchiv* in Potsdam and Merseburg constitute a considerable supplement to the official papers, and on occasion a valuable substitute for lost holdings. Yet losses resulting from the war are often very large. In some cases papers were destroyed by bombing or lost in the great confusion of the period just after the war.

The condition of the papers or files of political parties, of unions, or other political and economic organizations is even worse. The public archival establishments have just begun to collect them. The files of the German parties and organizations before 1933 present a particularly sad case, for during the interregnum of National Socialism political parties were prohibited and possession of such documents was risky. Thus much was lost. The private papers of leading politicians help occasionally, but not always, to fill gaps. The case of the German Social Democratic party is somewhat more favorable. In 1933 the party, sensing what was coming, gave the greater part of its archives to the *Internationales Institut für Sozialgeschichte* in Amsterdam. There the holdings are generally open for use, though special permission is required. A small part is still in the possession of the Social Democratic Party in Bonn. Many other party collections, such as the archives of the *Alldeutscher Verband,* found their way to the *Deutsches Zentralarchiv* in Potsdam, but much is irretrievably lost. Still, German archives, considering the extent of the war's destruction, are again in good condition. The war practice of storing the archival holdings in salt mines was generally successful in preventing losses by air raids.

Good libraries are, of course, also indispensable for successful historical research. In general the students will find their basic working materials in the special libraries of the history departments and research institutes. Well-stocked university libraries are also usually available. Libraries like the American or English, with more or less unrestricted admittance to the stacks, do not, however, exist in Germany outside seminar and institute libraries. While important handbooks and reference works are available in special reading rooms, a student cannot search the library stacks himself and for reading-room as well as outside use he must usually order books a day in advance.

The war tore large holes in the holdings of university libraries. And the high circulation resulting from the increase in number of students has aggravated the problem further. As a result, a student frequently is unable to obtain a desired book at once, though it is possible to order a book in advance or to obtain an inter-library loan. Large central libraries, similar to the Library of Congress in the United States, would provide the best access to books, but the Federal Republic has no such library. The *Deutsche Bücherei* in Leipzig which from 1912 collected all works in the German language is in the GDR. Its counterpart, the *Deutsche Bibliothek* in Frankfurt, was established only in 1946. The most important of German libraries, the Prussian *Staatsbibliothek* in Berlin, was torn in two in 1945 and many of its holdings were lost during the war. Most of its remaining holdings are in Marburg and administered by the *Stiftung Preussischer Kulturbesitze, Staatsbibliothek,* while a smaller part is in the old building of the former Prussian *Staatsbibliothek* (on the unter den Linden in East Berlin) now named *Staatsbibliothek.* Of the great German supra-regional libraries only the *Bayrische Staatsbibliothek* in Munich survived the war essentially intact.

Several special libraries are useful for historians working in specialized fields. Among these are the library of the *Monumenta Germaniae Historica* in Munich, the *Bibliothek für Zeitgeschichte* (*Weltkriegsbücherei*) in Stuttgart, the library of the *Institut für Zeitgeschichte* in Munich, and the library of the *Johann-Gottfried-Herder-Institut* in Marburg. The library of the *Institut für Weltwirtschaft* in Kiel possesses much important newspaper and magazine material. For the recent development of German parliamentarianism there is the *Bibliothek des deutschen Bundestages* in Bonn. For newspapers the *Institut für Zeitungs Forschung* at Dortmund may be of assistance.

VI. Tendencies and Emphases of Contemporary Historical Research

The era of National Socialism, not the end of the war, constitutes the deepest break in the development of German historical thought. From 1933 historical study was deliberately and systematically forced into the service of the ideology of totalitarian *Volkstum*. This ideology, arising in part out of the depths of *Völkisch* (folkish or racist) and anti-Semitic beliefs, had little or nothing in common with the traditions of German intellectual life. A historian who did not wish to lose his position or to leave the country could, it is true, avoid trouble by concentrating on learned specialties. Many historians, to their honor, took this way of "inner emigration." It is no coincidence that pioneering studies in modern regional and local research were made during these years. Nonetheless, National Socialist ideology deeply affected historical study. The pull of the popular ideology of the times was extraordinarily strong. Thinking in terms of historical continuity, not a few historians acclaimed Hitler and the National Socialist movement as the summit of a German national history stretching back to Martin Luther and Ulrich von Hutten. The Prussia of Frederick the Great was seen as a predecessor of National Socialism, as was Bismarck's statecraft. From Fichte, Hegel, Treitschke, Nietzsche, to Stefan George, the great personalities of German intellectual life were made to appear as the intellectual trailblazers for the National Socialist *Volkstumsideologie*.

This gross distortion of German history was partly the result of a vast self-deception, partly the consequence of the opportunistic desire to come quickly to terms with the ruling powers. National Socialist *Kulturpolitik* was not fastidious in its methods. The National Socialists not only systematically tried to claim or mobilize the traditions of German intellectual life for their own political aims but also to parade as their guarantor and executor. Almost everything held holy by the German cultured classes could be found in a conglomerate of contradictory postulates of the National Socalist program: the Kantian concept of duty, Fichte's idea of the German cultural mission, the romantic assumption of an organically organized *Volksgemeinschaft,* the idea of socialism, the "anti-capitalistic yearning" of broad elements of German intelligentsia, the anti-bourgeois sentiments of the youth. All of these, in perverted form, were fitted into a National Socialist ideology designed to capture bourgeois votes and legitimize the rule of the petit bourgeois leadership corps of the NSDAP that was in reality altogether devoid of geunine attachment to German culture. Upright and great German historians saw at once that this identification of National Socialism with the traditions of German history was a crude lie. But only a few dared to say so openly. The lie came to an end in 1945, but the harm was not easy to eradicate. As a result of the effective propaganda of the National Socialists, the entire German past seemed compromised. Where, the question was, could historical thinking resume again? Where was the firm ground on which one could build anew?

This was the great dilemma facing historical thought and study in Germany after the catastrophe of 1945. There appeared to be a deep and almost unbridgeable chasm between present and past. All the positive traditions of German history were broken or dissolved into nothingness, like the German Empire created by Bismarck. To this was added the German people's shock as they became aware of the full extent of the National Socialist regime of terror. This led to a "flight from history," to an exclusive preoccupation with the pressing problems of daily life. The nation's, as well as the individual's own, past was generally regarded as taboo and this, too, had an unfavorable effect on the development of historical consciousness. For, a short time, as Alfred Heuss demonstrated in a masterful study, there resulted a "loss of history."[11] The intellectual climate was thus unfavorable for the regeneration of German historical study. A considerable number of years had to elapse before history could find itself. This can be clearly illustrated by the nature of historical publication in Germany. Because the crisis made it difficult to find firm foundations for judgments based upon the whole German past, far more special studies were done and collections of sources published than great syntheses written. On the other hand, the situation in 1945 offered a favorable climate for new views. Thus, in 1953 Theodor Schieder in his "Erneuerung des Geschichtsbewusstseins" spoke of the need for a new "open history," receptive to new approaches as well as new methods.[12]

[11] Alfred Heuss, *Verlust der Geschichte*, Göttingen, 1959.
[12] Theodor Schieder, *Staat und Gesellschaft im Wandel unserer Zeit: Studien zur Geschichte des 19. und 20. Jahrhunderts*, Munich, 1959, p. 195.

Since 1945 efforts to attain new orientations in German history have been many and varied. These efforts, however, have not often produced much in the way of concrete results. German historiography still is (even after twenty years) in a period of transition and its study has not yet assumed definite contours. The sharpest trend is away from writing of history on national lines. The history of the German national state no longer constitutes, as it did for earlier German historians, the inevitable main theme. Insofar as the writing of national history continues, it often takes a self-critical or almost introverted form: an accusing settling of accounts with the German political tradition of the nineteenth and the early twentieth centuries. Even conservative and nationally oriented historians, as Gerhard Ritter, have not remained uninfluenced by the trend. The present bitter discussion about German politics before and during the First World War illustrates this, just as do the numerous monographs on the history of National Socialism.

There are also efforts under way to find forms of historical writing which are quite free of political prejudice. These strive for a comparative method which describes historical phenomena by means of "ideal types" modelled on the work of Jakob Burckhardt, Max Weber, and Otto Hintze. The numerous works of Theodor Schieder, Werner Conze, and Otto Brunner point in this direction. The concept of nation is no longer regarded as the guiding idea for historical thought, but is subjected to a critical, comparative analysis which seeks the numerous variations and forms of appearance of the idea of nation in European and non-European development and relates them to social movements.

Furthermore, there are strong efforts to replace the national- and European-centered historical consciousness with a universal historical consciousness. The programs of the German historical meetings, for instance, afford impressive evidence of this general trend. Some historians would like to put historical writing on a new basis or, at any rate, to make an attempt to write history in terms of European world civilization rather than along national lines.[13] In addition, there are attempts to write "theoretical history," partly on the model of Toynbee, partly in the form of historical sociology. All these beginnings, it must be admitted, are as yet but little more than

[13] In the sense of the famous work of Hans Freyer, *Weltgeschichte Europas,* 2 vols., 1948.

postulates. True universal history, if it is at all possible, has not been attempted in contemporary Germany. In Afro-Asian history, where attempts at this universal history might be first expected, research is only beginning.

For the development of German historical writing, the shift of research emphasis to the regional and local historical studies is of most consequence. German historians are no longer spellbound by the central authorities or the institutions of power. Instead, they interest themselves in the history of areas and regions. This is particularly true of medieval history, but it is also true of modern history. In fact, new perceptions from regional studies have substantially corrected and expanded preconceptions of general development.

Equally significant are those changes in methodological thinking connected with the development of regional research. Among these changes are the correction and modification of the terminology and the leading concepts of nineteenth-century and early twentieth-century historical writing. Otto Brunner, for example, has emphatically opposed the transference of the modern juridical concept of the "state" to the Middle Ages and the early modern times. Although his criticism has remained within the bounds of the traditional historical thought, he started an avalanche. The predominance of pure political history, since Ranke the almost automatic main concern of German historical thought, was challenged as soon as the modern concept of the state per se as a historical category was seen to be of relative validity.

Instead of questions concerning the nature and role of the state, new questions arose concerning the relationships of the state and society and the varying forms of domination in society. The central interest in medieval research is no longer in the royalty and the Empire as it was with the editors of the *Jahrbücher der deutschen Geschichte,* but the ruling elite of the European feudal nobles and the independent local roots of their domination of the land. A similar trend can be traced in recent research on the medieval orders and their role in medieval society. Scholars are no longer solely interested in the religious and intellectual motivations of the monastic movements but try to identify their social functions within the medieval society. A related question is that of the close personal relationships among the monastic orders and the local feudal nobility.

In modern history there is a similar trend. The political and social structure of society and its various organizational forms as well as its immanent trends begin to interest scholars more than the motives of statesmen and leading personalities. One example will suffice. Historians try to understand the political parties and other political associations not so much on the basis of the formulated programs and the ideologies they embody as through study of their social structures and organizational bases in the country. The actions of the leading statesmen are interpreted against the background of contemporary social and constitutional conditions. Historians, hence, are less and less satisfied with those traditional models of explanation which tried to relate the actions of statesmen as well as of political groups to specific religious or ideological convictions. There is general agreement on the necessity of putting political history on a broad basis through research on the changing patterns of the social and economic conditions of society.

Concrete research in social and economic history, however, still lags behind that being done in other western countries. In part, this results from the traditional organization of historical studies in Germany. For at most universities the discipline of economic history still belongs either to the faculty of economic and social sciences or to the faculty of law and governmental sciences and not to the philosophical faculty, and for this reason economic history has a fairly isolated position within the historical discipline. It is not customarily part of the training of most historians.

Social history suffers also from the traditional gap between history and the social sciences. As a discipline, long considered purely humanistic, history still has but few links to the social sciences and there are but very few students who try to combine the approaches of both the social sciences and the humanities. Insofar as social history is well established as a special discipline within the framework of historical studies at German universities, it is largely pursued through methods akin to those used in the history of ideas. The works of Alexis de Tocqueville and Otto Hintze still serve as guides for modern research. There are, hence, few studies based on systematic use of quantitative methods and statistical materials, the philological origins of history being still very much alive. A radical social historiography comparable to that of the French school of the *Annales* has, up to the present, scarcely found footing in Germany, though the work of this school is given much attention. In contrast to French practice, demographic studies are little pursued, and a historiography of the "common man" virtually does not exist. German historians try to supplement and to deepen traditional diplomatic and political history through social and structural historical concepts, but departures of the nature of the history of *"longue durée,"* in the manner of the *Annales* group, are not thought to be realistic. While German history is open to the methods of modern social sciences it holds fast, and for good reason, to the idea that the spontaneous actions of the individual or of individuals (though largely conditioned by ideal or material interests) are still the main themes of historical study, not the formulation of scientific generalizations for prediction and control, which is the task of the social sciences.

For these reasons it is not a coincidence that the history of ideas still occupies a favored position in historical research and instruction at German universities. But intellectual history as it was conceived by the American, Lovejoy, isolated from the history of the political and social developments, is almost completely rejected. Only at Berlin and Erlangen are there special chairs for intellectual history. Nevertheless, the history of political and social ideas is given much attention and the analysis of ideologies and the *Weltanschauung* forms an integral part of political history.

This brief survey of German historical study has omitted much of importance. A survey of the study of history in the GDR might have been included. But there historiography is forced to follow different laws for its main task is thought to be the fostering of communist ideas and justifying communist rule in this part of Germany. An analysis of it would have gone far beyond the range of problems dealt with in this introduction. This survey, nevertheless, has revealed that historical research and instruction at German universities again flourish on the basis of great traditions.

Selected Bibliography*

BRACHER, Karl Dietrich, *Die Auflösung der Weimarer Republik*. 3rd ed., Stuttgart, Ring, 1960.

* References listed here are in addition to those mentioned in the text.

BRUNNER, Otto, *Land und Herrschaft.* 4th ed., Vienna, Rohrer, 1959.

——, *Neue Wege der Sozialgeschichte.* Göttingen, Vandenhoeck and Ruprecht, 1956.

DEHIO, Ludwig, *Deutschland und die Weltpolitik im 20. Jahrhundert,* Munich, Oldenbourg, 1955.

DROYSEN, Johann Gustav, *Historik. Vorlesungen über Enzyklopädie und Methodologie der Geschichte,* 3rd ed. Hübner, Darmstadt, Wissenschaftlichs Buchgesellschaft, 1958.

ERDMANN, Karl, *Forschungen zur politischen Ideenwelt des Frühmittelalters,* F. Baethgen, Berlin, Akademie, 1951.

FISCHER, Fritz, *Griff nach der Weltmacht,* 3rd ed. Düsseldorf, Droste, 1963.

HEUSS, Alfred, *Verlust der Geschichte.* Göttingen, Vandenhoeck and Ruprecht, 1959.

LÖWE, Heinz, *Von Theoderich dem Grossen zu Karl dem Grossen. Das Werden des Abendlandes im Geschichtsbild des frühen Mittelalters.* Darmstadt, H. Genter, 1956.

MEINECKE, Friedrich, *Die Entstehung des Historismus,* Werke, vol. III, K. Hinrichs, ed., Munich, Oldenbourg, 1959.

MITTEIS, Heinrich, *Der Staat des hohen Mittelalters,* 6th ed., Weimar, H. Böhlau, 1959.

NÄF, Werner, *Die Epochen der neueren Geschichte,* 2nd ed., Aarau, Sauerländer, 1959/60.

RITTER, Gerhard, *Staatskunst und Kriegshandwerk,* 3 vols. Munich, Oldenbourg, 1959–1965.

SCHIEDER, Theodor, *Geschichte als Wissenschaft, eine Einführung.* Munich, Oldenbourg, 1965.

——, *Staat und Gesellschaft in unserer Zeit. Studien zum Geschichte des 19. und 20. Jahrhundert.* München, Oldenbourg, 1958.

——, ed., *Hundert Jahre Historische Zeitschrift 1859–1959.* Munich, Oldenbourg, 1959.

SCHNABEL, Franz, *Deutsche Geschichte im 19. Jahrhundert,* 4 vols. Freiburg im Breisgau, Herder, 1927–1936.

SRBIK, Heinrich von, *Geist und Geschichte vom deutschen Humanismus bis zur Gegenwart,* 2 vols. Munich, Bruckman, 1950–51.

Part Four

Historical Study
in
Great Britain

A. TAYLOR MILNE

I. Education and Training

A. The teaching of history in schools and universities

History of a sort is taught in practically every elementary and secondary school in Great Britain. The vast majority of boys and girls pass through the state-controlled or state-aided primary schools, where education is provided free of charge. They gain a very limited acquaintance with the past, at most one or two teaching periods of less than an hour each week from the age of 8 or 9 to the lowest leaving age of 15. Under the Education Act of 1944 all children pass at the age of 11 or 12 to various types of secondary school: "grammar," "technical," "modern," or "comprehensive," where they will stay until the age of 15, 16, 17 or 18, according to their aptitudes and chosen vocations.

In the grammar schools, to a greater extent than in the other types of secondary school, a reasonable proportion of time is devoted to history lessons, especially in the upper "forms," or classes, as the pupils begin to specialize in certain subjects. In the comprehensive school, the secondary technical school, and the secondary modern school, apart from those pupils preparing the subject for a school-leaving examination, history is tending to merge into classes on "civics" or "social studies." Nevertheless, the number of boys and girls offering history for the General Certificate of Education at the Ordinary Level and the Advanced Level is a high proportion on the Arts, as distinct from the Science, side in English and Welsh schools. In order to secure admission into any British university at present it is necessary to pass several subjects (not less than three) at the Advanced Level in the General Certificate of Education Examination, at about the age of 18. History is a strong favorite as an Advanced Level subject on the Arts side for the older universities, for London, and for the larger provincial universities in England. Although the terminology is slightly different, the pattern is similar for Scottish schools.

The so-called "public schools" stand outside the system outlined above. With the private "preparatory" schools, which are mainly concerned with preparing their pupils for entrance examinations and scholarships at the public schools, these expensive establishments depend to a large extent on fees and endowments, although many of them now receive substantial government grants on condition that they regularly submit to inspection by the Department of Science and Education. History, especially British history, is vigorously taught in preparatory and public schools. It is therefore not surprising that a high proportion of "open" scholarships, i.e., scholarships open to competition by all comers, are won each year at the Universities of Oxford and Cambridge by public-school boys offering history as their major subject. In addition, many of these schools have "close" scholarships at the older universities and so maintain a regular stream of their pupils to Oxford and Cambridge colleges.

The position in Scotland is somewhat different. There are few "preparatory" or "public schools" of the English type within its borders. Famous institutions such as Fettes College and Loretto College near Edinburgh are run on not dissimilar lines, but well-off Scottish parents who wish to educate their children outside the state system often send them as boarders to the private schools in England. As a result titled and landed gentry in Scotland are often indistinguishable from their English prototypes and this has done much to merge the governing classes in the two countries. The last two Conservative Prime Ministers, Mr. Harold Macmillan and Sir Alec Douglas-Home, are of Scottish origin, yet both were educated at English public schools and Oxford University. The great majority of Scottish boys and girls, however, start their education in the parish school and this is more frequently than in England followed by a secondary education at an academy or high school. Standards in the parish schools of Scotland are still noticeably higher than in the equivalent elementary schools of England, thanks to the prevalence of graduate teachers and a strong traditional respect for learning in all classes of the community. At the secondary school level, however, and in the universities, the same observation is no longer true. The teaching of history would seem to be below English standards, perhaps because the examination system in the Scottish universities does not encourage specialization to the same extent as in England, and there are thus comparatively few school teachers who have devoted themselves to the subject.

In addition to the "close" or competitive scholarships tenable at British universities, there is now ample provision for boys and girls of even moderate ability to obtain a university education without payment. Besides state scholarships, awarded for periods of anywhere from two to five years, there are county and other local awards which ensure that no youngster of talent fails to get a university education through lack of means. Indeed, the boot has shifted to the other foot. At the moment there are too few places in the existing universities for all those who seek entry. The plans for at least a score of new universities, in addition to those recently established, should take care of this problem in the near future. The Robbins Report on Higher Education[1] set as targets increases from the total of 216,000 students in full-time higher education in Great Britain during the academic year 1962–1963 to figures of 390,000 in 1973–1974 and 560,000 by 1980–1981. These objectives, together with some of the recommendations on financial and other means of implementing them, were immediately accepted by the last Conservative government, so that the figures represent the least that is planned and more is already being achieved in fact. The British Labour Party is pledged to go further and create sufficient additional institutions of adult education, going by the name of universities, to give every boy and girl who seeks higher learning the opportunity to obtain it.

The position of historical training in these developments is difficult to forecast, but the general result should be to increase the number of university graduates with history as their major subject, although the percentage in relation to other subjects may decrease. Several of the new universities started since 1946 anticipated some of the recommendations of the Robbins Report, viz.:

14. A higher proportion of students should receive a broader education for their first degrees.
15. There should be more courses involving the study of more than one main subject.[2]

---

[1] Committee on Higher Education. *Report of the Committee appointed by the Prime Minister under the chairmanship of Lord Robbins, 1961–63.* [Cmnd. 2154]. H.M.S.O., 1963.

[2] *Robbins Report*, p. 278.

These suggestions, for they are no more than suggestions, may affect the position of history in the syllabuses of the older universities as well as the new. Hitherto, the wide range to be covered both in time and in area has encouraged a tendency to make history, of all subjects among the humanities, the one to be studied with a minimum of interruption from other subjects. In the University of Oxford, the Honours School of Modern History has for many years attracted the greatest number of candidates for the Bachelor of Arts degree. The present syllabus includes:

1. The History of England, with some attention to Scotland, Ireland, Wales, India, and other Commonwealth countries "so far as they are connected with the History of England."
2. General History during some period selected by the candidate, for example, 1409–1559 *or* 1871–1939.
3. A Special Historical Subject carefully studied with reference to (printed) original authorities, some of which are likely to be in foreign languages.

Before they are admitted to the Second Public Examination in an Honours School at Oxford, candidates have to pass one part of the First Public Examination, which is usually taken a year after going up to the University. The Preliminary Examination for Modern History is usually the part chosen by those aspiring to an Honours degree in that subject. Candidates holding the status of senior student may be exempted from the First Public Examination. The qualifications for this status are "an approved degree at an approved university obtained after courses extending over three years at that university." The normal period of residence required before the Second Public Examination can be taken is nine terms (three years), but senior students may take it in less, according to their previous records. The candidate for an Honours degree has to sit as many as ten three-hour papers in this Examination, including two on his chosen "special subject," e.g., "British imperial policies, 1763–1783."

He will also have to undergo a viva voce examination to determine whether he receives First Class Honours, instead of Second, or Third Class. A man, or woman, with a First Class Honours degree in modern history at Oxford can usually count on an academic career, if he desires it. He may obtain a postgraduate studentship or a fellowship at one of the colleges, with or without tutoring responsibilities. In any case it is normal to expect some research work before plunging even the most brilliant students into university teaching. It may be added that some distinguished British historians from Oxford did not in fact pass through the Honours School in Modern History but the School of Literae Humaniores (popularly known as "Greats"). This is entirely devoted to the Greek and Latin languages, literatures, histories, and philosophies. Others have taken "Modern Greats"—a combination of philosophy, politics, and economics. A few well-known historical scholars have passed through more than one of these Schools.

At Cambridge University the Bachelor of Arts degree examination is known as the "Tripos," which derives its name from the three-legged stool, or tripod, on which the new B.A. sat to deliver a short, usually satirical, speech, when the results of the examination were read out. Today the Historical Tripos examination is normally taken in two parts, the first after a student has been in residence not less than four terms, the second after not less than seven terms. As the great majority of students come up to the University in the Michaelmas Term (starting in October) and the Tripos examinations take place in June each year, these provisions mean that normally three years are taken in preparation for them. Under certain prescribed conditions a student who has obtained Honours in another Tripos examination may be a candidate for Honours in the Historical Tripos (usually sitting the Second Part examinations). In Part I all Honours candidates have to write an English essay on a set subject and answer questions from five other papers chosen from eight syllabuses. The effect is to ensure that at least two papers in British history are taken and at least one in medieval or modern European history. Ancient history, the history of political thought, or the history of the United States of America may be chosen for two of the remaining papers. In Part II of the Tripos examination, the student has again to write an essay and answer questions from at least six other papers, including two on his "special subject." This has to be chosen from a variety of periods ranging from ancient history to the twentieth century. One of these two papers requires the study of printed texts, including some in foreign languages. A knowledge of Latin and at least one modern foreign language is required by students who are proposing to read history at Oxford, Cambridge, London, and most of the other British universities.[3] Postgraduate students embarking on research are thus able to read manuscript sources in classical or medieval Latin with a little practice and to consult essential books in French, German, or another foreign language bearing on their chosen subjects.

The History Honours courses for the B.A. examination in London are not dissimilar from those at Oxford, although no viva voce is involved. A larger number of options are given and a greater range of special subjects from which to choose. The older provincial English universities and the colleges of the University of Wales all have B.A. Honours History courses more or less on the "Oxbridge" or London model, but with fewer options, since they have fewer specialized teachers. The Scottish system is again somewhat different. There is no B.A. degree in any of the four old universities and most students are content with the "ordinary" M.A. degree, which involves examinations on several subjects during a three-year course. The few who wish to take Honours in History enroll for four years and begin to specialize in the subject in their second or third year. The effect is to limit severely the number of Scottish postgraduate students who go on to read for higher degrees in history.

Despite the precautions against over-specialization incorporated into all history syllabuses, as briefly indicated above, and similar safeguards for other subjects among the humanities, an influential number of university teachers have not been satisfied that they were sufficient. In the first new university established in Great Britain after the Second World War, Keele in North Staffordshire, a complete break was made from the prevailing system. At Keele the normal B.A. course extends over four years, during the first of which a wide range of subjects is studied, followed by three years studying two principal subjects to Honours level. One of these may be history. At the still newer universities of East Anglia, Essex, Lancaster, and Sussex, students may "major" in a particular subject but only in a broad scheme involving several related fields of study. At the University of East Anglia, for instance, a B.A. Honours degree will be awarded in the School of English Studies, with specialization in

---

[3] All students admitted to Oxford University must have a knowledge of two foreign languages. Cambridge is now content with one, but those reading for the History Tripos need two.

English history, but it entails study of and examination in English language and literature as well. At the University of Sussex, history may be a major subject for the B.A. degree in the School of English and American Studies, of European Studies, or Social Studies, or African and Asian Studies. The aspects of history taught vary according to the particular School and are accompanied up to the final degree examination by parallel subjects, such as English and American literature, economics, and so on.

It is too soon to judge the results of these experiments, some of which have barely started. Certainly a greater variety of training will be available to potential historians, but it may well prove that the best approach to thorough knowledge is through the Honours degree concentrated on one subject. Experience at Keele and other universities founded within the last few years would appear to indicate that, in the field of history at any rate, too general a basis for studies at university level is as unsatisfactory as over-specialization. No doubt graduates are being produced who possess sufficient acquaintance with the past to make them cultivated persons within whatever vocation they enter. But without much better qualifications they are not likely to become professional historians, capable of teaching the subject to adults or contributing to research. It is significant that the postgraduate students of history beginning to appear in the new universities are either graduates of other universities who have "majored" in the subject or graduates preparing for one of the recently instituted higher degrees by examination, which do not require original research and the writing of a dissertation. Nevertheless, all these new universities in Britain look forward to having research schools and some, notably Sussex, already have a respectable number of postgraduate students in history: nearly all of them of course drawn from elsewhere at the present early stage in development. For the moment it is in the conventional universities—Oxford, Cambridge, London, and the older provincial and Scottish centers of learning—that almost all advanced study and training for research in history are taking place.

B. *Postgraduate study in British universities*

Despite the extensive changes now taking place, postgraduate research, usually for a higher degree, is regarded as an essential feature of all university schools or departments of history in Great

Britain, even the youngest. The old universities still rely mainly on the individual scholar to guide, or at least advise, one or two chosen pupils preparing theses in the tutor's own field of study. Formal instruction is reduced to a minimum, although both Oxford and Cambridge have recently introduced one-year postgraduate courses with set syllabuses and written examinations. The Oxford B.Phil. course is "intended to provide a training in advanced work for those not yet fully equipped to proceed to original and independent work, and for those seeking a limited amount of further experience of academic work after the B.A." An Oxford man or woman who has been placed in the First Class in the Honours School of History is, however, normally regarded as ready to pursue independent research for the much more difficult D.Phil. degree under supervision, and will usually set about collecting material for a thesis soon after obtaining the B.A. Honours degree. Similarly in Cambridge, graduates with First Class Honours in at least one of the two parts of the History Tripos examination may embark immediately on research leading to the Ph.D. degree or to the less exacting M.Litt. degree. The newly-instituted (1963) one-year course for a Certificate in Advanced Historical Studies at Cambridge provides a certain amount of technical instruction for graduates in history, also introductory classes in sociology, comparative government, and special aspects of history, which may be varied from year to year. Papers in these subjects have to be written at the end of the course. At both the old universities the M.A. degree has long been a formality: it may be obtained, without examination, on payment of a fee "by Bachelors of Arts of Oxford, who have had their names on the books of a college or hall for a period of twenty terms." The Cambridge regulations are similar. In all other English and Welsh universities, the M.A. has until very recently been regarded as a research degree, although the historical theses presented, after one year's postgraduate work, for this degree in several of the provincial universities must be classed as academic exercises rather than original contributions to knowledge.

Very different has been the M.A. degree in the University of London, for which a minimum of two years preparation by full-time postgraduate students, or three years by part-time students, was required. The historical theses submitted for the London M.A. have frequently been of as high a quality, though not so lengthy, as those submitted for the Ph.D. degree. Partly as a result of the Robbins

Report it is already clear that the character of the London M.A. and provincial degrees of equivalent standing will change radically in the near future. For several years there has been in London a M. Sc. (Economics) degree by examination and this may be obtained in certain fields of modern history without any sort of thesis, after one year of postgraduate study. In the university session 1965–1966, a similar M.A. degree by examination was introduced, for history as well as for other Arts subjects, and the place of the old M.A. by thesis has been taken by a new M.Phil. degree, for which a full-time course of research for two years and the writing of a substantial dissertation will be required. Although these changes may be regretted, there are good reasons behind them. Perhaps the main consideration is the overloaded syllabus for the B.A. degree and the reluctance of university authorities to extend for a further year the normal three-year course, which already brings most candidates for a first degree to the age of 21. Many of them without a special vocation for history or another academic subject do not wish to pursue learning further. Others, it is thought, will be content with a further year of more intensive study, with the reward of a Master's degree at the end of it. In most of the new universities the M.A. or B.Litt. degree by examination has accordingly been established from the outset and the older provincial universities are quickly following suit. The general effect throughout Britain may be to reduce the numbers of those prepared to face the rigors of historical, literary or linguistic investigation represented by typical Ph.D. courses and to a lesser extent by the new M.Phil. in London.

As has been indicated above, the standard of research theses varies considerably, although not so widely perhaps as in some other western countries. The D.Phil. degree at Oxford and the Ph.D. at Cambridge are still, in the opinion of those who have acted as examiners for several universities, of a higher quality than the equivalent degrees of other British universities. The number of students who achieve either of these distinctions is very small: during the year 1966 in all fields of history 22 students obtained the D.Phil. at Oxford and 27 the Ph.D. at Cambridge. Rather more students secure the Ph.D. in history at the University of London—there were 78 successful candidates in 1966—and the standard was not far below that of the older universities. Elsewhere in Britain the attempt to keep up to "Oxbridge" levels for research degrees is not always so evident. All of these doctoral degrees depend on a thesis, anything from 60,000 to 120,000 words long, making an original contribution to knowledge. An oral examination of the candidate normally follows the reading of the thesis by his own supervisor, by another expert in his own university and by an external examiner from another university. Unless all three are satisfied the student may be failed or "referred." In the latter case he is required to present the thesis again, within a given time limit, improved in specified ways.

C. Principal places of training

The long tradition of "amateurism" and the tutorial system at the old universities have until very recently tended to discourage anything like organized training of historians at Oxford or Cambridge. The great names of the nineteenth century—Macaulay, Carlyle, Froude, Freeman, Stubbs, and others—were either not university teachers at all, or did their major work outside their academic duties. They had few, if any, research students. Continental and American influences made some impression in the early twentieth century. Paul Vinogradoff tried without much success to introduce into Oxford the seminar method by which he had himself been trained. Sir Charles Firth ran into serious trouble with his attempts to centralize historical studies in that university and the echoes of the controversy have not yet died down. The present Regius Professor of Modern History at Oxford, Mr. H. R. Trevor-Roper, alluded pointedly to it in his inaugural lecture of 1957, on "History, Professional and Lay." His predecessor, Professor V. H. Galbraith, took a rather different view of the question, after much previous experience of supervising research students in Edinburgh and London. Soon after his retirement from the same chair, the late Sir Maurice Powicke saw the opening of the new Faculty of History Library in Merton Street (1957). He and a few sympathizers in Oxford wished to make this a center for advanced work in history, comparable to the Institute of Historical Research in London. It has indeed become a convenient place for the holding of a few seminars and introductory courses in such subjects as palaeography, but the attempt to confine it to postgraduate students has been abandoned and the nature of the historical library it contains will inevitably change.

The picture is not dissimilar in Cambridge. In his short career as Regius Professor of History there, Lord Acton had little time to spare for research students, although he was a firm believer in collaboration and the seminar method of instruction. The Acton Collection, which he left to the university library, has provided the nucleus of materials for advanced study in history, but it is still far from comprehensive. Students preparing for a higher degree in Cambridge have a supervisor who may or may not be a tutor in their own college. If they are medievalists they will be able to attend university courses in palaeography and diplomatic where they will meet other medievalists, but there is no single center within the university for all advanced students of history. The Seeley (Faculty) Library caters to undergraduates as well as to postgraduates. Such group instruction as postgraduates receive is usually within the college of a don keen about a particular subject, who has gathered several disciples to work under his guidance.

It was actually at Owens College, now the University of Manchester, that the first successful English seminar in history was run, although it was an Oxford man, Professor Thomas Frederick Tout, who organized it early in the twentieth century. Many well-known medievalists came under his influence, either as postgraduate students or as colleagues at Manchester: Sir Maurice Powicke, Professor V. H. Galbraith, Sir Goronwy Edwards, Professor C. R. Cheney, to name but a few. The amount of original research which could be done in Manchester was severely limited and Tout's contemporary, Albert Frederick Pollard, was quick to realize the unique position of London as a center for advanced work in history.

In his inaugural lecture as Professor of Constitutional History at University College in 1904, Pollard advocated the establishment of an Institute of Historical Research in London, not only for University teachers in the metropolis and their postgraduate students, but also for scholars coming to London from other British universities and from abroad. It was not until the year 1921 that the offer of a free building site behind the British Museum and an initial grant of £20,000 from a wealthy friend gave Pollard the opportunity to realize his dream in the shape of the famous "Tudor Cottages" erected along Malet Street as a temporary home for the newly-founded Institute. After the Second World War a wing of the new Senate House of the University of London on the Bloomsbury site was allocated to the Institute and the move into its permanent quarters was made in September, 1947. By that time the Institute had become well established and it has since grown very rapidly, both in the number of users and in the scope of its activities. In 1939 there were 349 registered readers; in 1949 there were 489; by 1967 the number had risen to 1,597, of whom 352 were students preparing theses for higher degrees of British or foreign universities.

Although primarily intended for London graduates and for London university teachers doing advanced work in history, the Institute from the start threw open its doors to scholars from every part of the world. The advantages of such a meeting place close to the British Museum and within easy reach of the Public Record Office and many other repositories of documents were obvious. Since the Second World War especially, other British universities have sent many of their best historical students to the Institute to read in the library and attend introductory courses or seminars. At the present time all the universities in Great Britain and Ireland pay annual subscriptions to the Institute and have the right to nominate a fixed number of postgraduate students to free places and also to claim admission without fee for members of their staffs engaged on historical research. A growing number of universities abroad also subscribe, particularly those in Commonwealth countries and the United States. For most of its income, the Institute, like all other parts of the University of London, depends on annual grants from the Senate. The money comes eventually from the University Grants Committee, a quasi-independent body which distributes funds voted by Parliament to all the universities of the United Kingdom.

The Institute has no teaching staff of its own, excepting the Director. Apart from any classes he may give, all the "introductory courses" and "seminars," covering many fields of medieval and modern history, are conducted at the Institute by some of the numerous history specialists (more than 200 in 1967) attached to the various Schools and Colleges of the University of London. For purposes of instruction and study, the Library of the Institute, containing nearly 100,000 volumes, is divided into a series of "seminar libraries," comprising the main printed sources of British and foreign history, together with bibliographies, guides to libraries and archives, and other essential works of reference. There are special collections for British national and local history, for France, Germany, Italy, the Netherlands, Spain and Portugal, and other European countries, for the countries of the British Commonwealth, for the United States of America and Latin America, for Byzantine History, Military and Naval History, and International Relations. It should be added that some other institutions of the University of London are especially well equipped for certain fields of history, for example the London School of Economics and Political Science, the School of Slavonic and East European Studies, the School of Oriental and African Studies, the Institute of Advanced Legal Studies, and the Institute of Commonwealth Studies. Postgraduate students of these subjects naturally use the most appropriate institution as the base for their studies.

A yearly pamphlet giving details of the University of London School of History contains a prospectus of the Institute of Historical Research, and an *Annual Report* on its activities is made to the Senate. The principal publication is the *Bulletin,* which is issued twice a year in May and November. The annual *Theses Supplements,* one recording "Theses Completed" in the previous year, the other "Theses in Progress" on the first of January will have started to appear as a separate publication under the title, *Historical Research for University Degrees in the United Kingdom* (May 1967—). Another annual publication of the Institute is a comprehensive list of *Teachers of History in the Universities of the United Kingdom* (latest edition, January, 1968). A number of research enterprises are carried on at the Institute, the biggest of which is the *Victoria History of the Counties of England,* usually referred to as the *Victoria County History.* This is managed by a special Committee, of which the Director of the Institute is chairman. The total administrative staff of the Institute, including the editorial office of the *Victoria County History,* consisted, in late 1967, of 25 persons. Accommodation is provided in an Annexe to the Institute for the staff (more than 20 graduates) engaged on the biographical *History of Parliament,* sponsored by the House of Commons, and for other historical projects.

Every summer there is held at the Institute an Anglo-American Conference of Historians, attended by scholars from both sides of the Atlantic but not confined to British and American history. Papers are read on subjects ranging from Europe in the "Dark Ages" to contemporary international relations. A plenary conference, lasting a week, takes place every five years, the latest in July, 1967. Other congresses are held at the Institute from time to time, notably "Les

Journées franco-britanniques," sponsored by the Comité français des sciences historiques and the British National Committee, and in recent years several successful Anglo-Soviet conferences. In 1963 the Bureau of CISH (Comité international des sciences historiques) and the Assemblée Générale held their meetings at the Institute and the British National Committee affiliated to CISH regularly meets there. The traditional Thursday Evening Conferences started by Pollard still go on, although less frequently in these busier days. At them distinguished scholars discuss with their colleagues their own special researches. Visitors from abroad have frequently been invited to address British historians on these occasions. In these and many other ways the Institute of Historical Research is striving to fulfill the wishes of its founder and even serving to some extent as an international center for advanced work in history.

The only other British university which has anything comparable is the new one at York, where the Borthwick Institute of Historical Research was founded in 1953. Although on a much smaller scale than its prototype in London, it does several of the same things. The Borthwick Institute is housed in St. Anthony's Hall where there are kept the archives of the Province and Diocese of York, and so is particularly serviceable to students of English ecclesiastical history. It also has rich local records to draw on, but of course is distant from the great national collections so readily accessible to research workers in London. Students of Welsh and Scottish history have special advantages in Aberystwyth and Edinburgh respectively, where the national archives of the two countries are to be found, insofar as they are not contained in the Public Record Office, and where there are the National Library of Wales and the National Library of Scotland. Both these libraries are entitled to copies of all British copyright books. The Bodleian Library at Oxford and the Cambridge University Library are also copyright libraries. Each contains great collections of manuscripts, while many of the colleges possess priceless documents. Elsewhere in Great Britain there are important archives or collections, so that all the provincial and Scottish universities are places which research students interested in a particular field of history will be well advised to visit. There are, for instance, special opportunities for studying Romano-British history at Newcastle-upon-Tyne, English local history at the University of Leicester, Jacobite history at Aberdeen, business and industrial history at

Birmingham, Leeds, Manchester, or Glasgow, maritime history at Bristol, Liverpool, or Southampton, educational history at Leeds or Sheffield, and so on. The University Grants Committee is encouraging the establishment of special centers for advanced work in universities outside London. Books, newspapers, and documents of value to historians have already been collected at the Birmingham Centre for Russian and East European Studies, at the Durham School of Oriental Studies, the Edinburgh Centre of African Studies, the Liverpool Centre for Latin American Studies, and the Manchester Department of American Studies, to name only a few. Up-to-date information is briefly given in a *Guide to Research Facilities in History in the Universities of Great Britain and Ireland,* by G. Kitson Clark and G. R. Elton (New ed., Cambridge Univ. Press, 1965).

II. Practicing Historians

A. Teachers in schools and universities

To estimate the number of those engaged in teaching history in British schools brings in a qualitative factor. The total number of schools of all kinds for children (excluding nursery schools) in the United Kingdom is not far short of 50,000. In most of them there is likely to be at least one member of the staff paying special attention to history. In English public schools, grammar schools, comprehensive schools, and secondary modern schools there are always anything from two to a dozen specialists who teach nothing but history or very little else. Scotland has fewer specialist teachers but, allowing for this, one may say that not less than 20,000 persons are engaged in teaching the subject in British schools. Of these perhaps a third are specialists who give instruction in secondary schools to a satisfactory level for boys and girls in their teens.

As regards adult education a distinction must be drawn between the universities, chartered by the crown, and the numerous colleges for training teachers, clergy, scientists, and technicians of all kinds, craftsmen, artists, businessmen, servicemen, and so on. All of these have been until very recently outside the university system and on the whole have had lower standards in such subjects as history, which play a minor part in their syllabuses. The Institute of Historical Research issues a useful annual list of *Teachers of History in the Universities of the United Kingdom.* In the 1968 issue the total number listed was over 1,160 persons. By far the largest history "schools" (or departments) were those in Oxford where some 200 teachers of the subject are noted, in Cambridge where the teachers numbered about 127 and in London where the number was over 200. Every Oxford and Cambridge college has its history dons and the principal institutions of the University of London have in each of them well-staffed history departments: University College has 28 professors, readers or lecturers in the subject; King's College, 19; and the London School of Economics and Political Science, 33, if one includes the political scientists. All of these teachers are preparing undergraduates for Honours Degrees in History and most of them are "recognized" as competent to supervise and examine research students preparing for higher degrees. In addition, London provides an advisory service for postgraduate students preparing for "external" degrees not requiring attendance at classes. Only graduates who have taken a first degree at London either internally or externally may submit a thesis for an external higher degree. Moreover, the Extramural Department of the University of London and similar departments in other universities employ many full- or part-time lecturers and tutors in history who conduct classes or courses leading to Diplomas, equivalent to a pass degree. London, for instance, has a Diploma in History, awarded after a final examination at the end of an evening course extending over four years. Selected periods of ancient and modern history are covered in the first three years, with an examination at the end of each year. In the final year, evenings are devoted to studying the nature and use of historical evidence and the students write a short thesis based on original sources as part of their essay work. There are other Diplomas of London University, in British history, and in English local history, and also courses on paleography, diplomatic, and other auxiliary sciences.

There are sizeable departments of history in several of the older municipal universities: Birmingham (52 teachers), Manchester (40), Liverpool (36). The four colleges which up to now have together constituted the University of Wales (Aberystwyth, Bangor, Cardiff, and Swansea) each have small but very active history schools, with specialized teaching in Welsh history and important chairs in several other fields. In Scotland the biggest school of history is at the

University of Edinburgh, where there are 59 teachers of the subject; Glasgow comes next with 43, and St. Andrews and Aberdeen have 31 and 24 respectively. One of the newest Scottish universities, Strathclyde, although primarily concerned with science and technology, has started off with a small department of history. As mentioned earlier, most of the professors, readers, and lecturers in Scotland are mainly engaged in preparing undergraduates for their first degrees and have little supervision of research, although the great majority of them are themselves engaged on advanced historical work of one kind or another.

Besides the chartered universities, old and new, there are a considerable number of "Colleges of Further Education," or "Higher Education," which aim to reach similar standards and indeed prepare some of their students for university degrees. There are also hundreds of other institutions devoted to adult education in the United Kingdom, many of them, even colleges of science and technology, offering classes in history, or at least an historical approach to vocational subjects, and maintaining one or more history specialists on their staffs. Under the plans being formulated in accordance with the Robbins Report, a considerable number of these institutions of higher learning will be raised to the status of universities, or more closely associated with existing universities than in the past. All in all, the opportunities of a career for young men and women with a flair for historical study or teaching are far more extensive than ever before in Britain and few adults of ability are likely to be missed. In the view of some observers the danger may be rather in the direction of encouraging too many young people with inadequate equipment to enter the historical profession at the academic level. If, however, those doing so can be put through the testing mill of research for a higher degree before being let loose on students, the danger may be lessened. During the present period of expansion in Britain it is rather too easy for young men and women to get into well-paid teaching posts in universities or other institutions of adult education without having undergone this chastening experience and with little incentive to keep up their advanced studies of history.

B. *Independent research*

Although not normally obliged to do so, a great number of university teachers in Great Britain are in fact actively engaged in research. The days are gone when the award of a college fellowship at Oxbridge could mean a not-too-strenuous life of delivering one or two lectures a week during three brief terms and the personal tuition of a few undergraduates. It was a wasteful system which gave a few men, who were conscientious as well as able, the leisure to produce an occasional masterpiece, while the rest simply enjoyed the leisure. The only place where it survives is at All Souls College, Oxford, whose fellows include several distinguished historians active as University teachers although without pupils in the College. A proposal in January, 1965, to admit thirty postgraduate students was abandoned and a scheme for visiting fellows substituted. The Franks Commission, set up by the University of Oxford itself to investigate higher education within its college walls, has been critical in its *Report* (May, 1966) of the "infirmity of purpose" shown by All Souls, which may soon lose its privileged position. By contrast with the old, carefree times, present-day dons complain that the number of lectures they have to give and the number of students with whom they have to deal prevents them from getting on with the thesis or the book which is really the dominant object in their lives. It is true that higher degrees are still not regarded as a criterion of ability in some quarters at the old universities. Many college fellows and tutors at present in office have in fact not themselves proceeded to a doctoral degree and some are inclined to discount the educational value of the D.Phil. or Ph.D. Nevertheless, an increasing number spend a high proportion of their time in preparing articles for learned journals and writing substantial books, occupations which involve the same sort of discipline as that undergone by the postgraduate student writing a thesis. College fellowships are rarely awarded for life nowadays and indications that a holder is a scholar as well as a competent tutor are increasingly demanded by those responsible for renewing them. Many senior fellows are also university lecturers, and thus incidentally add to their earnings. They must, hence, keep abreast of current ideas and obtain fresh information about their special subjects. Personal investigation of their own particular interests often follows as a result.

University teachers in London have fewer tutorial duties, although several colleges have recently introduced something not unlike the Oxbridge system. They certainly have more lecturing and essay reading to do than their colleagues at the older universities. They are usually required by the terms of their appointments to engage in advanced work as well as to direct postgraduate research when required. Almost to a man they are investigating original sources in the Public Record Office, the Department of Manuscripts at the British Museum, or in Lambeth Palace, and other repositories of ecclesiastical documents, in the Guildhall Library, the halls of City Companies, the archives of chartered companies and modern business houses, the records of the Bank of England and other banks, and all the other accumulations of documents which make London the Mecca of historians.

Publication of the results of research undoubtedly helps the young British scholar to obtain promotion and the complaint is less often heard than it used to be that there are too few periodicals to receive all the learned articles being written on historical subjects. Nor is publication in book form so difficult now that university presses and learned societies are able to obtain subsidies for works which are valuable to scholarship but not economically viable. All the well-established universities in Britain have their own presses, journals and specialist periodicals for particular departments. A greater number of new books per head of population is published annually in Great Britain than in any other country and historical works are a high proportion among them. In July, 1967, the number of new British historical publications issued during the previous twelve months and listed in the catalogue of the book exhibition at the annual Anglo-American Conference of Historians totalled more than 700 separate works. This figure did not include school or college textbooks, or popular writings of ephemeral value. Among the works listed were many publications of national or local societies whose place in the British scene is considered below.

The writers of these very varied publications are far from being all of them university dons, although a high proportion are certainly university graduates. Only a few of the books are revised versions of doctoral dissertations; even fewer are mature works of scholarship. Rather more are monographs on special topics, not always written within the walls of a college. Many deal with local affairs in the past, with social and economic conditions, with particular industries and individual institutions, with families and personalities. A surprising amount of such work is still issued not only in book or pamphlet form, but also in magazines and newspapers by non-professional writers. The "amateur historian" is still very active in Britain: he has a periodical with that title devoted to his interests and recently taken over by the National Council for Social Service, a body with public money to spend on deserving objects. It has materially helped the Standing Conference on Local History, which in turn has encouraged the setting up of committees or societies for the study of local history throughout the counties of England and Wales. Many of these new societies and the older antiquarian ones maintain libraries and so do numerous professional associations, business organizations and social clubs which have well-equipped reading rooms where the reading and, if so desired, the writing of history can be carried on. Famous institutions such as the Inns of Court, the Bank of England, the Athenaeum, and the Reform Club in London, and similar bodies elsewhere have fine libraries well stocked with historical books and periodicals.

Apart from the free municipal and county libraries there are numerous other libraries, some easy of access, some charging substantial fees. In such great collections as the London Library in St. James's Square, the John Rylands Library at Manchester, or the Mitchell Library in Glasgow, the independent historian can find much of the printed material he needs and original manuscripts still requiring investigation. The non-academic scholar is much scarcer than he used to be, but he is often to be found at work in such places. The unskilled amateur is far more plentiful than he ever was. If he is content to speak to, or to write for, a limited circle of acquaintances he does no harm, but a great deal of bad history unfortunately appears in print from local enthusiasts. As in so many other fields, better educational facilities, including the excellent historical programs put out by the radio and television authorities, should correct this danger, which is somewhat in evidence at the moment.

C. *Institutes and centers*

Apart from the Institute of Historical Research, whose role has already been described, there are few national centers for advanced study of history in Britain and most of them are concerned with special aspects of the subject. All of them have very small staffs and operate on budgets which are infinitesimal by transatlantic standards. Although the British Academy annually dispenses substantial sums put at its disposal by the government, in order to assist scholarship, it has no proper library of its own and the Raleigh Lectures in History given in its rooms at Burlington House are prepared elsewhere. The Society of Antiquaries of London is another matter. It has a valuable library of printed works and manuscripts at Burlington House with a much wider range than archaeological pursuits. The lectures and publications of the society are concerned with many periods of history, although mainly confined to the visible remains of the past. To be a Fellow of the British Academy is as great a distinction on the Arts side of learning as to be a Fellow of the Royal Society is on the Science side. Fellowship of the Society of Antiquaries is also a considerable distinction, conferred only on those who have published work which is regarded as significant by the electing Fellows. The same is true *mutatis mutandis* of the Royal Historical Society. Yet the paid staffs of each of these eminent institutions could be counted on the fingers of one hand. The truth is that much of the work is done—as in so many other fields of British activity—by Honorary Directors and Honorary Editors, preparing for publication the results of voluntary labors by the Fellows. Another institution which is independent of the universities, although it receives occasional government grants, is the Royal Institute of International Affairs, which has done invaluable work for contemporary history. Not only its publications but also its library, lecture rooms, and studies in St. James's Square, London, have made "Chatham House" famous. The editorial and research staff, who get through a prodigious amount of work in gutting foreign magazines and newspapers, preparing factual reports and topical pamphlets, do not total more than a dozen persons. Here again unpaid working parties of experts produce some of the most useful surveys of the recent past.

Many other institutions concerned in part with history, or with special branches of the subject, flourish in London and other towns. Essentially most of them are national or local societies supported in the main by the subscriptions of their members. Their place in the study of the subject is considered below (section IV). Here it should simply be noted that the two principal ones are the Royal Historical Society, which at present has its offices in Bloomsbury, and the Historical Association, which is on the other side of the river Thames in Kennington. The former is the more learned body and in its latest

List of Fellows, Associates, etc. (1967), over 800 names are included. Most of these are British scholars and nearly all are university graduates: a high proportion are university teachers, so that their names appear in other categories already considered in this essay. The Historical Association, which has no qualifications for membership, except an interest in the subject, now totals over 12,000 members. Many of the same names of university dons appear, but the largest element are schoolteachers, with no pretensions to original scholarship but nevertheless deeply interested in history and well informed. As for the hundreds of other national and local societies described below their combined membership must run into several hundreds of thousands, albeit a large proportion of those participating in their activities could not be described as "students" except in the most general sense of the word.

III. *Where Historical Research is Done*

A. *Universities*

The preparation of historical dissertations for higher degrees in Britain is partly done in the libraries of the colleges and other institutions of the various universities, partly in archive repositories and other places where sources may be found. As indicated above, the Institute of Historical Research in London serves as a center for such systematic training as is at present offered in Great Britain and a high proportion of research students and more mature scholars from other universities, who are doing advanced work in the subject, take advantage of its facilities. The University of London Library, a comparative newcomer among national libraries, has grown very rapidly in less than fifty years and will soon contain a million volumes. They include a respectable number of *incunabula* and many other literary and historical rarities, among them a big range of pamphlets on economic and social subjects in the Goldsmiths' Library. The manuscript collection of the University is small at present but already contains valuable historical material.

Almost as large are the libraries at University College, London, and at the London School of Economics and Political Science. The former was the original library of the University and houses not only Jeremy Bentham's manuscripts, but those of Lord Brougham and of

the Society for the Diffusion of Useful Knowledge, and other interesting collections. "L.S.E." is strong in economic, social and legal
literature; it also has many papers of members of the Fabian Society and other personal manuscripts of importance for recent times.

The University of Oxford is fortunate in having the Bodleian
Library, which is one of the copyright libraries, with the right to a
copy of every book published in the United Kingdom. Established
150 years before the British Museum was opened, the Bodleian possesses a number of printed works never acquired by the Museum. In
the great series of Western Manuscripts, and in many other collections deposited on loan, it has original material for many periods still
only partially explored by scholars. At Rhodes House, which contains
part of the university library, are placed acquisitions of more recent
manuscripts and works concerning colonial and imperial affairs, past
and present. There are a number of specialized institutions within
the University of Oxford, such as the Ashmolean Museum, which
contain important archaeological, artistic, and scientific material of
great value to the historian. Most of the colleges have their special
collections of books, their ancient muniments and personal papers
of *alumni,* presented to them by the families of deceased celebrities.
All Souls College, for instance, has, in addition to its own rich archives, several modern acquisitions, such as the papers of Sir Charles
Vaughan, British Minister to the United States, 1825–1935. Christ
Church has at the moment, deposited by the present Marquess of
Salisbury, the Papers of the 3rd Marquess, the Conservative Foreign
Secretary and Prime Minister. Cambridge University Library also
has copyright privileges, so that virtually all books published in
Great Britain since the eighteenth century are to be found there.
Like the Bodleian, it possesses many rare books dating from the
early days of printing and several important manuscript collections.
Corpus Christi College, Trinity College, and several other old foundations in Cambridge have some of the finest medieval manuscripts
surviving, while the Pepys Library at Magdalene has a remarkable
variety of old books, pamphlets, manuscripts, prints and drawings, as
well as the famous *Diary.* For some fields of history it is hardly necessary for the researcher to go outside Oxford or Cambridge for all
he needs. In Edinburgh the University has the advantage of the
National Library of Scotland and its own fine collection of books
and manuscripts. Aberystwyth has the National Library of Wales.

The other British universities are not so fortunate as to have copyright libraries near at hand, but provincial towns have some great collections of their own, for instance, the Brotherton Library at Leeds, which is part of the University, and the John Rylands Library at Manchester, which is not. Distances in Great Britain are short and nearly everyone engaged on research can easily get to London, to Oxford, to Edinburgh or Aberystwyth, in order to see the books not available in his own university town and the manuscripts he needs to consult or collate.

B. *Libraries and archives*

Among the great libraries of Britain, pride of place must naturally be given to the British Museum, which contains more books, pamphlets, periodicals, and other forms of literature than any other institution in the world, with the exception of the Library of Congress. Even the Division of Manuscripts at Washington cannot vie with the superb collections in the various departments of the British Museum, which house unrivalled documentary treasures from specimens of the earliest writing known to the personal papers of statesmen and other celebrities not long dead. Clay tablets from ancient Babylon, papyri from ancient Egypt, inscriptions from Greece and Rome, parchments from medieval scriptoria; many of all these have gone into the British Museum either as part of the foundation collections of Cotton, Harley and Sloane, or in the Royal, Egerton, Lansdowne, and other collections of manuscripts added later, together with the vast category of "Additional Manuscripts." This last great series in itself embraces the hundreds of volumes containing the Newcastle, Liverpool, Peel, and Gladstone Papers, not to mention scores of other personal records of national and international significance. London has many other libraries, large and small, and innumerable muniment rooms. Besides the various libraries of the University already mentioned, there is the library of the Greater London Council (formerly the London County Council Members Library). It is especially concerned with London history and so is the Guildhall Library, but each has much of more general interest. Many of the metropolitan boroughs have large libraries containing works of a miscellaneous character, usually including a special collection for the history of the locality, very often the archives of the borough and other manuscripts as well. The Muniment Room of the Guildhall and the Corporation Records Office have magnificent original material for the administrative, legal, and financial history of the capital and the realm as a whole. Many of the records of the City livery companies and modern business houses have survived. The Bank of England and the other national banks have their own libraries and archive offices, so have Lloyd's Register of Shipping, the Port of London Authority, the Hudson's Bay Company, and many other chartered institutions too numerous to mention.

Leaving aside for the moment the Public Record Office, one should note that since the sixteenth century Parliament has kept its own muniments, which are housed in the Victoria Tower of the Palace of Westminster. Many early records of the House of Commons were destroyed in the Fire of 1834, but fortunately the House of Lords had copies of some of them and preserved its own documents intact. Another official body which has retained its own records is the College of Arms, whose heraldic documents go back into the middle ages. London is rich in ecclesiastical records—Lambeth Palace, Westminster Abbey, and St. Paul's Cathedral all have rich archives and fine old libraries. Many parish churches within the metropolitan area have preserved their records and all nonconformist religious bodies have valuable material: the Baptists, Congregationalists, Methodists, Presbyterians, Roman Catholics, Society of Friends, and Jews all have their muniment rooms in London. Sion College and Dr. Williams's Library have much ecclesiastical material in print or in manuscript, so have various church organizations: the Church Missionary Society, the London Missionary Society, the Society for the Propagation of the Gospel in Foreign Parts, the Society for Promoting Christian Knowledge, the Church Army, the Salvation Army and many others. Nor should propagandist bodies be forgotten—the Anti-Slavery Society, the West India Committee and the rest. Then there are the various museums and galleries, not only the well-known National Gallery and Tate Gallery, but those concerned with particular aspects of art and containing books, prints, and other historical material as well as pictures—the London Museum, the Imperial War Museum, the National Maritime Museum, the Post Office Museum, the Science Museum, the Railway Museum, and the Victoria and Albert Museum. Many specialist societies and professional organizations have their headquarters in London and have built up splendid libraries: the Royal Society itself, the Royal Institution, the Royal Society of Arts, the Royal Commonwealth Society, the Royal Institute of British Architects, the Society of Antiquaries, and so on. Every one of these bodies, and scores of others which could be named, possesses manuscripts, as well as many books, and all are frequently visited by scholars in search of historical data.

In the end, if not at the beginning, of research almost everyone concerned with western history goes to the Public Record Office in Chancery Lane, London. No other country has series of official documents so continuously preserved over so long a period as England. The records of the medieval Exchequer begin with Domesday Book, the two parchment volumes looking in their showcase as fresh as in the years they were written (1085–1087). The series of Pipe Rolls of the Exchequer started in the next century and the great series of Chancery rolls, on which are enrolled Charters, Letters Close, and Letters Patent, began before the end of the eleventh century and were kept going until the eighteenth, nineteenth, and in some cases the twentieth century, with hardly a break. The numerous series of State papers created by the new officers of the Crown since the sixteenth century are now deposited in the Public Record Office in vast quantities; so are the medieval and modern records of the royal courts of law. A glance at the revised *Guide to the Contents of the Public Record Office* (2 vols. H.M.S.O., 1963) will suggest the inexhaustible wealth of information contained in the various series, not only about the British Isles in the past, but about many other countries also: in the days of Britain's imperial greatness almost every country in the world. The gloomy Victorian-Gothic building in Chancery Lane has become a place of pilgrimage for scholars from far and near, so that the cramped search-rooms are barely able to provide seating space for those who want to spend laborious days in them. Unless more records are moved away from central London, as has already happened on a small scale, a larger building will be needed, both to house the constantly expanding series of documents and to give research workers better conditions in which to use them.

What has been said about the multifarious libraries and archive repositories in London could be repeated on a smaller scale for the sister capital in Scotland. The Scottish Record Office occupies part of H.M. General Register House in Edinburgh. Its contents are particularly valuable for the local history of the country. The National

Library of Scotland in Edinburgh has rich collections of manuscripts, foreign as well as British; so has the National Library of Wales in Aberystwyth. Nearly every town in Britain of any size has its municipal library and its muniment room. Many have excellent museums and art galleries, reading rooms, and well-equipped community centers. Local government records are an indispensable source for national as well as regional history since they so often illustrate the practical working out of legislation passed at Westminster. Every English and Welsh shire nowadays has its county record office into which have gone the countless parchments and papers written by many generations of local administrators: lord lieutenants, sheriffs, above all those justices of the peace who virtually ruled England for so many centuries. Town and county record offices also receive masses of manorial, estate, business, family, and other personal documents deposited by individuals or institutions with no facilities of their own for keeping records. Well-run record offices like those in Essex, Kent, Middlesex, and Surrey have a great deal to offer the investigator and the contiguity of these particular ones to the capital gives their collections in many instances a wider significance.

Parish documents have often found their way into county record offices; yet there remain plenty of parish chests which still hold registers of baptisms, marriages, and deaths, churchwardens' accounts and vestry minutes—the very stuff of local history. And one must not forget the old houses, large and small, which cling to their ancestral possessions, frequently including family papers of the first importance. Lawyers' offices and the strongrooms of banks often conceal ancient documents of value: title-deeds of property, of charitable bequests, and pious endowments. A few years ago the Wiltshire editor of the *Victoria County History* found the medieval records of a nunnery in a solicitor's office in the very modern town of Swindon. And the author of this essay has examined fifteenth-century deeds of a local charity in the very small strongroom of a suburban bank. More and more of these hidden treasures are coming to light through the vigilance of the National Register of Archives, whose work is sketched below. If documents are old enough to have lost their legal significance, most solicitors and bank managers are willing to place them in the custody of the county and municipal repositories now readily accessible.

A recent list of *Record Repositories in Great Britain* (H.M.S.O.,

1964, 2nd ed., 1966) was prepared by a joint Committee of the Historical Manuscripts Commission and the British Records Association. It includes: national and local repositories of public records; libraries, museums, and societies which possess substantial holdings of manuscripts and make regular provision for students; repositories maintained by the Church of England and other religious denominations; repositories maintained by public bodies which are not government departments (e.g., the British Railways Board); libraries of universities, colleges, and schools which have manuscripts accessible to students, business houses, banks, and other institutions including societies which have their own repositories but make their documents available for research. The introduction to this useful publication calls attention to organizations which provide assistance in finding record material. The greatest of these is the Historical Manuscripts Commission, which since its first establishment in 1863 "has issued over 200 printed volumes of Reports upon privately owned records, with indexes of places and persons." An up-to-date list of these reports is issued by H.M. Stationery Office from time to time as *Sectional List 17*. Those who have worked on English history need no reminding that the *Calendars* (précis or extracts) of documents, which started as appendices to the Commission's Reports, are now a major contribution to learning. The *Calendar of Manuscripts preserved at Hatfield House* already extends to nineteen volumes (H.M. S.O., 1883–1966) and has dealt only with Cecil papers of the sixteenth and early seventeenth centuries. The Sidney family papers at Penshurst are another voluminous series which has been calendared. The Historical Manuscripts Commission is mainly concerned with collections in private hands which are of national importance; the Second World War brought home to officials and civilians alike the urgent need to record and preserve smaller collections of historical interest. Starting as a temporary inquiry in 1945, the National Register of Archives has now been permanently established in the offices of the Commission at Quality House, Quality Court, Chancery Lane, London. In the short space of twenty years the small staff of the Register have produced nearly a thousand reports (mostly duplicated from typescript) upon privately owned records. These reports are not calendars but detailed lists, and they are being further extended by elaborate indexes of places, persons and subjects, kept at Quality House and freely available to inquirers. The annual *Bulletin* of the

National Register of Archives selects for special attention the most important collections noted during the year, and an annual *List of Accessions* calls attention to new material which has arrived in record repositories. All in all, the H.M.C. and N.R.A. are doing splendid work for the historical investigator in Great Britain: saving him endless time in discovering the existence and whereabouts of documents, encouraging owners to make known their family or business papers, guiding many valuable collections into local record offices. A striking instance was the great Wentworth-Woodhouse Collection, which had been inaccessible until the Registrar persuaded the Fitzwilliam family to deposit it in the Sheffield City Library. At Quality House are also kept the *Manorial and Tithe Documents Registers,* which note the whereabouts of these invaluable sources for many fields of English history.

An influential organization in the preservation and use of historical material is the British Records Association, founded in 1932. Its membership of well over a thousand brings together archivists and historians for fruitful discussions, especially at its annual conference. The Association's journal, *Archives,* is highly informative, and the Association has also published a considerable number of useful reports and memoranda of various kinds. More specialized and operating in only a small way at present is the British Archives Council, which issues a quarterly *Bulletin* and occasional other publications. The Society of Archivists is a professional body, but its *Journal* contains first-rate articles of value to the historian. There exist also in Great Britain a considerable number of "record societies," founded specifically to print texts or calendars of historical documents. Some representative ones are noted below in the general consideration of learned societies.

Encouragement, financial assistance, and occasionally even direction of advanced work in many fields is given by the state to an ever-increasing extent. The Department of Education and Science organizes weekend courses and summer schools in which history often finds a place. The Ministry of Town and Country Planning permits the spending of public money, for instance, by county councils, on preserving and publishing local records. The Ministry of Works has a large staff engaged in inspecting and preserving ancient monuments in the custody of the state, including most of the old castles and many historic mansions. Permanent Commissions, such as the three

Historical Monuments Commissions for England, Wales, and Scotland not only schedule old buildings or earthworks which must not be destroyed, but are publishing splendid descriptions, county by county, of the structures they have listed. London has its own Survey Committee doing similar work within the extensive boundaries of the metropolitan area. The work of the Historical Manuscripts Commission has been described above. It should be added that there are quite a number of independent organizations, sometimes enjoying government subsidies, engaged in the work of preservation from the National Trust to the "Friends" of various cathedrals and churches, towns and villages, libraries, museums, and art galleries. Many of these voluntary bodies publish excellent historical monographs or magazines.

IV. Historical Societies

In a recently issued list of *Historical, Archaeological and Kindred Societies in the British Isles* (2nd ed., Institute of Historical Research, 1968) the compiler, Mrs. Sara E. Harcup, notes well over 800 existing organizations seriously concerned with the subject. She gives only the date of foundation, the latest known address and an indication of whether the society issues any publications. The handbook of *Scientific and Learned Societies of Great Britain* (latest edition, 1964) goes into more detail, but is highly selective, noting in the section devoted to archaeology and history no more than 115 associations. Those named in the more comprehensive list have been founded for a variety of objects. Some simply aim at arranging lectures or visits to places of historic interest. Others publish their proceedings, limited perhaps to papers read to members; others again occasionally also print original manuscripts. Record societies confine their publications to texts or calendars of documents. English and Welsh ones have been fully listed in E. L. C. Mullins, *Texts and Calendars: an analytical guide to serial publications* (Royal Historical Society, 1958). The Society of Antiquaries of London (founded in 1707 and next to the Royal Society the oldest learned society surviving in Britain) performs several functions. It organizes archaeological investigations. Its library is of the first importance for scholars. The *Antiquaries Journal* contains articles, reports, occasional texts, bibliographies, and reviews of books. *Archaeologia* gives accounts of excavations and other investigations. The Royal Historical Society (founded in 1868) prints in its *Transactions* the papers read to the members. In the *Camden series,* which it took over from the Old Camden Society (founded 1838), only texts are printed. Other publications of the society are the useful *Guides and Handbooks* series and the annual bibliography of *Writings on British History.* This started with the year 1934 but has now been carried back to the year 1901, so that all significant publications on British history, whether in book or article form, from the beginning of the century until the end of the year 1945 are on record and plans to bridge the gap from that date to the present are well advanced. The *Annual Bulletin of Historical Literature,* issued by the Historical Association, is a highly selective but nonetheless valuable bibliography of works on all periods and aspects of history, with critical appraisals by experts. The Association's journal, *History,* is considered one of the best in the field. Its articles are scholarly, its reviews highly respected. The "General" series of *Pamphlets* issued by the Association are authoritative historical revisions, written by specialists, while the *Teaching of History Leaflets* are designed to meet the needs of schools. The Association also took over a few years ago the series entitled *Helps for Students of History,* for which it has issued new titles and reissued some old ones. The annual conferences of the Historical Association, while not on the scale of its American namesake, bring together university dons and schoolteachers in representative numbers each spring.

These are the historical societies of most general scope in Great Britain. Two societies less recondite than the Society of Antiquaries of London but concerned with similar pursuits and publishing journals and books are the British Archaeological Association and the Royal Archaeological Institute of Great Britain and Ireland, both dating from 1843. There is also a Society of Antiquaries of Scotland (founded 1780) almost exclusively concerned with activities within that country. The Scottish History Society (founded 1886) is largely concerned with publishing texts, and there are also a Scottish Record Society and a Scottish Text Society doing parallel work. Wales has the Cambrian Archaeological Society (founded 1846) which issues an important journal, *Archaeologia Cambrensis,* containing historical as well as antiquarian articles and texts of documents. More specifically concerned with history is the long-established Honourable Society of Cymmrodorion (1751), which publishes articles on the Welsh past in its magazine *Y Cymmrodor* and documents in the *Cymmrodorion Record Series*. Ireland has a flourishing Irish Historical Society founded in 1936 by the merging of separate bodies in Dublin and Belfast, who had for some years previously been jointly producing the first-rate journal, *Irish Historical Studies*. Among other features the regular lists of "Writings on Irish History" are the best guide to the subject. The Committee which handles this valuable publication includes Catholics and Protestants from both parts of Ireland, a triumph for scholarship over political and ecclesiastical controversy.

There are some fifty societies in existence exclusively concerned with printing texts or calendars of historical documents in Great Britain. Mention of a few will suggest the range of their interests. The Anglo-Norman Text Society (1938) is concentrating in an even earlier field than the Early English Text Society (1893). The British Record Society, like the Harleian Society (1869), issues lists and calendars of parish registers, ecclesiastical and heraldic visitations and other useful local material. The Canterbury and York Society (1904) prints bishops' registers in the original Latin: some county record societies, such as the fine one at Lincoln (1910), devote many of their volumes to such registers. More typical is the Buckinghamshire Record Society (1937) which has already issued a variety of material bearing on the history of the county. Religious bodies have published many of their manuscripts through societies, for instance, the Catholic Record Society and the Huguenot Society. The Alcuin Club (1897) and the Henry Bradshaw Society (1890) have made available liturgical and other ecclesiastical texts. Exploration and colonization may be studied in the many volumes issued by the long-established Hakluyt Society (1846) or in the more limited area covered by the Hudson's Bay Record Society (1938). The Navy Records Society (1893) has no exact equivalent for the British Army, although documents are occasionally published by the Society for Army Historical Research (1921). The Pipe Roll Society (1883) has supplemented the work of the Public Record Office by editing this difficult series of exchequer documents. Texts for legal history have been issued in England by the Selden Society (1887), in Scotland by the Stair Society (1934). A few English towns have published their archives through the medium of societies: more often municipal authorities in England and Scotland have sponsored publication. Even London, many of whose literary treasures have been published by the Corporation, has only recently acquired a London Record Society (1964).

Much more varied in character, of course, are the hundreds of societies which publish nothing, or not much more than reports of lectures. The list of them starts with the Abertay Historical Society at Dundee and ends with the Yorkshire Society for Celtic Studies at Leeds. Some, however, have national and even international significance in their special spheres: the Economic History Society, the Georgian Group and the Victorian Society, the British Society for the History of Science, the Newcomen Society for the Study of the History of Engineering and Technology, the Royal Numismatic Society, the Society of Genealogists, the Walpole Society for the history of art, and the Wedgwood Society for the history of ceramics. Many counties and some towns still have old antiquarian, natural history, and field clubs side by side with the recent "local history groups" and record societies. Famous ones are the Chetham Society (1843) at Manchester, the Surtees Society (1834) at Durham, the Sussex Archaeological Society (1846) at Lewes, the Old Edinburgh Club (1908) and many more, not to mention the numerous societies for studying the history of science and its practical application to industry, commerce, railways, tramways, and other forms of transport. Not a week passes but some new society is formed for at least the discussion and usually also for the investigation of a particular area, or a particular activity in the past.

V. Principal Journals or Reviews

Nearly every historical journal in Great Britain is issued by a society or university institution. Strangely enough the most important of all is a commercial enterprise, financed since its establishment in 1886 by a well-known publishing house, Longmans of London. The *English Historical Review* has had a series of distinguished editors from Mandell Creighton, bishop of London, at the start to Wallace-Hadrill at the present time. It appears four times a year and

attracts the most scholarly English work being produced in periodical form, although neither contributors of articles nor reviewers of
books are paid. This is true also of *History*, the magazine of the Historical Association, of the *Historical Journal*, sponsored by the Cambridge University Press and originally called the *Cambridge Historical Journal*, and indeed of almost all other periodicals concerned
with the subject, except *History Today*. This illustrated monthly
magazine is designed to interest a wider audience than the professional student or teacher, yet it contrives to maintain high standards
without being dull. A connection with the Historical Association,
whose members get special subscription rates and which is represented on the board of directors, should help to preserve its characteristic features. *History Today* has a much larger circulation than any
other British periodical devoted to the subject—at the present time
over 32,000 copies a month, compared with some 6,000 copies of
History (issued three times yearly) and fewer still of the other journals mentioned. The *Bulletin of the Institute of Historical Research*
appears only twice a year. Its articles and bibliographical features are
of high quality but it contains no reviews. *Past and Present*, now
issued by the Past and Present Society, has recently become respectable after a tendentious start. North of the Tweed, the *Scottish
Historical Review*, published by Nelson's since its revival in 1947 is
providing excellent service not only by significant articles, but by
regular archival and bibliographical information. In addition to
y Cymmrodor there is a new *Welsh History Review* and many other
historical journals, for particular counties or special subjects, most
of them sponsored by societies. The National Library of Wales is
responsible for the standard annual bibliography of Welsh history:
Bibliotheca Celtica and also for a *Journal* in which appears some of
the best work, especially of a documentary kind. The Board of Celtic
Studies has its own *Bulletin* and has issued important series of texts
in Welsh and English. Besides *Irish Historical Studies*, Ireland has
other excellent journals: notably the *Irish Ecclesiastical Record*,
mainly concerned with Roman Catholicism but including articles of
much wider significance. Taking into account the *Transactions* and
other publications of the learned societies of the four countries—
England, Wales, Scotland, and Ireland—there must be at least six
hundred serials concerned with history coming out at regular or ir-
regular intervals in present-day Britain and Ireland.

VI. Major Trends

During the present century British historians have shared with their colleagues in other western countries a greater awareness of the subjective element in all their work. The philosophy of Benedetto Croce has found echoes in many English writers, notably R. G. Collingwood (died 1943), one of the most influential interpreters of historiography in our time. The often misunderstood saying of Croce that "all true history is contemporary history" is generally accepted in its true meaning by British writers, who are conscious that present conditions and personal prejudices determine their attitude towards the past. Some, like Geoffrey Barraclough and E. H. Carr, face the fact boldly and urge historians to state their views and draw their morals. Arnold Toynbee has gone even further in his huge work on *The Study of History.* He offers explanations for the whole of man's story on earth, has seen "patterns" repeating themselves, similar "challenges" meeting with similar "responses," some overall plan working itself out. It should be emphatically stated that there is virtually no Toynbee "school" in Britain, nor indeed any other observable school of historical philosophy. Even the considerable number of younger historians who are socialist in politics differ widely from one another in discussing such controversial subjects as the English Civil War, the Industrial Revolution, the ruling classes at various periods. It would seem indeed that most British historical writers today, young as well as elderly, have their own personal philosophies, while sharing a diffidence about coming to conclusions, which is strikingly different from the cocksureness of the Victorians. There are exceptions, of course, and one could name well-known scholars who do not hesitate to judge as well as explain, to condemn as well as describe, the actions of statesmen, soldiers, clergy, and administrators even in recent times, when the evidence is far from complete.

Perhaps because bureaucracy is so much with us nowadays there has been a growing interest in "administrative" history, both central and local, in Britain as in other countries. It is often accompanied by the analytical methods employed so successfully by the late Sir Lewis Namier in his breakdown of *The Structure of Politics at the Acces-*

sion of George III, and by Sir John Neale in his detailed study of *The Elizabethan House of Commons.* The cooperative *History of Parliament,* now beginning to appear in print, and owing much of its shape to these two scholars, is essentially an amassing of biographical facts about all the members which, it is hoped, will reveal influences and pressures not hitherto appreciated. T. F. Tout is sometimes given the credit for initiating this movement with his *Chapters in Medieval Administrative History.* He has certainly had many imitators in both the medieval and modern periods. Writers are no longer content with political and constitutional explanations of public events. They look behind the "front men" for the "back-room boys," who really formulated policy as well as having to carry out the decisions of their chiefs. Doctoral dissertations and books based on them deal in increasing numbers with government departments, pressure groups, and individuals behind the scenes, although economic and social conditions remain favorite topics as well.

Other fresh interests have sprung from contemporary circumstances. Much of good quality is being written in Britain about Africa, about the Near East and the Far East. The two world wars have not only begotten official histories but stimulated comparatively novel subjects like "Military Studies" (for which there are chairs of history in several universities and a special Institute in London). Far more attention is being given to the history of the United States, which figures now in many school syllabuses, as well as in the Honours courses of most, if not all, universities. The British Association for American Studies has done much to promote the subject and among other activities has published *A Guide to Manuscripts relating to America in Great Britain and Ireland* (1961). There are now an Institute of United States Studies in London and flourishing departments for the subject in several other universities. Latin American studies are also developing in the same way and so are Slavonic studies. With so many aspects of history contending for notice the problem is to fit them into school and university syllabuses. One answer has been to allow a wider choice of "optional" and "special" subjects in Honours degree courses; another is the regional basis adopted for the Honours degree in several of the older universities and most of the new. At the School of Slavonic and East European Studies in London, for instance, one may obtain a B.A. Honours degree in Slavonic Studies, the examination for which includes literary and linguistic papers as well as historical ones. Until very recently the writing of contemporary history in Great Britain was severely hampered by the "fifty-year rule," which closed to scholars public records of less age. Despite it a good deal has been written on the events of the last fifty years, although as A. J. P. Taylor points out in his recent book, *English History, 1914–1945,* "the period has as yet to be studied almost entirely in printed sources." Fortunately, the rule has now been changed to thirty years by the Public Records Act of 1967. It will soon be possible to present the British evidence in many international affairs as well as that already available from, for instance, the captured German documents to the end of the Nazi period (1945) and American official papers which are open to accredited students to a recent date indeed.

VII. Problems of the Profession

From all that has been said above it will be appreciated that, among what are described as the humanities, the study of history is more widespread than it has ever been in Great Britain. At the present moment there are too few teachers of quality to meet the demand in schools and universities. The expansion of adult education now taking place should do much to overcome this difficulty within the next decade or so. In the meantime everyone of standing in the profession is bombarded with requests for articles, books, broadcasts, or television appearances. Although tempting fees are offered and although costs of living continue to rise, it cannot truthfully be said that young historians are driven to accept such invitations by dire necessity. Thanks partly to scarcity value, partly to pressure exerted by such bodies as the Association of University Teachers, the salaries of even junior lecturers in universities and colleges of further education compare favorably with those received in other professions and in ordinary commerce. No don of course can ever hope to enjoy the income of a company director or an outstanding barrister, unless his books sell on the scale of G. M. Trevelyan's *Social History of England.* Academic salaries in Britain are determined by scales approved by all the universities in consultation with the University Grants Committee. Scientists and medical men have higher scales in all grades than non-scientific professors, readers, lecturers, and assistant lecturers. Those employed in the capital are given a special London Allowance to meet the higher cost of living. Oxford and Cambridge do not fit tidily into the pattern as the saving of expense by residence in a college, the system of college fellowships, additional employment done as librarians, bursars and so on, very often result in considerably higher real incomes than those of even their London colleagues.

No profession is ever satisfied with its emoluments and conditions of work. History teachers in universities can with reason complain that they have much more to do, not only in the classroom and the study, but in committees and at office desks. Attempts to devolve such duties onto full-time administrators have not proved very encouraging. Control of policy is lost, mistakes are made through ignorance of academic requirements, the wrong persons are consulted. Reluctantly the present-day historian, like his colleagues in other disciplines, has to pay the price of responsibility by spending at least half his time in administration. Examining greater numbers of students, both undergraduates and postgraduates, often in more than one university, eats into his vacations. Supervision of research and the reading of several theses every year further curtail the time he has at his disposal for his own reading. As a consequence many university teachers live under considerable strain. Time, which will produce more manpower in the profession, would seem to be the remedy.

For many fields of history, travel at home or abroad is essential if the scholar is to keep abreast of his subject, continue his researches in foreign libraries and archives, consult colleagues in other countries, attend conferences, and so on. British historians are still in a less favorable position than scholars in other western countries in the opportunities for getting abroad. Grants for comparatively short visits are few in number and often difficult to obtain. Far more young scholars would embark on the study of foreign countries if there were more travel scholarships available for long or short periods. The sabbatical year's leave is only just being introduced in a few British universities as a concession rather than a right. With their small staffs it is difficult to arrange in Oxford and Cambridge colleges and in some of the smaller universities. Larger institutions, such as the London School of Economics, have been pioneers in this regard, perhaps because their comparatively large staffs have made the absence of a few members each year easier to handle. "Study leave," with or without pay, for periods of six months or less, is much more common and there are benefactions, such as the Leverhulme Trust, which make special provision for scholars who have to find a substitute, or do without their pay, while on leave of absence to complete a piece of research.

These are some of the practical difficulties confronting academic historians at the present time. If Britain remains financially strong and able to stand the very much greater expenditure on adult education contemplated for the coming generation, problems of staffing, salaries, travel, and study leave should gradually resolve themselves. Burdens of administration will be lightened and a better balance achieved between hours devoted to teaching and research. There are some university teachers who almost resent the lecturing and tutorial side of their duties and would gladly reduce them to a single lecture a week (an objective actually achieved by some professors of history). The majority of British historians are, however, not of this view. They appreciate that the necessity to put their facts and ideas into order for teaching purposes is salutary and aids rather than hinders the formulation of research work. The eternal student, who would happily go on investigating an historical subject for as long as he can find the funds to sustain him, has received some encouragement from the generosity of the State and private benefactors in recent years. He does not often produce the best results; sometimes he produces no results at all. Most postgraduate students are content with the three years of uninterrupted research they can usually count on while preparing for a higher degree in history. Once involved in university teaching or administration, or some other scholastic pursuit which occupies the greater part of their time, they do indeed find it difficult to produce another substantial piece of original work based on documents. For such reasons study leaves, research fellowships for mature scholars and other devices for releasing them from their normal duties serve the best interests of the historical profession. There are very few scholars in Britain today rich enough to emulate an Edward Gibbon by devoting their full time for many years to a major work. This is regrettable in some ways but there are compensations. Writing is not the only way of conveying historical discoveries to an audience. Teaching in all its forms, whether in the lecture room, the seminar or the television studio, has a sobering effect on judgments and at the same time an exhilaration lacking in private study. And it may produce better books, as the many historical works of high quality now appearing in Great Britain would seem to suggest.

Selected Bibliography

Anglo-American Conference of Historians, *Bibliography of Historical Works Issued in the United Kingdom, 1946–56, 1957–60, 1961–65,* compiled by Joan C. Lancaster and W. Kellaway, 3 vols. London, Institute of Historical Research, 1957, 1962, 1967. Annual supplements.

AUSUBEL, H., BREBNER, J. B., and HUNT, E. M., eds., *Some Modern Historians of Britain, Essays in Honor of R. L. Schuyler.* New York, Dryden, 1951.

British Council and Association of Commonwealth Universities, *Higher Education in the United Kingdom, A Handbook for Students from Overseas.* London, Longmans, 1966. Biennial pubn.

BUTTERFIELD, H., *The Present State of Historical Scholarship,* Inaugural Lecture. London, Cambridge University Press, 1965.

ELTON, G. R., *The Practice of History.* New York, Crowell, 1968.

FIRTH, Sir C. H., *A Plea for the Historical Teaching of History.* Oxford, Clarendon Press, 1904.

FURBER, Elizabeth Chapin, ed., *Changing Views on British History: Essays on Historical Writing since 1939.* Cambridge, Mass., Harvard University Press, 1966.

GALBRAITH, V. H., *Albert Frederick Pollard, 1869–1948,* reprinted from *Proceedings of the British Academy,* vol. XXXV [1949].

———, *Historical Study and the State: an Inaugural Lecture.* Oxford, Clarendon Press, 1948.

GOOCH, G. P., *History and Historians in the 19th Century,* 2nd ed. London, Longmans, 1952. Chapters on British historians.

Great Britain. London, Public Record Office, *Guide to the Contents of the Public Record Office,* 2 vols. H.M.S.O., 1963.

HALE, J. R., ed., *The Evolution of British Historiography. From Bacon to Namier.* New York, Macmillan, 1967.

HARCUP, Sara E., *Historical, Archaeological and Kindred Societies in the British Isles. A List,* 2nd ed. London, University of London, Institute of Historical Research, 1965.

HEPWORTH, P., *How to Find Out in History. A Guide to Sources of Information for All.* London, Pergamon Press, 1966. Addressed to beginners in Great Britain.

Historical Association, *Annual Bulletin of Historical Literature.* London. Annual since 1922.

BARLOW, G., and HARRISON, B., eds., *History at the Universities: a comparative and analytical guide to history syllabuses at universities in the United Kingdom.* London, Historical Association, 1966. New edition in preparation.

Historical Manuscripts Commission, *Record Repositories in Great Britain. A List Prepared by a Joint Committee of the Historical Manuscripts Commission and the British Records Association.* H.M.S.O., 1964; 2nd ed., 1966.

KITSON CLARK, G. and ELTON, G. R., *Guide to Research Facilities in History in the Universities of Great Britain and Ireland,* 2nd ed. London, Cambridge University Press, 1965.

MILNE, A. T., comp., *Writings on British History. A Bibliography of Books and Articles on the History of Great Britain . . . published during the year(s) 1934–45,* 8 vols. London, Royal Historical Society, 1937–1960. Continuation in preparation. Vols. for 1901-33, ed. H. H. Bellot, in press.

MULLINS, E. L. C., comp. *Texts and Calendars: an Analytical Guide to Serial Publications.* London, Royal Historical Society, 1958.

OMAN, Sir C., *On the Writing of History.* London, Methuen, 1939.

Oxford University. Hebdomadal Council. Commission of Inquiry (Franks Commission), *Report,* 2 vols. Oxford, Clarendon Press, 1966.

Parliament, House of Commons, *Higher Education. Report of the Commitee appointed by the Prime Minister under the Chairmanship of Lord Robbins, 1961–63,* Cmnd 2154. London, H.M.S.O., 1963.

POLLARD, A. F., *Factors in Modern History,* 3rd ed. London, Longmans, 1948.

POWICKE, Sir F. M., *Modern Historians and the Study of History. Essays and Papers.* London, Odhams, 1955.

TREVOR-ROPER, H. R., *History, Professional and Lay: an Inaugural Lecture.* Oxford, Clarendon Press, 1957.

University of London, Institute of Historical Research, *Historical Research for University Degrees in the United Kingdom.* Annual lists issued in two parts: *Theses Completed* and *Theses in Progress.*

———, *Teachers of History in the Universities of the United Kingdom.* Annual list.

WINKS, Robin W., ed., *The Historiography of the British Empire-Commonwealth.* Durham, N. Car., Duke University Press, 1966.

Part Five

Historical Study
in
The United States

BOYD C. SHAFER

I. A Short Historical Sketch

Interest in history was high when the modern study began in the United States of the 1880's. George Bancroft was making the final revision of his patriotic and popular *History of the United States,* begun fifty years before, and Francis Parkman, finest of American stylists, was culminating his four decades of work with *Montcalm and Wolfe* and *A Half Century of Conflict.* In colonial times Americans, especially the Puritans, had written and read history. During the nineteenth century literate Americans read not only the works of their own historians, Parkman, Bancroft, Prescott, and Motley, but also Gibbon, Macaulay, and J. R. Green. Nevertheless, the nature of historical study was changing. During the last quarter of the nineteenth century, currents of thought similar to those stimulating professional studies in western Europe were flowing in the United States.

These currents, strongest in Germany and France, and a little later in Britain, arose in large part out of romantic and nationalist sentiment. But their direction and force were influenced both by the growing interest in scientific methods and, especially in the United States, by the spread of belief in popular government and the desire to make "good citizens." The truth about men's past, it was increasingly thought, could be discovered through the use of scientific methods, in somewhat the same way physicists could describe the phenomena and formulate laws of the physical world. And lessons from the past could be used to educate citizens just as they had once been used to instruct princes.[1]

Basic "scientific" ideas for the study of history had been developing in Germany since at least the 1820's and the writings of Barthold Georg Niebuhr and Leopold von Ranke.[2] Discussed in France and

[1] See above, p. 5.
[2] See above, pp. 17–18, 79–81.

Britain from about the 1860's, they were transmitted to the United States largely through young American scholars trained in Germany and through the correspondence of American scholars with those of Britain and France.

Until the 1880's few systematic rules for research or criteria for interpretation had been formulated in the United States; no profession of history, similar to those in theology and law, had developed; and in the universities little attention was paid to history. Those indispensable institutions for historical work, libraries and archives, seldom existed and nearly all the necessary bibliographical tools were yet to be forged. Though much history had been written and history had many readers, the primary purposes of most American historians had been to tell a tale in literary form, to win an audience, and to point out moral lessons from the past.

These three purposes would not disappear, but two others were arising which would become of first importance: (1) to reconstruct the past as accurately and fully as research in primary sources would permit, and thus (2) to increase citizens' understanding of the present through affording them knowledge of the past. These newer purposes meant that scholarly standards had to be set, that students had to be methodically trained, that the resources for study had to be organized, that historians would wish to organize in order to establish communication among themselves and set professional standards for their study—just as craftsmen in many other fields were beginning to do, and that instruction in the schools, colleges, and universities had to be expanded and improved.

The growing professional emphases led to or were reflected in a series of actions which would strengthen the study of history. Among these were: (1) the establishment of graduate training in history, especially at the Johns Hopkins through the work of German-trained Professor Herbert Baxter Adams; (2) the related founding of undergraduate courses in history and the accompanying creation of professorships and departments of history in most universities and colleges; (3) the publication of scholarly studies and book reviews which set standards, particularly in the *American Historical Review,* beginning in 1895 under the editorship of J. Franklin Jameson; (4) the organization of scholarly societies, especially the American Historical Association in 1884; (5) the improvement of libraries during the quarter century between the report on *Public Libraries in the United*

States . . . (1876) by the United States Bureau of Education and the appointment (1899) of the scholarly Herbert Putnam as Librarian of Congress; and (6) the publication by Charles Kendall Adams of a *Manual of Historical Literature* (1882) which was not only a bibliography but an instructive introduction in the German manner to the study of history.

The new professional historians of the late nineteenth and the early twentieth century produced few major works to rival the best books of the gifted amateurs who were passing, or at least few that attracted as wide an audience. The new professionals usually were, as the historians' historian, J. Franklin Jameson, described himself, makers of "bricks without much idea of how the architects will use them." They prized original research more than a well-turned phrase or flowing narrative, and critical attitudes toward the sources and the work of others more than creative insights into or fertile hypotheses about the subjects of their inquiries. If they had a patron saint it was Leopold von Ranke whom they elected the first honorary member of the American Historical Association. While they failed to understand Ranke's basically intuitive approach,[3] they wanted to understand and to write history in terms of his famous phrase, *"wie es eigentlich gewesen"* ("how it actually happened"). They thought they could be "scientific": evolve universal methods for objective inquiry which would lead to accumulation of historical knowledge and finally to definitive books. They were opposed to philosophical or theoretical schemes for the interpretation of history. Historians, they believed, should delve into documents and manuscripts, critically and according to rules (as those of Bernheim and later Langlois and Seignobos) evaluate the first-hand evidence, and then reconstruct the past as it actually was. For them the monograph which exhausted the sources on a narrow subject was a first requirement and only after long years of exhaustive research and analysis, when a pattern would reveal itself, should synthesis be attempted. An historian, as the young Edward Channing of Harvard declared, "should get all the facts by hard study of original materials and the work of his predecessors," in reflection "pass all this matter through his brain," make the mass of facts part of himself, and only then try to "reveal to others that which the past revealed to him."

The early professional historians' interests were restricted, not

3 See above, pp. 17–18, 79.

as narrowly as later critics would assert, but still restricted. Wanting above all to show how the American nation was achieved and freedom won, they concentrated upon the development of the colonies and the British Empire in America, upon political constitutions and social institutions, upon diplomacy, and, more specifically, upon the American Revolution and the Civil War. Few engaged in research on modern Europe, still fewer if any on Asia or Africa except as their histories touched those of America.

Though they partly realized their limitations, again more than later critics would grant, they were not as objective as they thought. They were not as blatantly nationalistic or as democratic as Bancroft had been, but their writings revealed their deep commitment to American democratic ideals. While they generally rejected theology and ignored philosophy, they, like John Fiske, usually accepted evolution (Darwinism) and progress, and formed their histories upon these concepts as if they were universally true. They were also men of conscience who recognized their duty to society: to inform their fellow citizens, to teach their students, to improve the schools of the nation. Most of them were teachers in the growing colleges and universities and spent most of their time in instruction. A purpose of their research, then, was not only to discover truth about the past but also to impart that truth to their students and their fellow citizens.

Their histories, their public addresses, their many letters, and their "confident memoirs," may seem prosaic to a later generation, but they labored for the causes in which they believed. For the most part New Englanders or New Yorkers, they held themselves and their work in high esteem and they intended to build solid foundations for the historical work of the future, vigorous, democratic America. Andrew D. White, the first President of the American Historical Association, was not only a pioneer teacher (at Michigan) of history and an academic administrator (at Cornell), but a public servant. The greatest of the founders, J. Franklin Jameson, though basically a shy man, presented a frosty exterior to all except intimate friends as he strove mightily to establish the scholarly bases for historical study. Herbert Baxter Adams, the organizer of the AHA and of historical work at the Hopkins, was ambitious and pedestrian but he devoted most of his life to the promotion of solid historical work by others.

White, Jameson, Adams, and a few dozen others tilled the soil for later major scholarly achievements. One of the early harvests was the first scholarly collaborative series covering the whole history of the United States, *The American Nation* series (28 volumes), edited by Albert Bushnell Hart of Harvard and published chiefly from 1904 to 1907. Of the 24 authors 21 were professors of history in universities and 22 had had graduate training in history.

To later generations the founders passed on their critical attitudes, a thirst for original sources, the monographic form of book that exhausted the subject (and too often the few readers), and a belief in the possibility of progress that would somehow survive two world wars, a major depression, and shattering psychological revelations about the irrationality of man. After and because of them other historians would take care to "get the facts straight," to document their statements (sometimes endlessly), to avoid plagiarism, and to try (without full success) to avoid moralizing.

Later generations would term much of their writing "second rate and devoid of genius"—indeed, Jameson thought this unavoidable and even desirable at the beginning. As the work of the first generation of professionals neared its end about 1910, Jameson asked a long series of probing questions, questions that each succeeding generation persisted in asking. That these in 1910 still had to be given largely negative answers should not hide the fact that the ground had been prepared if the harvest was yet meager.

What stage [he asked] of progress have we reached in the accumulation of printed materials for history in our libraries, or of unprinted materials in our archives? . . . What is the quantity and what the quality of our output of historical monographs? What is upon the average the mental calibre and what the training of those who make them? How do we stand with respect to the publication of histories of a higher order . . . ? How deep or how copious is American thought on the theoretical or philosophical aspects of history? . . . What are the present purposes, nature and effects of American historical teaching, elementary, secondary, collegiate, or university? . . .

In our universities what is the status of research? How are our historical societies and journals performing their function? What is the character of those books of history which most hold the public attention—so far as the public attention can be said to be held by any books whatsoever?

Each succeeding generation of American historians has attacked though not repudiated its predecessors. Probably this occurred both because each new generation sought an independent identity and because each generation, living under different conditions, viewed the past from different perspectives and asked different questions. In any case, by 1910 or 1912, revisionist tendencies were clearly appearing. New, though often but slightly younger, historians demanded "new history." While they usually were trained and taught in the east (especially Columbia), they often came from the middle west and reflected the reformist views of their progressive age. The New Englander Jameson, a scholar whose scholarship transcended doctrinal schools, remained the real head of the profession, but younger scholars now sometimes spoke disparagingly of "the establishment." They wanted more vigorous history, a wider and more useful history that would help solve the social problems then becoming obvious.

The program of the "new history" was not very new. It was not true, as a critic in the *American Historical Review* commented, that the new generation had "largely abandoned scientific history." It was true that once complacently accepted "certainties," in values, methods, and expected results, were challenged. Some of the new men, "at once reformers, meliorists, optimists, and idealists," were dissatisfied with the earlier work, and with the attention paid to history and likely to themselves as serious scholars. Some of them might have agreed with Theodore Roosevelt that historians had been "conscientious, industrious, painstaking little" pedants who believed that "if they only collected enough facts . . . there would cease to be any need hereafter for great writers, great thinkers." Historians, a good many began to believe, might make significant contributions to society by formulating and pursuing hypotheses and by utilizing the methods and findings of the arising social sciences. The chief spokesman of the "new history," James Harvey Robinson of Columbia, "flogged many a dead horse" but he pleaded, like Henri Berr in France, for a genetic point of view, for the inclusion of "every trace and vestige of everything man has done and thought" within the scope of history, for less collecting of unimportant data, and for interpretation that would reveal the social, scientific, and intellectual progress leading to the present. Whether or not in answer to Robinson's pleas, American historians did extend the range of their researches and began to arrive at "new viewpoints."

If there was no less collection of data among historians at large, there were different interpretations as the works and teachings of

Frederick Jackson Turner, Charles Beard, Vernon L. Parrington, and Carl Becker testify. Basically the new generation, though not Marxist, adopted an economic interpretation of history. Though they knew little and cared less about Hegelian dialectic, the most influential among them saw the past in terms of conflict—Jeffersonians versus Hamiltonians, debtors versus creditors, farmers versus bankers, the people versus the "vested interests," the democratic west versus the aristocratic east, the plantation south of slavery versus the industrial north of capitalism.

In consequence their fields of interest differed from those of their predecessors. They continued to be interested in the American colonies but gave more attention to the place of the colonies in the British Empire (Charles M. Andrews) and to the American Revolution (Claude Van Tyne and Carl Becker). They (as Frederick Jackson Turner) increasingly studied the influence of the sections of the United States, particularly the west and south. They (like Charles A. Beard) demanded and gave more emphasis to social and economic history—an emphasis that was to be realized later in the thirteen-volume series, *A History of American Life* (1927–1948) edited by Dixon Ryan Fox and Arthur Schlesinger. They (Vernon Parrington and James Harvey Robinson) were much more interested in the history of ideas (intellectual history), but despite their fondness for science they did little to write its history, though a few (Victor S. Clark) gave attention to technology. During and after World War I they wrote more on European history, especially the French Revolution. Occasionally they spoke of modern Asian and African history but they did little research in these fields. No more than their predecessors were they interested (until later) in either grand schemes concerning the meaning of history or in the philosophic bases of historical knowledge. Though some of them listened to and applauded Karl Lamprecht when he appealed for a socio-psychological approach to what he called the collective consciousness of humanity, they ignored the disturbing probings of Wilhelm Dilthey into the nature of historical understanding.[4] While they pleaded for more interpretation, many of them would not have disagreed with the progressive ex-Senator turned biographer, Albert Beveridge, who thought "the facts when justly arranged interpret themselves."

So simple a conclusion was bound to be unsatisfactory. It begged

[4] See above, p. 24.

so many questions. Through the 1920's few historians publicly examined the philosophical bases or implications of their knowledge,
as Henry Adams had done a little earlier. By the 1930's, however,
the disillusionments of the late war and the current depression and
growing awareness of recent findings of psychology brought serious
doubts and much self-examination in the United States, just as they
did in Europe. Was human progress so probable? Was man capable
of rational thought and action? Some American historians once more
turned to their European colleagues both for their critiques and
their formulations—in particular to Benedetto Croce, Karl Heussi,
and, later, R. G. Collingwood. They were aided in their search by
emigrés from Europe, by, for example, the son-in-law of Beard, Alfred Vagts.

Again there was continuity with past historical work in America. A few historians continued to write in the fashion of historians
in the nineteenth century, though few wrote as well. Perhaps the
most renowned American historian of the mid-century, Samuel Eliot
Morison, wrote narrative history in the grand manner and as if philosophic doubt and methodological dilemmas did not exist. Most historians did not discard the "scientific" precepts of the first generation
of professionals and on occasion an individual rose to defend them.
The "new history," which encompassed everything, was no longer
thought new, and in fact became orthodox. Revisionism within the
earlier frameworks, of course, continued, the most hotly debated
issues being the responsibility for the World War of 1914—about
which Sidney Fay, Bernadotte Schmitt, and Harry Elmer Barnes
wrote big books, and the influence of the American frontier—about
which dozens of books and hundreds of articles were being written.

Still fundamental doubts were arising, with older men once
identified with the "new history" being the leaders. Becker and
Beard, with their many able disciples, asked whether the past could
be fully and objectively recreated. Their answer was "no": there
was an actual past but the historian could not recapture it. He was
conditioned by his time and place, the general climate of opinion
(Becker), and his own frame of reference (Beard). He was limited by
the nature of his own mind and the inadequacy of the documents.
The best that could be hoped for was honest, subjective, and selective interpretation. To the question of what further principles
should guide this interpretation they had few answers except the

pragmatic one of usefulness in understanding how the past became the present and, even more important, the future.

While the philosophic foundations were being examined, the subjects of study were expanding. From the late 1920's more significant work was being done in modern European history: the *Journal of Modern History* was founded at Chicago in 1929 and the multi-volumed series, *The Rise of Modern Europe* (still incomplete), was initiated in 1934 by William L. Langer. A few men began to study modern Asia, though almost none studied modern Africa except in relation to the British Empire. By the mid-1930's the most popular and growing field of American history was intellectual history, though the big books of Ralph Gabriel and Merle Curti, two leaders who trained many students, were just being prepared. Works of synthesis covering big subjects and including economic history, were becoming more respectable, though few (for example, Tenney Frank and Michael Rostovtzeff in ancient history) tried them on any large scale.

Except for a new interest in military history, the period of World War II saw no startling new developments in either methodology or subject matter. The energy and thought of historians were diverted to other tasks. But the war and its immediate aftermath led to major developments both in the scope of historical investigation and in the breadth of understanding.

The war brought the whole world not only to American diplomats and soldiers but to American historians. Both the war and the totalitarian regimes preceding and accompanying it once more revealed deep irrational forces within men, not only to psychiatrists but to historians. In consequence, the widening and deepening of historical study continued, though now in different ways and directions. By the 1950's and 1960's, multiplicity and diversity were the most descriptive nouns that could be applied to historians and their work. No distinct and dominant school of historical interpretation developed, though individual professors across the nation, at Harvard, Columbia, North Carolina, Wisconsin, Chicago, Texas, and California (Berkeley), for example, each won followers.

Few postulates, concepts, hypotheses, or even subjects were discarded as new ones were added. In more than one sense the whole past of the human world became the domain of historians. Though some were "alienated" by their own society, little of man's experience now was alien to them. And not only little of it was alien but much of it attracted them. Hence more and more of them attempted to reach out to, to have empathy for, to get inside of their subjects— whether these be individuals or institutions, classes or occupational groups. As they did so, some of them attempted to use methods and insights evolved by social scientists, especially by social psychologists and anthropologists, and those social scientists who would, by the 1960's, be called behavioralists. Sometimes, as in the Social Science Research Council *Bulletins* 54 and 64 (1946 and 1954), they seemed to be exhorting each other to use the methods and findings of other disciplines more than they themselves actually used them. Their success in wresting viable insights varied. Quantitatively their pro- duction steadily mounted—more books, more articles, and more re- search in progress.

Only a small proportion of the 12,000 or more historians in the United States of the early 1960's were actually productive scholars— even a rough estimate of 20 percent may be high. Generalizations even about the work of this questionable 20 percent are difficult, their research and their publications were so different.

There is no quantitative way of measuring the relative signif- icance of the many ideas that influenced the research and views of post-World War II American historians, nor of precisely determin- ing the importance of the various approaches they tried or interpre- tations they evolved. Again they drew on germinal concepts of Euro- pean scholars. A few gave attention to Friedrich Meinecke's his- toricism—"the idea of the inimitable, unique individuality" to be comprehended only by "the totality of all spiritual powers." More were influenced by Max Weber's analyses of the role of ideas (as those of Protestantism) in history and by his use of "models" (as for bureaucracy). The insistent demand of Lucien Febvre and Marc Bloch that historians examine *all* the varied experience of men, including the mythological, won wide acceptance. Some American historians learned, too, from Raymond Aron who out of his analysis of German philosophic schools asked for sympathetic reconstruction "of the consciousness of others," from the incisive insights of Lewis Namier as he minutely described the personal motivations of eight- eenth-century English politicians and thus deflated the significance of issues and political parties, and from Edward Carr who, from a relativist position, thought conceptions of the future determined interpretations of the past.

Though American historians seldom probed deeply into philosophical theories, some of them (like Lee Benson and Richard McCormick) evolved new analytical approaches to and quantitative (chiefly statistical and sampling) ways of arriving at generalizations. Though they were influenced by Marx's economic interpretation, they usually refused to accept either his political programs or his monolithic class interpretation of history. Psychoanalytic and anthropological insights of the kind symbolized by the names of Sigmund Freud and Franz Boas attracted more of them than the dialectic of Marx, as they, men such as Richard Hofstadter, Henry Nash Smith, C. Vann Woodward, and Carl Schorske, examined American or European history in terms of myth, psychological frustration, or social status.[5]

But there was no common approach or dominant center of interest. In an older American historical tradition Arthur Schlesinger, Jr., tried both to educate his fellow citizens and to find the vital center of American history in numerous books and articles on recent American history. In the tradition of the eighteenth-century enlightenment, though with different methods and sometimes comparative approaches, Robert Palmer, Joseph Strayer, Louis Hartz, and others examined major movements and ideas in western civilization, for example, democratic revolutions, feudalism, and nation-building. The always strong interest in the American Civil War intensified during the years of its Centennial. While much of the writing about it catered to popular tastes, Allan Nevins and Bruce Catton were engaged on large-scale histories that were based on new reading of sources, and Kenneth Stampp and David Davis were doing careful studies of slavery that afforded new interpretations.

When American historians sought new interpretations, they did not, of course, discard the traditions of their craft or of the American past. To recreate the past, particularly the political past, *wie es eigentlich gewesen* remained a vague goal. Though few historians thought they could attain it, some, if judged by their publications,

[5] But it is important to note that most writing on psychoanalysis and history has been done by scholars who are not historians. See, for example, Bruce Mazlich, ed., *Psychoanalysis and History*, New York, 1963.

still pursued their studies as if they could. Nor did belief in the possibility of democratic progress disappear. While not many publicly defended the presuppositions of their democratic faith, these presuppositions continued to supply basic frameworks for much historical interpretation and teaching.[6] Somehow, in some way, the United States, western societies, and even the world were evolving toward the liberal, democratic civilization envisaged by Condorcet and Jefferson, and later perhaps by the Fabians, H. G. Wells and George Bernard Shaw, and by the American Presidents Woodrow Wilson, Franklin D. Roosevelt, and John F. Kennedy. Most American historians, here apparently sharing the belief of other American educators, still hoped that through education and through knowledge acquired by empirical research a more prosperous, freer, and more peaceful world could somehow be achieved.

This heritage of hope from earlier generations was indeed questioned. For many scholars who had matured in the disorderly and confused world of the twentieth century, human progress seemed at least doubtful and, in any case, it could hardly provide *the* basis for selection and evaluation of historical phenomena. As Becker and Beard themselves came to doubt the universality of the faith, so did their disciples and other still younger historians. Not only war and totalitarianism, but findings of psychoanalysis undermined faith in rational man and the possibility of rational societies. The invention of "the bomb" and the danger that it would be used to destroy men and their civilizations brought further doubts. Doubts about the future brought doubts about the past. Was it possible to postulate that continuity in history which an earlier leader, Edward P. Cheyney, had thought a basic law of history? And if this were not possible, was there any value, except that of entertainment, in historical study?

Though prophets of doom like Oswald Spengler were uncommon in America, increasing numbers of its historians were critical of the popular American belief that the United States was a garden (Henry Nash Smith, David Noble) or that its people were "innocent" (Henry May). Perhaps this realization meant that historical study was finally maturing in the United States. Perhaps it meant that historians could now get above (or below) the surface of the striking American

---

[6] This is a conclusion of this author after reading about 1,500 essays submitted (1953 to 1963) to the *American Historical Review* in hope of publication.

material advances into the nature of those individual and mass motivations or those underlying social forces, if any, which had seemed to some philosophers to determine the course of history. There was no agreement but searching argument and much questioning.[7]

A diminishing proportion of historians continued to write rather conventional political, economic, constitutional, and diplomatic history. More of them were now interested in cultural and intellectual history, as the founding of the *Journal of the History of Ideas* (1940), the publication of many books as those of Perry Miller and Bernard Bailyn on the American colonies and Revolution, and the appearance of textbooks on western or world "civilizations," like that by Brinton, Christopher, and Wolff, gave evidence. Even when the still "newer" historians wrote political history, they conceived of politics in the context of the wider culture. A few of the ablest men (Charles Gillispie and Thomas Kuhn) turned to the history of science; the number was small, both because the field was new and because of the technical knowledge required. At least half the historians continued to specialize in the history of their own nation, especially its recent history. Within American history there was much more attention to quantitative (Samuel Hays) and psychological analysis (Martin Duberman), much more to biography (Arthur Link on Woodrow Wilson and Frank Freidel on Franklin D. Roosevelt), and somewhat less to sectional interpretation. Under the auspices of the National Historical Publications Commission, a number of able historians, for example Julian Boyd and Lyman Butterfield, were devoting their lives to the scholarly editing of the papers of famous Americans, such as those of Thomas Jefferson and members of the Adams family, and of the basic documents of American history, e.g., those concerning the ratification of the American Constitution. The proportion professing modern and recent European history did not decline, but fewer worked in English history and more (like Richard Pipes) in Russian. While most historians agreed on the necessity and desirability of continued study of ancient and medieval history, so few devoted themselves to these fields that colleges and universities could not find enough specialists at the level of the

[7] Particularly in the journal, *History and Theory*. See, for example, the article of Hayden White, "The Burden of History," vol. V, No. 2, 1966, pp. 111–134. But the questioning also increasingly appeared in the more orthodox *American Historical Review* from about 1956.

Ph.D. to teach their courses.[8] In part because of increasing interest in and in part because of the availability of foundation grants, the number though not the proportion of students in Asian and African history increased swiftly. But, in spite of major works being published by scholars such as John Fairbank, Edwin Reischauer, and Philip Curtin, these latter fields remained comparatively undeveloped.

Diversity, then, characterized the work of contemporary historians in America. But they, like the American society which supported them, seemed to agree on some fundamentals in their approach to history. They, like their immediate predecessors, were usually empirical and pragmatic. If historians could not arrive at full or objective truth about the past, or even parts of it, they could find semblances of past reality in the documents and the resulting historical knowledge, when meaningfully interpreted, could be a useful instrument in understanding the present and the possibilities of the future. If there could not be full agreement among historians on major issues, at least there could be partial consensus for a time —until new views arising out of new cultural needs brought new perception of the meaning of old evidence or discovery of new evidence gave rise to differing interpretations.

Some of the keenest of the contemporary historians sought to go further. Total objectivity, total recapture of the past, was, of course, not possible. Perhaps it was not even desirable. But if historians knew more of psychology and anthropology and of literature and philosophy, they could get "inside" their subjects and imaginatively understand experience in ways earlier historians had not. Analysis of feelings of guilt and alienation (Christopher Lasch) and of the desire for social status (Richard Hofstadter) might, for example, provide more meaningful insights than examination of devotion to ideologies or social ideals. This meant that historians would have to dig deeper, become more "involved" in the minute details of individual, "unique" experience as they used sharper intellectual instruments to gain understanding of this experience.

That this attempt to get "inside" was desirable few denied, though there was little agreement on the best ways of doing so. Most historians in the United States would likely agree with the generality that application of the "heuristic concepts and methods" of the so-

8 See below, p. 204.

cial sciences is of great value in historical inquiry, but nearly all would also likely agree with another generality, historians should use any concepts and methods that prove useful in wresting understanding. Louis Gottschalk expressed a common view when he wrote, "The world has room and the profession has need for all kinds of historians," and this is true whether the historians be narrative, analytical, quantitative, behavioral, or nomothetic.

Most American historians, however, still paid little attention to all but the most obvious of the philosophical problems of acquiring knowledge and many of them still scoffed at philosophies of history. But whatever their attitudes, they were involved not only in the acquisition of knowledge but in the meaning of what they found. Once more questions of value seemed to become important; for some these became even more important than the traditional mining of details from the traditional kinds of sources. The founding of the journal, *History and Theory,* in 1960 reflected the belief of a growing minority that historians could no longer ignore theory or philosophy if the study of history was to continue to be fruitful.

II. Who Are American Historians?

Those who make the teaching or writing of history their principal work probably number about fifteen thousand. This estimate could easily be increased by definition. It does not include the more than sixty thousand or more high school teachers who have classes in history, those who teach history in colleges and universities under a different title (as classics or literature), advanced students in history still in universities though they may be teaching part-time as assistants, or the considerable number of archivists and librarians who perform historical tasks. The number does include those who teach in colleges and universities, a small number who are employed as historians in governmental agencies, and the few who, like the talented "amateurs," Catherine Drinker Bowen and Barbara Tuchman, devote a major part of their time to historical research and writing but do not belong to academia.

Compared to what is known about several other professional groups in the United States, little precise information is available on the social origins or views of its historians. In recent years, however, some information has been systematically compiled about their training and their teaching.

Probably seven out of eight historians teach history in the colleges and universities. Most of those who teach, over 65 percent, possess a Ph.D. degree. And most of those who teach devote most of their time to teaching rather than to research. About half of the historians teach United States history, almost a third European, and not more than 10 percent Asian, African, or Latin American history. The specialties of some cannot be geographically classified as their subjects, the history of science or economic history, may cover more than one traditional historical field or geographic area. In the big universities and increasingly in small colleges, historians specialize in a field, as American or European, in a time period, as early modern European or recent American, and in one aspect of history, as political, economic, or intellectual. Both for research and for teaching, historians tend to devote themselves primarily to the history of one nation, but in smaller institutions they more likely will teach courses in two or three fields and cover the history of several nations or even areas.

Most historians live and do most of their work in the eastern part of the United States, east of the Mississippi and north of the Ohio River, though increasing numbers are employed in California. Of the 12,880 active members of the American Historical Association in 1964, over half, 7,760, resided in the seventeen New England, North Atlantic and North Central states and the District of Columbia, about 1,765 in the thirteen most western states (1,120 in California alone), only 1,455 in the ten southeastern states, and but 1,301 in the tier of eleven west central states stretching from Minnesota to Texas. The geographical distribution of the historians reflects in part the concentration of colleges and universities in the United States. It reflects also the greater stress of eastern institutions on the humanities and of the midwestern and mountain institutions on "practical" subjects.

Firm information on the political affiliation or class origins of historians is unobtainable. They are, judging by unsystematic observation, usually liberals (in various twentieth-century meanings), internationalists, democrats (small "d"), and Democrats (in political leanings). Very few are Marxists, and still fewer are political Marxists. Few actively participate in state or federal politics, possibly more because of personal inclinations than social and institutional pressures. But in 1967, two United States Senators had a Ph.D. in history and a good many Congressmen had majored in history in undergraduate school. Few of the historians are rich, or sons or daughters of rich or high "status" families. Most are from and regard themselves as being members of the large American middle class. Without doubt most are from and, if measured by economic income, remain members of the lower middle classes. Most of them live on their salaries as teachers. A rare historian, perhaps the author of a successful textbook, has a sizeable income from his writing; very few possess inherited wealth of consequence.

Most historians have received their undergraduate education as well as graduate training at large universities. However, a greater percentage of the graduates of small liberal arts colleges go on to graduate work. A large proportion teach in the large universities, public and private, and these tend to dominate the profession and set its standards. But at least as many teach in independent liberal arts colleges, in what used to be called teachers' colleges (though now often called universities), and in junior or community colleges.

In their social origins, American historians mirror the society of which they are a part. In religious background most of them are Protestant while perhaps a fifth are Catholic and a seventh Jewish. Though a good many of them attend church, not many play active religious roles. Geographically, a comparatively large proportion still come from New England and the North Atlantic states, though the numbers and percentage of those coming from other sections of the nation, particularly California, seem to be increasing. Those with "Anglo-Saxon" names and backgrounds no longer are as pre-dominant as was once true, while descendants of later immigrants, German, Irish, and now eastern Europeans, have gained increasing prominence. From the beginning, the study of history in the United States has been enriched by emigrants from Britain, a Goldwin Smith, a Gilbert Highet, or a Lawrence Stone. After 1917, 1933, and 1945, a considerable number of central and eastern European historians emigrated to the United States and enriched historical study. Among these emigrés were Michael Karpovich, Michael Rostovtzeff, George Vernadsky, Felix Gilbert, Hajo Holborn, Ernst Kantorowicz, Stephan Kuttner, Hans Kohn, and Ernst Posner; each of these historians made important contributions to historical study and two of them were elected President of the American Historical Association. A surprising number of younger and rising historians are also emigrés or sons of emigrés. Though there is little racial prejudice among American historians, only a few Negroes have entered the profession and a rare few have become prominent. Until recent years Negroes in America have not often had equal educational opportunities or had the desire to enter the professions. The percentage of women in the profession has increased but little, if any; about 90 percent of the practicing historians are men, partly because of lack of interest on the part of women, partly because college and university history departments, chiefly composed of men, may not wish to employ women.

No way has been devised to measure the intelligence and scholarship of historians in relation to these qualities of scholars in other fields. Older historians long complained, as did William E. Dodd about forty years ago, that history had to take "in the main the poorest material." The incomplete and sketchy studies now available do not bear out Dodd's pessimistic observation. But as these studies reveal, certain other academic fields, such as mathematics, physics, and literature, probably do attract higher numbers of brilliant students—if brilliance can be measured by standard academic tests.

American historians now generally think of themselves as members of a distinguished profession. But they do not constitute a profession in the sense that lawyers and medical doctors do. They have established neither the rigid and often legally set standards for their profession nor the tight and exclusive organizations. Customarily historians are employees of public and private institutions and subject to the (usually but not always lightly exercised) jurisdiction of the state governments (not the federal government), to boards of trustees, and to the administrative officers, the presidents, chancellors, and provosts, appointed by these governments or boards. On the other hand they are seldom considered civil servants, as in France, and they are not, as in France, protected by civil service rules. Nevertheless, because they follow a responsible calling and have had professional training, they believe themselves entitled to the privileges and status of professionals. In practice and by custom they have acquired certain of the freedoms and some of the prestige. These they enjoy not because they are historians but because they are members of academic communities. A sizeable number of historians, like other American academic scholars, belong to the American Association of University Professors which endeavors to set standards of academic employment and freedom.

Neither the conditions of work nor of freedom are uniform throughout the United States. Much of the variation depends upon the wealth and traditions of the institutions and of the localities in which they are located. Through the late 1950's and the early 1960's, salaries mounted at the rate of three to seven percent annually until the real incomes of historians were higher than at any previous time. They still remained much lower than the average ($18,000) received by medical doctors. Moreover, geographical and institutional variations were wide, the salaries in southern and in some midwestern and mountain states and in most small colleges being comparatively low.[9] Within the academic world, historians fared about as well as members of other humanistic disciplines but not as well as those in the natural sciences. In 1967 an instructor in history might receive, for the school year of nine to ten months, a salary of $7,000 to $8,500, an assistant professor $7,500 to $10,000, an associate professor $8,000 to $13,000, a professor $12,000 to $20,000 and, infrequently, more— up to $25,000 or very rarely $30,000. To these base salaries, "fringe benefits" were nearly always added, the most usual being retirement insurance toward which, on a variable matching basis, the employing institution added five to fifteen percent of the salary. Other "fringe benefits," not always given, included medical and modest life insurance and sabbatical or research leaves. Historians who were engaged in research might, in addition, obtain foundation grants, though these were fewer and lesser in amount for historians than for scientists.

The conditions of teaching also varied widely. Young men and teachers in most small undergraduate institutions normally taught twelve hours a week, though nine was slowly becoming the standard. In large and graduate institutions the teaching load was more likely to be less, perhaps five or six hours (one course and one seminar), but graduate teachers, in addition, usually had to supervise the work of graduate students in the preparation of theses and dissertations, and sit upon their examining committees. Like other American

[9] Statistics on academic salaries are published each spring in the *Bulletin of the American Association of University Professors,* but no exact figures on the salaries of historians are available.

academicians, academic historians were much plagued by committee work, both within their own departments and in their institutions. Though American faculty members had little authority, except in matters of curriculum, for the administration of their institutions, their administrators often thrust much institutional responsibility on them, at times even for student morality.

Like scholars in other academic disciplines, historians were also increasingly expected to do research and to publish. But only in the best graduate schools and colleges did the phrase "publish or perish" describe reality. In many small and less acclaimed institutions even a full professorship might be attained without substantial publication and "non-publishers" could obtain and retain positions, perhaps even be promoted. As remarked above, relatively few historians have published books or articles which could be considered, in any real sense, "contributions to knowledge," though many more engage in some kind of research. Probably no more than ten percent ever presented scholarly papers at the several annual national meetings of historians, though all but the least articulate were called upon to lecture occasionally to outside study and social groups in their communities.

Upon receiving a Ph.D., and sometimes before, young men could usually obtain a first position as an assistant professor; because of the high demand for teachers, the rank of instructor seemed to be disappearing, except in the largest and strongest universities. To obtain an associate professorship and tenure usually required, at least at the better institutions, from five to seven years or longer, as well as publication of serious work and demonstration of ability in teaching. For a professorship at least as many more years of experience were necessary, and at the better institutions a substantial record of publication. Few historians reached the rank of professor before the age of 40 but if they achieved this goal they usually did so before the age of 50. Of course, a professorship at Harvard or one of the other great and prestigious universities ranked much higher and afforded much more status than a professorship at lesser or less well-known institutions.

American historians were as free and as restricted as their colleagues in other fields to express their views. Only occasional violations of academic freedom occurred, but they did occur, especially in times of national stress. Few American historians, it is true, expressed unpopular or radical opinions (the "New Left" of the 1960's is an exception) and therefore tests of their freedom infrequently occurred. Because of their own sense of propriety or public and institutional pressures, it is likely that a good many did not feel completely free to speak on current issues (in the south on race questions, for example) or, in some instances, to express historical views which were unpopular. Once, however, a scholar had acquired tenure (usually by serving a number of years or by becoming an associate professor), he could not, in most institutions, lose his position except for demonstrated incompetence or a moral offense.

In their own institutions and in the wider academic community of the nation, historians and their subject were accepted and generally given high place. A comparatively (in relation to other disciplines) large number became deans and presidents of universities and colleges. Students filled their classes and often history ranked second (after literature) or third in comparative enrollments. Frequently students were required by the colleges to "take" a survey course in history. Within their institutions, historians nearly always formed strong departments which had control over the courses in history, limited funds for library purchases and sometimes for secretarial service, and considerable power to recommend promotions and salary increases for departmental members.

The status of historians with the larger public was probably not as high. If this status depended upon the number of readers of their works, then they ranked quite low. Only a few historical volumes by trained historians, for example, Samuel Eliot Morison, Garrett Mattingly, or Arthur Schlesinger, Jr., sold well and appeared to be read by many people. And only a few historians, like Allan Nevins, Henry Steele Commager, and Barbara Tuchman, were asked to contribute to commercial magazines and newspapers. Still, state legislatures and private boards of trustees, both of which reflected public opinion, modestly supported historical departments and historical teaching and research. Among the humanities, history generally received more financial support than other disciplines except literature. But, of course, the natural sciences received more acclaim than the humanities and historians' salaries and research grants were much less than those available for physicists and biologists, or, for that matter, economists and psychologists who could, more often than historians, obtain positions in government and business.

III. How Historians Are Trained

American students obtain their first formal introduction to history in elementary and junior high schools. This introduction, often in the fourth and seventh grades, is elementary indeed, with simple readings on local history, simple biographies, popular stories, and field trips to local points of interest filling a large part of the time. In senior high school (grades 9-12 or 10-12) nearly all students are required (sometimes by state law) to take a year (or a two-year) course in American history, most often offered in the eleventh grade. Over half of them have another year course in world history, usually in the tenth grade. In rare cases at the best high schools, as that of New Trier (Winnetka, Illinois), a few more have specialized courses, for example, in Russian history. The high school courses are almost without exception survey courses, with the reading chiefly done in well-illustrated, simple textbooks. In most cases history is part of the general social studies requirement, and social studies or even current events may be more emphasized than history. As nearly all American boys and girls are required by state laws to attend school to the age of 16–18 (or graduation), there is no selection of students as in Germany and other European nations and the variations in levels of ability and of achievement are enormous.

The high school teachers are not, for the most part, professional historians and many have but little training in history. During the early 1960's in Indiana, which is not untypical in this respect, only 34 percent of the teachers had an undergraduate major in history, and 30 percent had no graduate training at all. Few American high school teachers of any subject engage in research and the history teachers are not exceptions. Perhaps more shocking is the fact that many do not read widely.

High school teachers seldom give formal lectures. More often they conduct recitations by asking students questions about their reading or conduct discussions based on the textbook and upon outside readings. Frequently they also assign or provide for special projects in hope of encouraging interest—essays on specific or general topics, short biographical sketches, map studies, debates on controversial subjects, and visits to sites of historic significance. The students' grades in each course are based upon tests (which are usually "objective"), infrequent essays, and their responses in class. There is no required general examination at the conclusion of high school, though more and more students now take the College Entrance Examination Board aptitude, or less frequently, achievement tests. The "Board" scores constitute one criterion for admission to many colleges; in general the more prestigious the college, the higher the "Board" scores it requires.

College and university historians, as academicians in other fields, generally decry the quality of high school work in history, believing it to be quite inadequate and superficial. Most of them admit that there are some good high schools and some fine high school teachers, and that a few exceptional students enter college well prepared in history. Since 1957 the American Historical Association has tried to assist in the improvement of high school teaching through its Service Center for Teachers.[10] Since 1964 National Defense Education Institutes have been established for high school history teachers. At these six- or seven-week summer institutes, attended by over 4,300 teachers in 1966, college and university historians help high school teachers deepen their knowledge and acquaint them with results of current research in American and world history. But relatively few historians take an active interest in the schools and relatively few high school teachers make strenuous efforts to keep up with scholarship in their fields of teaching.

In many colleges and universities and in nearly all liberal arts undergraduate schools, students are, as remarked above, required to take or voluntarily take one basic course. Usually this is a general survey of American history, of western civilization, or of modern Europe. These cover, on a more advanced level, much the same subject matter as the high school courses. In all the "survey" courses the role of ideas tends to be more and more emphasized. Generally the lecture method is used, though formal lectures are not always prepared or given and a third or fourth of the time may be allotted to discussion. But it should be noted that the "civilization" courses are frequently patterned on the one first given at Columbia University in 1919 and involve much reading and strenuous discussion. The one basic survey course may afford the only formal introduction to history American college students obtain and some do not obtain even

10 See below, pp. 000.

this introduction. Only a minority of those who major in other fields go on to take one or more elective and advanced courses in history as well.

History departments in their undergraduate courses devote most of their endeavors to their "majors." Students majoring in history ordinarily take thirty or forty semester hours of course work.[11] Among their eight or more history courses, however, they may have an independent reading course or two, and they may, though this happens infrequently, be introduced to the seminar method. A few departments in the best colleges require or encourage their advanced majors to have a course in historical methods or in historiography (including in rare cases philosophies of history). In general, the instructor lectures, assigns readings, and holds discussions. Sometimes the students give reports in class and receive comment and criticism from both their instructors and their fellow students and often they are required to write short or long ("term") papers which their teachers read, criticize, and grade. Ordinarily the student receives grades only in the specific courses he completes, though again several of the best colleges also require final written or oral examinations covering the areas of the student's concentration.

In 1965-1966 the number of history "majors" graduating, that is receiving the Bachelor of Arts (B.A.), or equivalent degree, totaled 26,421 (17,128 men and 9,293 women). A few of them also won "honors" in history. This usually meant both that they had received high grades in their history courses and had written a special paper, based on considerable reading, and in some cases, on original research in primary sources.

Professional training in history begins in graduate school which most students enter in hope of obtaining the degrees of Master of Arts (M.A.) and Doctor of Philosophy (Ph.D.). To enter, students usually must have an average grade of "B" or higher in their undergraduate school and have made an acceptable score (upper fourth or higher) on a Graduate Record Examination taken during their jun-

---

[11] The American system of "credits" is, of course, quite unlike any procedure in European universities. If, for example, a student successfully completes a course meeting three hours a week for a semester he receives three hours credit toward graduation. If he completes ten three-hour courses, he will have thirty hours credit toward the 120–132 semester hours normally required in all subjects for the B.A. degree. As many institutions are on the "quarter" or trimester system, the arithmetic of credits is often confusing.

ior or more likely their senior year in college. As every American undergraduate knows, the more prestigious the graduate school the more likely it is to receive applications and to admit only students who have high grades and scores.

Requirements for the Master's degree in history vary with each of the more than 200 universities and colleges offering the degree. Usually the student must take at least twenty-four semester hours of course and seminar work and receive a grade of at least "B" in these; often he must write a thesis based on research; and usually he is required to take an oral or written examination (or both) covering the chosen field or fields of study. A recent variation of the Master's degree is the Master of Arts in Teaching (M.A.T.), now widely offered. For this degree a student enrolls for a fifth year or more of work in Education and in an academic subject, such as history, in order to prepare himself and meet the legal requirements for teaching in high school.[12]

Both the requirements for and the qualities of training for the Master's degree so vary that it is impossible to determine its worth except by examination of the individual student's record. In 1964–1965, 3,161 students (2,258 men and 903 women) obtained the degree in history. Most of them were qualified to teach history in the secondary school, but only those going on for further graduate work could aim higher.

Truly professional training starts with work for the Ph.D., the degree which in history has become almost necessary for permanent positions in colleges and universities and for subsequent advancement in the profession. Training for the doctorate in history began in the 1880's. The requirements then established by Johns Hopkins University, which were based on German practices, provided the basic model.

As with the Master's degree, present requirements as well as qualities of training for the Ph.D. differ, but again, as with the Master's, there are common features. Almost always two years in residence beyond the Master's degree is required, as well as successful completion of additional courses and especially seminars, a reading

---

[12] A large number of students who hope to enter secondary school teaching take work for the Master of Education or Master of Arts in Education degrees. The first usually requires more pedagogical preparation (Education courses) than the MAT.

knowledge of one or two foreign languages, the passing of one or two comprehensive examinations covering at least two fields of history, and completion of a dissertation requiring intensive research. To these common requirements, departments frequently add others, particularly for individuals but sometimes for all their students. A student of medieval history, of course, needs Latin as well as modern European languages and, as most students will eventually teach, they may be asked to participate in a course devoted to problems of instruction as well as to demonstrate their own ability by delivering lectures or leading discussions.[13]

Training for the doctorate has three major purposes: to provide (1) thorough knowledge of history, or rather of important but limited areas of history, (2) intimate knowledge of and experience in research, and (3) beginning acquaintance with the problems of teaching. Of these three the last has been least stressed, even though successful candidates will likely devote most of their efforts to teaching. In graduate preparation the master in research is preferred to the master of teaching.

Departments normally expect students, on entrance, to have had an undergraduate major in history and often the Master's degree, and therefore to be acquainted with several fields of history. Increasingly they also expect knowledge of at least one foreign language. A few institutions give qualifying examinations to test the student's abilities and his previous achievements; most rely upon the student's previous work in undergraduate school and for the Master's degree —if this has been taken. During the first year, the student usually takes several lecture or directed reading courses and a course in historiography or historical methodology if he has not previously had them. At this stage, however, research training is considered more important than further acquisition of information, and he will likely participate in one or two seminars organized in the traditional manner. Ideally the seminar consists of six to ten students sitting under a master historian, examining with him source materials in his special field, writing papers of thirty to fifty pages (or more) on restricted subjects, and receiving from him and their fellow students both helpful suggestions and rigorous criticism. In actuality the

---

[13] A sizeable number obtained limited experience in teaching as graduate assistants in large survey courses.

seminars are both smaller and larger and the student papers vary in quality from superficial essays to original, publishable studies.

Sometime after the first year, possibly at the end of the second year or more likely during the third or fourth year, the student faces the first major hurdle, the general examination. This is always written and usually oral as well. The student must pass it in order to be admitted to "candidacy" for the doctorate. Variously known as the general, preliminary, qualifying, or comprehensive examination, it tests the student's knowledge in two or more fields of history, and particularly in the principal or major field he has chosen for concentration. Definitions of "field" are not uniform. Some universities, which narrowly limit the fields, may require the student to offer six, while others, which broadly define fields, may demand competence in but two or three. United States history may be divided into two, or three, or more fields, European into three or four. Often one of the fields must be outside the field of history, for example, political science. Normally a student concentrates on a phase of the history of one nation, but he is also expected to demonstrate achievement in both breadth and depth of historical knowledge.

The written examination, usually given in several parts, may last from four to twenty-five hours and is read by at least the major professor and one or two others. A departmental committee, varying in size from three to five professors (with perhaps one from outside the history department) conducts the oral examination (if given) of two to three hours. Both examinations concentrate on the major or "first" field, but questions about subject matter and bibliography covering almost any aspect of the fields offered may be and are usually asked. The student is judged on "how he answers" as well as what he knows, though there is not full agreement among professors either on the nature of the questions or on how the answers should be judged. The examinations are expected to push the student to his best efforts. The student knows this and prepares himself accordingly. The percentage of failures is not known but it is not inconsiderable. Generally those students who pass do so on the first or second attempt and some universities do not permit more than two attempts. Many students themselves decide that they are not prepared or are so told by their advisors, hence never take the examination and "drop out."

At or before the time of the general or preliminary examination the students must usually present evidence (by taking tests) that they are able to read two foreign langauges (in some cases statistics may be substituted for one language). Regrettably, in the opinion of most historians, American students are weak in languages and the requirement is followed more often in the letter than in the spirit.

Once the student has successfully passed the "prelims," he is admitted to candidacy. Ordinarily in his second and third years he has taken part in two or more seminars (one in his major field), listened to lectures in other courses, read independently or under supervision, and he may continue to attend seminars and courses. But the big task before him after the general examination is the dissertation. He is now working under a "major" professor who supervises his studies (sometimes closely) and who must formally approve a dissertation topic, suggested either by himself or by the candidate.

For many years the dissertation was supposed to make a "contribution to knowledge" and culminate in a published book. Occasionally it still does. Now the sights are more modest and the dissertation is normally considered "a training experience and evidence of scholarly attainment in research, critical analysis, and writing." The dissertation is seldom published, at least in its original form, though in most cases an abstract of it is printed in the University of Michigan publication *Dissertation Abstracts* and the complete dissertation is microfilmed and thus made available to readers.[14] Nevertheless, the dissertation is generally of book length—300 to 400 typed pages is considered an optimal length, and prepared as if it were to be published, with all the scholarly paraphernalia of uniform footnotes and a formal bibliography. The topics are nearly always restricted in scope and monographic in nature. Too often, it is generally agreed, the dissertations are also pedestrian in style and dull to read. Only later and after further research and much revision are the best ones publishable as books, though parts of a good many more provide bases for articles to come. A large proportion never get beyond

14 The American Historical Association has long published, at two or three year intervals, a *List of Doctoral Dissertations in History in Progress or Completed at Colleges and Universities* . . . ; the 1961 edition contains a bibliography of earlier lists.

the typed stage of the copies deposited in the university libraries and the abstract mentioned above.

Upon completion of the dissertation the candidate must usually again undergo another examination. The dissertation has been carefully read by the major professor and, perhaps less carefully, examined by the members of the candidate's committee, all or a majority of whom must approve it. The committee examines the candidate orally for perhaps two hours. But this examination, in which the candidate "defends his thesis," is, unlike the practice in France,[15] customarily little more than an inherited formality, for de facto approval of the dissertation precedes the examination and rarely does the examination cover more than the subject and quality of the dissertation. A few departments no longer require it.

Theoretically, three or four years of graduate work (including that for the M.A., if it is a prerequisite) are required for the doctorate. Actually, most students in history needed or took much more time; during the late 1950's and early 1960's seven to nine years were more likely. Few (perhaps eight percent) achieved the degree in less than four years, and in spite of university statutes of limitation on time, about a third spent more than nine years. Up to half the Ph.D. candidates completed all the requirements for the degree except the dissertation and then taught full- or part-time while they continued to work on their dissertations. Almost as many doctoral candidates were "off campus" as in residence at any one time. For many reasons, including anticipation of increased demand for teachers, some departments about 1962 began to "speed up" training and thereby reduced the time between entrance into graduate school and the award of the degree.[16] This policy and the increasing number of fellowships made it likely that fewer years would be needed.

The number of Ph.D. degrees granted in history has climbed more or less steadily from the late 1940's and increased swiftly from 1962. More students desired and would work for the degree; more institutions were offering it; more fellowships were becoming avail-

---

[15] See above, pp. 44–46.

[16] The pressure for trained teachers of undergraduates has led Yale University to offer a degree, "Master of Philosophy," to students who have completed all requirements except the dissertation, and the University of Michigan a certificate to students who have reached the status of candidate.

able; and more positions in history were open. In 1941, 58 institutions offered a doctorate in history and 158 degrees were granted; in 1960 the comparable figures were about 80 institutions and 365 degrees, and in 1964, 106 and 507. By 1966, 116 were offering the degree and the number of degrees had increased to about 560.[17] The annual production was now nearing the total number of Ph.D.'s in history who were living in 1925 and within the last twenty-five years the number of institutions offering the degree had doubled. More Ph.D. degrees were being awarded in history than in any of the social sciences and in any of the humanities except English.

Over 50 percent of the candidates of the mid-1960's gave their chief attention to American history—whether because of native interest, availability of sources, or language qualifications. About a third worked in European history, particularly in the period since 1815. Few specialized in ancient and medieval history: in 1964 only eight degrees were awarded in the former and sixteen in the latter. Though the number in Asian and African history remained small, it was swiftly increasing. The number and percentage of those in Russian and east European history were mounting but the percentage in English history was declining. The recent Ph.D.'s worked more often in cultural and intellectual history than had their predecessors, an appreciable though small number were specializing in the history of science and in military history, and a growing number were interested in quantitative and behavioral studies.

There was no common denominator for the Ph.D. across the nation as a measure of knowledge, skill, or demonstrated ability. The quality of the degree (and hence its reputation) depended not only on the individual but also on the institution and the "major" professor. Undoubtedly the degree, wherever it was awarded, did guarantee that the possessor had acquired a good deal of information in the fields of his concentration and knew something about the techniques of research. But that an historian had attained the degree did not prove he was or would become a productive scholar or a stimulating teacher. His scholarship and teaching ability remained to be proven in the future.

A few institutions and departments had acquired high reputations and often large enrollments. Among these Harvard stood

17 Statistical sources do not permit more than approximations. If "American Civilization and Culture" is included, then the number in 1966 was about 576.

out, but several other universities (here listed alphabetically) were outstanding: California (Berkeley), Chicago, Columbia, Michigan, Princeton, Stanford, Wisconsin, and Yale. And among other institutions offering widely recognized work in particular fields were Cornell, Johns Hopkins, and Pennsylvania on the east coast; Illinois, Indiana, Minnesota, and Northwestern in the middle east; Duke, North Carolina, Texas, Tulane, and Virginia in the south; and the University of California in Los Angeles and the University of Washington in Seattle on the west coast. The reputations of these and other departments vary from year to year and in the several fields of history. Over the years Harvard and Columbia granted the most doctorates; in 1964 Harvard awarded 52 and Columbia 42.

That graduate work in history was well established in the United States did not mean it was not criticized. Critics within the profession still thought the calibre of students too low, the standards too loose, the training too lax. More often repeated were the complaints that graduate training did not train students to write well and that while it taught them to write unexciting monographs on insignificant topics, it did not stress imaginative thought and historical insight. Too often, the critics asserted, young authors were unwilling or unable to understand their subjects in context—their relation to what came before or after, or their place in the total culture of the period. A seminar paper or a dissertation on the life of an obscure Civil War politician (or on any subject) might be based on voluminous primary sources, it might have a hundred or a thousand footnotes and a long bibliography, but its prose might be awkward, its insights few, and its contribution negligible.

The most often heard censure of graduate training concerned its failure to teach men how to teach. Here the system in the United States revealed its origins in Germany—the stress on research which ran counter to traditional aims of American undergraduate education. American colleges were usually committed to liberal education. Professional or vocational education was not normally or professedly their primary goal, but rather the general education of young men and women between the ages of 18 and 22, education which might prepare them for later professional training but whose first aim was acquisition of general knowledge, ways of thinking, and attitudes of mind rather than research skills. The stress on research and publication in graduate schools meant, so the arguments ran, that college teachers put research before teaching and specialized knowledge before general understanding, and that therefore they did not or could not interest enough students in liberal learning. The arguments, of course, over-simplified a complex problem rooted deeply in the pragmatic nature of American culture. But even American educational administrators sometimes failed to understand the fundamental and vital relationship between knowledge acquired through research and learning obtained in the classroom. Probably no one as yet was asking questions that were sharp and urgent enough to demand effective solutions.

The criticisms of graduate training all had weight and were seriously discussed, not as revealing insurmountable difficulties but, in the American tradition, as problems to be solved. One long-time need was finally being met, the inadequacy of financial aid—fellowships and research and travel grants to permit students to pursue their studies without serious interruptions. Several late nineteenth-century educators, as Charles W. Eliot of Harvard and David Starr Jordan of Stanford, had vigorously opposed "paying students to come." Nevertheless, more and more financial assistance was given to the natural sciences and enormous sums were to become available for the training of young scientists. History, like the other humanities and most of the social sciences, fared poorly until the late 1950's. Individual institutions—especially the major state universities—offered many graduate assistantships but few fellowships in history. Shortly after World War II, Fulbright student fellowships for study abroad became a boon to young potential scholars. Predoctoral grants from the Social Science Research Council and later from the American Council of Learned Societies, though limited in number, helped. But in comparison to the sciences, few graduate fellowships of any kind were established in history; these few carried lower stipends than the large number in the sciences, and they were seldom open to first-year graduate students. Available evidence indicated that for financial reasons many able students were unable to enter or to continue in graduate school and that some of these would have become historians. By the mid-1960's, however, several hundred fellowships for one to three years of study were being awarded through the Woodrow Wilson Foundation and the National Defense Education Act. Through 1967 over 1,500 students had been awarded

Woodrow Wilson fellowships in history and about 1,000 NDEA fellowships; but after 1967 the annual number of Wilson awards was drastically reduced.

New questions were arising. Would history, in the competition with other disciplines and especially the sciences, continue to attract its proportion of able students, and could history departments both expand and maintain a high quality of training? With the enormous number of advanced history students, over ten thousand in 1963 and over sixteen thousand in 1966, and the prospect of doubled enrollment in ten years, these questions will shortly require answers.

IV. Organizations and Periodical Publications

In the United States the study of history has its deepest traditions along the Atlantic coast, and especially in Massachusetts and New York. Until the twentieth century, American historians, with a few important exceptions, concentrated on American subjects, the explorations and settling of the continent, the tribulations of religious groups, the winning of national independence, the making of the new government, and the Civil War. Now the study is carried on throughout the nation; new strong centers exist in the south, the middle west, and along the Pacific coast, and historians have expanded their interests in time and space to almost every conceivable aspect of life everywhere that could possibly interest anyone. The expansion is reflected in the efforts of historians to provide for their craft through organization.

Filled with the excitement and importance of new independence, state and local societies began to record their communities' achievements soon after the American Revolution. The Massachusetts Historical Society was founded in 1791, the New York Historical Society in 1804, and the American Antiquarian Society in 1812. Through the nineteenth century, citizens formed many other state and local organizations. Professional as well as national organization began with the establishment of the American Historical Association in 1884. At that time "there were apparently only fifteen professors and five assistant professors of history" in all the colleges and universities of the country, and "amateurs" outside the academic cloisters wrote most of the history. But just as members of other professions were forming "associations" to care for their interests, historians believed they also should promote theirs.

In September, 1884, 41 interested individuals, inside and outside the academic world, gathered at Saratoga (New York), on the invitation of a committee of five, three of whom were academic historians, Charles Kendall Adams of Michigan, Moses Coit Tyler of Cornell, and Herbert Baxter Adams of Johns Hopkins. From the beginning, Herbert Baxter Adams took the lead. He thought the new Association should not simply be composed of historians devoted to scholarly endeavors, but an association of public-spirited citizens and historians capable of influencing the government and enhancing the reputations of its members. Issues arose that have persisted. Was the Association to be small and composed chiefly of academic historians, or large and open to any citizen—especially those of prominence? Was it to stress "scientific" studies, or popular history which would be read? Was it primarily to devote itself to study of the past, or should it help correct evils in American life? In each case the decision went eventually to the first alternative, but not without argument and not conclusively. While the AHA now devotes itself almost exclusively to the promotion of historical knowledge in all fields, membership is open to anyone interested enough to pay its dues, and its members often ask that it take stands on public issues—which it seldom does.

The purposes of the Association were (and are) otherwise fairly clear. To do "good for the common cause," it was to provide for an interchange of historical knowledge through meetings at which scholarly papers were read, to enable publication of these and other historical studies, to set forth and promote standards for historical research, and, though no document specifically so states, to afford enjoyable social relationships and status for its members.

At the first meeting, several papers, both scholarly and didactic, were read—a practice which continued, though their number increased and they would be less obviously didactical. The assembled members elected the German-trained President of Cornell, Andrew D. White, the first Association President. They decided to hold annual meetings and inaugurated the series of volumes called the *Papers of the American Historical Association*. During the next years, until 1895, the Association usually met in Washington, D. C., and after that in various cities from New York to Madison (Wisconsin) to New Orleans. Not until 1965 did it meet on the west coast.

From the beginning some members of the Association, led by Herbert Baxter Adams, hoped for an official connection with and aid from the federal government. In 1889 the Association, the only learned society to so do, obtained a charter from the Congress and became, in legal terms, a "body corporate and politic" for the "promotion of historical studies . . . and for kindred purposes in the interest of American history, and of history in America." Though the AHA was then (and now) required to report annually to the Secretary of the Smithsonian Institution "concerning its proceedings and the condition of historical study in America," it remained independent. While the Smithsonian still prints the Association's *Annual Report* (generally two volumes) at government expense and though the Association, like other educational groups, is "tax exempt," the Association has not received direct financial assistance from the federal government, nor has it suffered from serious governmental control or interference—though great danger arose in the McCarthy era when the Association, along with philanthropic foundations and other scholarly societies, was subjected to the investigations of the Reese Committee of the House of Representatives. On the other hand, the federal government paid little attention to historians' and the Association's pleas for the preservation of documentary materials. The early efforts (1894) for federal creation of a national Historical Manuscript Commission failed and the Association had to set up its own Commission (1895). Four decades passed before the Association, largely through the efforts of the early leader, J. Franklin Jameson, succeeded in persuading Congress to establish The National Archives and another three decades before Congress (1964), through the National Historical Publications Commission, appropriated funds for the systematic editing and letter-press publication or microfilming of important governmental documents and the papers of leading Americans.

The funds of the Association have always come largely from its membership dues, supplemented by the interest from its capital funds (over $1,200,000 in 1967), occasional and usually small individual donations, editorial and other fees collected from the joint publisher (Macmillan) of the *American Historical Review* in New York, and from the mid-1950's by grants from foundations for specific purposes, such as the microfilming of documents, the editing of bibliographies, and a study of graduate training.

Though its title began with the adjective "American," the Association from its origin included all history within its purview. The Charter's phrase, "of history in America" has always been given a liberal interpretation, though in the early days papers concerning religion were heard but not published, though political partisanship has nearly always been avoided, and though the Association has seldom been involved in discussions of current affairs. Some historians have always been unhappy that the Association has played so small a part in public affairs. In 1904 Theodore Roosevelt wrote to an English friend, "In a very small way I have been waging war with their kind (pedants) on this side of the water for a number of years. We have a preposterous little organization which, when I was just out of Harvard and very ignorant, I joined." In 1912, however, Roosevelt became President of the AHA, probably more because of his political prominence than the history he wrote.

Through the years the Association, within its restricted sphere, has carried on significant historical activities. From its beginning it sponsored or encouraged bibliographical enterprises and later it would become responsible, by way of example, for the annual volume of *Writings on American History*, for the second *Guide to Historical Literature* (1931), and for the third, now titled the *American Historical Association's Guide to Historical Literature* (1961). It has acted to lessen governmental restrictions on freedom of historical study—to liberalize, for instance, governmental regulations on the use of archival material. Through the years it has offered prizes both for unpublished and published historical studies, hoping thereby to encourage high standards of research and writing. From the 1890's to the 1920's and again from the 1950's to the present, it has sought to improve "instruction in the schools." The Report of its Committee of Seven on the *Teaching of History in the Secondary Schools* (1899) provided the basic high school curriculum in history for many years, and its Service Center for Teachers of History, established in the late 1950's, attempts to bridge the gap "between high school teachers and professional historians" through the publication of pamphlets[18] summarizing late historical research in many fields of history and through the sponsorship of institutes of short dura-

18 By early 1965 over 1,000,000 of these pamphlets had been sold or distributed.

tion in which high school teachers confer with professional historians.

The chief activities of the Association remained two, the holding of the annual meeting of three days (before 1954 two or two and a half days) and the publication of historical studies. Over five thousand historians now register for the meetings (held in large hotels) and around 120 to 150 scholarly papers are read. The hotel corridors, bars, and private rooms are jammed by historians "talking shop," by younger men seeking first positions, by older men hoping for better places, and by departmental representatives interviewing candidates. So much time was devoted to "jobs" that the term "slave market" was coined and the Association, in 1954, created a Professorial Register in an attempt to introduce some kind of system into the chaos.

Originally the Association published only its own *Annual Report* and *Papers*. When the *Papers* were discontinued, the *Annual Report* continued to publish both the Association's *Proceedings* and primary historical sources—diaries, letters, etc.—until 1940. But neither publication supplied the opportunities American historians desired. Through the 1880's and early 1890's they were demanding a "Review" comparable to the *English Historical Review* or the *Historische Zeitschrift*. Independently a small group, acting with the Macmillan Company, established the *American Historical Review* in 1895. This *Review* soon came to be the unofficial and later (1916) the official "organ" of the Association. Some members of the Association looked forward to a time when the Association would publish many books. This hope has not materialized. Neither the funds nor the staff of the Association has been large enough to enable substantial publication. The Association has granted subventions to assist in the publication of a limited number of those volumes to which it has awarded prizes; it has published a good many documentary volumes, and, from 1957, about seventy Service Center pamphlets to aid teachers. Most serious historical books are now published by university presses, a few by commercial publishers (by Alfred Knopf, for example), and not infrequently authors themselves must contribute or guarantee part of the costs of publication. Since 1908, when the Yale University Press was founded, university presses have increasingly assumed the burden of scholarly publication.

The AHA is governed by an elected Council, as it has been

from the beginning. The Council, nearly always, is composed of prominent historians from major universities. The annually elected President of the Association is, nearly always, an historian noted for his publications, but his power depends upon his inclination and on his prestige, for his chief duties consist of presiding at Council meetings and giving the major address at the annual meeting. Responsible to the Council are the Executive Secretary and Managing Editor (combined offices from 1940 to 1963) who, with a small office staff and numerous committees, carry on most of the actual work.

The AHA in most instances is recognized as the official representative of historians in the United States. It, for example, is represented in the American Council of Learned Societies, and the Social Science Research Council in the United States, and in the International Congress of Historical Sciences. When the voice of historians is desired by governmental agencies, the AHA is customarily consulted.

The number and variety of historical organizations in the United States fit the multiple and diverse interests of its historians. Over two thousand societies or associations of one kind or another were in existence in 1966.[19] Three or four of the national, as the AHA, and many of the state associations or societies, as that of Wisconsin, were highly organized—with a central administrative staff, membership dues, planned activities, and an annual budget. Some societies, particularly the local, did little more than hold occasional meetings to hear genealogical or patriotic lectures and engage in pleasant antiquarian discussions. Others, national, state, and local, existed only on paper—though they nearly always elected officers. Only a small proportion, not more than one in twenty, gave first attention to significant historical work.

While American historical groups cannot be neatly classified according to their nature, they generally arise out of an interest in a geographical area or in a particular subject. The Organization of American Historians (formerly the Mississippi Valley Historical Association) devotes its attention entirely to American history. It is firmly established (founded 1907) and by 1967 had a large membership—about eight thousand individual members, most of them aca-

[19] For an almost complete list see the *Directory of Historical Societies and Agencies in the United States,* the last edition being that for 1965–1966, published by the American Association for State and Local History.

demic historians. Organized on the model of the AHA and governed by an elective Council, it holds an annual meeting at which around fifty to sixty scholarly papers are read and it publishes a well-edited and well-known quarterly, the *Journal of American History* (formerly the *Mississippi Valley Historical Review*). At another extreme in organizational arrangements, though not in scholarly purpose, is the Conference on Modern European History, which holds one session during the AHA meeting, a luncheon at which a scholarly paper is read, and cooperates with the University of Chicago Press in the publication of the *Journal of Modern History*.

The dozens of national and hundreds of state and local groups may then be elaborately or little organized and engage in much or little actual historical study. Among the most important are the historical societies or associations organized in each of the states for study of their state's or their region's history. Though a few, like the Massachusetts Historical Society are independent, most receive some, though inadequate, financial support from their respective state governments. They occasionally possess valuable libraries and well-kept museums, and, in addition, several, such as the State Historical Society of Wisconsin, have skilled, full-time administrative and editorial staffs. Nearly always they publish quarterly journals or reviews,[20] similar in format to those sponsored by the most important of the national groups, and some, in addition, publish books and documents. Nearly all of them hold at least some kind of annual meeting, open to all members and perhaps to the public. The papers given at most state meetings are, or purport to be, scholarly, but the reminiscences and tall stories of old citizens may still be heard and occasionally predominate.

Even a cursory examination of American historical organizations reveals how they reflect the amazing variety of historical interests. The Southern Historical Association and the Pacific Coast Branch of the AHA, for example, concentrate upon their areas of the United States but hold sessions at their meetings on other areas of history, while the Society for French Historical Studies and the three (geographically organized) conferences on British history exist for reasons obvious in their titles. Little that could have historical

---

[20] The *Directory* just noted lists these. For a basic list see Eric H. Boehm and Lalit Adolphus, eds., *Historical Periodicals,* Santa Barbara (Calif.) 1961, pp. 486–523, which includes nearly all historical periodicals in 1961.

interest escapes attention. Historians and historically minded citizens organize for the study of their nationality (as the Ukrainians or Poles), their religion (as the Catholic, Presbyterian, or Jewish), or because of their interest in a field, a branch or time period of history —whether this be Middle Eastern history, economic history, the history of education, or the history of science. They also form and belong to interdisciplinary societies, for example, the Mediaeval Academy and the American Studies Association. It is safe to generalize that nearly all historians join at least one organization and that many are members of three or four. And it is equally safe to predict, as Lord Bryce did for all Americans, that if a dozen or more American historians have a common special interest but no organization to promote it, another organization will soon be established and will sponsor a publication.

For many years historians complained with reason of the difficulties in finding media for the publication of their books and articles. As early as 1889, Charles Kendall Adams thought the "most important need of advanced historical instruction" to be "such a publication fund as will enable the university to give to the world in academic form the results of thorough and advanced instruction." During the 1950's the then Executive Secretary of the AHA pleaded often and usually in vain for foundation funds to enable publication of worthy books. That the difficulties were real and at times insurmountable cannot be denied, though commercial publishers sometimes replied, also with reason, that historians did not write to be read and that their books did not sell.

Because the United States has become affluent and possibly also because historians write a little less prosaically, more scholarly studies can now be published.[21] Few books by professional historians become commercial successes but the sales of many may cover actual printing costs and the subsidized university presses may carry other expenses for those books they publish. But it is also true that there are more historians and that more are writing and therefore hoping to publish. During the mid-1960's from 200 to 300 volumes (the number depending on the definition) of serious historical writing

---

[21] The "paperbook revolution" has now enormously increased the sale and availability of these studies and some books are now published only in "paperback."

were published each year, and several hundred volumes of historical documents and source materials as well.

Few American historians care or have the ability to write for commercial magazines and few commercial magazines publish historical articles as they once did. The result is that historians chiefly publish in their own professional journals. Most historical journals are published by societies, either national, or state and local, as pointed out above. A few very good ones, for example, the *William and Mary Quarterly* (devoted to American colonial history), are sponsored and published by institutions or university presses.

The almost 600 journals differ enormously in quality. While the *American Historical Review* ranks with the most scholarly historical reviews and is perhaps the world's most catholic and comprehensive scholarly historical review, many other journals, catering to their subscribers, publish chiefly anecdotal or antiquarian little pieces, and one, *American Heritage,* frankly and successfully appeals to the "literate public" with its well-written, beautifully illustrated, and generally romantic and patriotic narratives. The scholarly journals follow the pattern established in Europe and Britain in the late nineteenth century, brought to the United States on the establishment of the *American Historical Review,* and put into practice by the first editor of that *Review,* J. Franklin Jameson.

The *Review* and most other national quarterlies place more stress on reviewing books than on publishing articles. This emphasis grew out of the early need for high standards of scholarship. Compared to European historians, however, the Americans are more genial, their reviews are less destructively or constructively critical, and hence the reviewing has not been as effective in stimulating scholarly work as the best historians have hoped. For its articles the *Review* has tried to "display the largest catholicity possible" and to avoid becoming an "organ of any school, locality, or clique." Catholicity has sometimes led to wide variety rather than to high quality and occasionally readers deplore the miscellaneous nature of the published essays. Jameson established early the criteria for acceptance of articles that he and later editors have tried to follow: "they shall be fresh and original in treatment; . . . the result of accurate scholarship; and . . . have distinct literary merit." Since 1953 only about ten percent of the articles submitted, in the editors' opinions, have met these criteria. The *Review* also devotes considerable space (thirty to forty pages in each issue) to lists of recently published articles in all fields of history and, until the Association established a separate *Newsletter* in 1962–1963, it gave ten to twenty pages or more to news concerning historians and historical work throughout the world.

Other journals, as the *Journal of Southern History* and *French Historical Studies,* restrict their articles, reviews, bibliographies, and news to their special fields. Several, as the *William and Mary Quarterly,* the *Journal of American History,* and the *Journal of Modern History,* uphold the highest standards of scholarship but others are less critical, less carefully edited and sometimes neither their articles nor their reviews seem to add to knowledge, to deepen insight into the past, or to exemplify rigorous scholarship.

V. Some Problems of the Profession in the United States

Several basic concerns seem universal among historians whatever their country: materials for research, time for research and writing, the historian's position in his society, divisions over professional issues, and the kinds of contributions historians should make to their societies. Certainly these are among the major concerns confronting American historians. But there are differences of degree and of context.

Opportunities for research have expanded enormously in the United States since the 1880's. The great libraries, the Library of Congress, the Widener Library of Harvard, and the New York Public Library, have each collected several million volumes and have become centers to which historians must go. But there are many other important libraries in the major cities and at the large universities of the nation, for example, in Boston, Cleveland, and Los Angeles and at Yale University, Columbia University, the University of Michigan, and the University of California (Berkeley). For special subjects, as Byzantine history, Tudor and Stuart England and the American colonies, or the history of the American mid-west, there are excellent more or less specialized libraries, the Dumbarton Oaks Research Library in Washington, D.C., the Huntington Library in

San Marino, California, as well as the Folger Library in Washington, D.C., and the Newberry Library in Chicago.[22]

For an historian's purposes no library is better than its catalogues. In the United States these have been developed on such a grand scale that they are better or at least more convenient than those of libraries in other nations. The Library of Congress prints its catalogues in both card and book form and these are available throughout the nation. The printed books held by several hundred libraries can be ascertained by consulting the *National Union Catalog* also compiled by the Library of Congress.

Hundreds of libraries throughout the nation have collected, preserved, and ordered manuscripts and a few of these collections are huge. For the study of American history few serious scholars can afford to overlook the papers in the Manuscript Division of the Library of Congress, the New York Public Library, and the Houghton Library at Harvard and many must examine one or more of the more than 2,500 collections at universities and public and private libraries. Long-needed general guides to the manuscript collections of the nation are just beginning to appear, the National Historical Publications Commission's *A Guide to Archives and Manuscripts* . . . , edited by Philip Hamer, in 1961, and the multi-volumed *The National Union Catalog of Manuscript Collections* prepared by the Library of Congress and beginning in 1962.

For historians there are never enough books, manuscripts, or guides. American historians are no exception. Even in American history much remains to be done before these resources for historical study are developed as historians desire. Archival development began late in the United States; not until 1934 did the federal government organize and establish The National Archives. Before that time, with notable exceptions, archival collections, federal, state, and local, were in deplorable condition. In some states they still are, though there has been remarkable progress, most recently in the creation of Presidential libraries (Hoover, Franklin Roosevelt, Truman, Eisenhower, and Kennedy). The best archival establishments,

---

22 For an historian's purpose there is no one satisfactory guide to libraries, but see, Eleanor F. Steiner-Prag, comp., *American Library Directory*, 24th ed., New York, 1961; Anthony T. Kruzas, comp., *Director of Special Libraries and Information Centers*, New York, 1963.

including some of those of the states,[23] have also prepared detailed guides or inventories, but some of these are out of date and others are incomplete. For its vast collections of records The National Archives issues *Preliminary Inventories* and other finding aids, e.g., the *Guide to Federal Archives Relating to the Civil War* (1962), and the *List of National Archives Microfilm Publications* (1963).

While the library book collections in the United States provide indispensable information on most historical subjects, the archival resources, as might be expected, cover chiefly the American Colonies and the federal and state governments. The National Archives has slowly been able to collect, order, and make available a large proportion of the federal records—by 1964 it and its fifteen Record Centers held over nine million cubic feet. For the states the archives are spotty. Those in some states, as Virginia and North Carolina, are excellent; several in other states, as Arkansas and Louisiana, are little organized and incomplete. For most topics in modern European history, American historians must go to the Public Record Office, the Archives Nationales or other great European depositories. In medieval history as well, the records in Europe must be searched. Nevertheless, arduous collecting and in recent years micro-reproduction have made much available in several fields of history, e.g., the Vatican materials in St. Louis, the monastic manuscripts at St. John's University (Collegeville, Minnesota), and the microfilms of World War II German military records in The National Archives. The National Archives, too, contains much (and much unused) information on European history, as the reports and materials gathered by American officials on the Siberian fur trade and on local revolutions in Switzerland in the 1830's.

Bibliographies of basic books and articles have now been prepared for most fields and if one is not yet in existence, then one or more soon will be. Americans are often excellent bibliographers.[24] For American history there are not only the current lists of books and articles in the reviews but since 1902, with the exception of the

[23] The best and only recent survey is that of Ernst Posner, *American State Archives*, Chicago, 1964.

[24] A standard United States general guide to basic reference books is Winchell, Constance, *Guide to Reference Books*, 7th ed., Chicago, 1954, with supplements; see also the *Bibliographic Index: a Cumulative Bibliography of Bibliographies*, New York, 1938 ff.

years 1940–1947, the annual though slowly published volumes of *Writings on American History*. To list major volumes for other fields is not possible, but two of the most comprehensive general bibliographies are the *Harvard Guide to American History* (1954) which covers the whole field and the *American Historical Association's Guide to Historical Literature* which, with twenty thousand items, samples the world's history. Nevertheless, again, much remains to be done and the American Historical Association is making a major study of the needs.[25]

For many years American historians have complained of inadequate support for research. They still do, though fellowships and grants have increased both in number and in amount. Through grants from foundations, the American Council of Learned Societies and the Social Science Research Council offer a limited number of fellowships and travel grants to historians each year. The Guggenheim Foundation awards several much prized fellowships, and the American Philosophical Society and other educational and philanthropic agencies offer small grants-in-aid for research. Aided by Fulbright fellowships, several hundred historians have been able to study in Europe and elsewhere. In 1966 a new National Foundation on the Arts and Humanities, financed by federal funds, began to give awards to artists and to humanists, including historians. But much more money for research continued to go to scientists than to humanists both from the federal government and from private foundations, and historians envied their good fortune.

Quite possibly historians in most other countries envy the comparative affluence of their American colleagues. But Americans are not certain that they have more opportunities for creative work than their European colleagues, at least those in western European universities. They teach more hours each week, and within their society they do not often have the privileges European historians customarily enjoy in theirs. Still, in the opinion of some American university administrators, American historians, especially those in the graduate schools, are so often "off campus" on research projects that their students are neglected.

25 The first results of this study appear in the critical analyses of resources and needs contained in Dagmar Horma Perman, ed., *Bibliography and the Historian*, Santa Barbara, Clio Press, 1968.

Many, if not most, American historians are torn between their desire to teach and their interest in research and writing. This is a professional issue of great concern, much debated among academicians in all fields. More and more historians wish to devote their energies chiefly to research, while their colleges have traditionally stressed good teaching and students still demand it. First honors in the profession and the best positions go to productive scholars who publish their findings.[26] The graduate institutions reflect this valuation as they train their students in research more than they prepare them to teach undergraduates. Yet most historians devote, must devote by the nature of their positions, most of their time to teaching and preparation for it. This conflict of interest has led to severe tensions. So concerned did a number of historians become that the American Historical Association sponsored a comprehensive study of graduate training in 1959–1961. The principal authors, John Snell and Dexter Perkins, of the resulting volume *(The Education of Historians in the United States,* New York, 1962), and the distinguished committee advising them thought teaching as important as research and recommended experience in teaching for all Ph.D. candidates who planned to teach. Yet the emphasis on research continues.

The reasonable view, put forward by the committee, that good teaching is based on experience in research and knowledge of its findings and that uncommunicated research has little value, is often overlooked or termed unrealistic. Young historians believe they must make a choice and the most dedicated scholars usually choose to emphasize research and publication. With the present state of demand for historians few perish but the highest rewards do go to those who publish. The acclaim of students is heart-warming but recognition by professional colleagues is more highly valued and monetarily rewarded.

Another professional debate divides historians into generalists and specialists, those who, in the argumentative phrases, engage in "sweeping" general studies and those who concentrate on "narrow" specialties. If, as seems likely, American historians since the 1880's have erred, they have erred on the side of specialization. An able few, like James Breasted, Charles Haskins, and Robert Palmer, have

---

[26] See above, p. 194.

written big books on big subjects. Most have been content with less ambitious monographs.

Few American historians cling to the old myth that thousands of detailed studies in the first-hand sources will finally permit definitive syntheses to be written. Yet they recognize the ever-present danger of generalizing too soon and from too little evidence. No American historian denies that examination of primary sources is the basic duty of an historian, that history more than poetry or sociology deals with the particular—what Alcibiades did and suffered. On the other hand, none disagree with Pirenne's observation that every effort at synthesis, if honestly offered, "cannot fail to react usefully in investigations." In actuality American historians give recognition to both specialists and generalists—if they are good. And now and then an historian, as Crane Brinton of Harvard who has written on several large subjects, is able to combine the two approaches. The dilemmas remain, as the recent volume, edited by Louis Gottschalk, *Generalization in the Writing of History,* well demonstrates. At what point can an historian legitimately generalize *and* at what level? No one has answers on which everyone or even a majority will agree.

A related concern is the place of history in the realm of knowledge. Is it one of the humanities or a social (or even behavioral) science? A majority of the historians think of it as a humanity. History, they say, humanizes as it brings understanding of the play of chance or probability, folly or wisdom, irrationality or rationality in human affairs and the lives of individuals. But a minority, who think of history as scientific in method and purposeful in objective, consider it a social science which could lead to the discovery of constants or general laws in human behavior. The argument is as old as the nineteenth century. Is history art or science? Most American historians agree that it is both—humanistic in purpose, more or less scientific in method. But most believe it also to be *sui generis,* a field of knowledge, a discipline with its own *raison d'être* and its own methods. And this remains true even though a growing number are attempting quantitative studies with the aid of computers.

Those who believe history to be primarily a humanity, in the manner of Herodotus and Burckhardt, emphasize the pleasure and understanding its study affords. Those who believe it a social science, followers in a way of Bentham and Comte, not only emphasize the discipline of systematic historical thinking but the usefulness of historical knowledge for intelligent political and social action. The humanists tend to stress past experience and to value historical knowledge primarily for the depth of human insights it brings, while the social scientists more often regard historical data as guides for present national and international policies—to guide, for example, Supreme Court decisions in the United States on the crucial questions of racial integration or State Department and White House decisions in foreign relations. Nevertheless, few are certain that history teaches any certain lessons and most would agree with Burckhardt's judgment that history is "on every occasion the record of what one generation finds worthy of note in another."

This judgment helps explain why another, and now dying, issue arose, that of the need for historical revision by each generation. It is now commonly agreed that time is the enemy of "definitive" books and that each new generation of historians will seek new answers because new questions arise out of their time and because of their desire to establish their own identities (the generation's gap). Few older historians are surprised, then, when the younger attack the interpretations of their predecessors—even the magisterial construction of Frederick Jackson Turner on the American frontier and Charles A. Beard on the role of economic interests.

Still another issue concerns the best form for written history, narrative (literary) or analytic (scientific). Each variety has its advocates and practitioners. The "professionals" generally have used the analytic approach, the "amateurs" the narrative. But now and then an historian with professional qualifications, as Allan Nevins, stoutly defends the narrative, while "amateurs" like Bray Hammond, who left governmental service to write history, publish excellent analytical studies. Both "amateurs" and "professionals" write big biographies, as Douglas Southall Freeman who wrote on Washington and Samuel Flagg Bemis who wrote on John Quincy Adams. The issue is no longer as heatedly debated as it was a generation ago. Insofar as opinion can be sampled, it seems to hold that there is no one best way to write history, and that the form chosen should depend upon the subject and the historian.

On many problems, some more fundamental than those just outlined, there is basic though never complete agreement among American historians. They seldom divide on fundamental ideologi-

cal issues and but few bitter controversies arise among them on sub-
stantive historical questions. They generally agree with the modest
claim of Carl Becker that history prepares men "to live more
humanely in the present, and to meet, rather than to foretell, the
future."

But they also believe that their society does not properly appreciate either their subject or those who teach and write it. Here they
may share the values of American culture more than they realize.
They want, on occasion desperately, to have the value of historical
knowledge recognized in the deliberations of the councils of the
nation, as it seemed to be during the administration of John F.
Kennedy. They hope, probably in vain in the present technological
society, that they themselves will be accorded the social and economic status American scientists now possess. Nevertheless, most
of them will not cater to popular tastes and write and teach those
romantic varieties of history their fellow citizens would most avidly
applaud and reward. As American historians have had to do since
the 1880's, contemporary American historians must consider the
tastes of at least three audiences, those of their own colleagues, their
students, and the nebulous "reading public." If they are to satisfy
the first, they must write critical and documented history however
dull it may seem to laymen; if the second, they must make history
"come alive" and thus face the accusation of "presentism"; if the
third, they must provide entertainment or foretell the future (and
thus deny their own principles) or brilliantly illuminate the past
(like a rare Garrett Mattingly). As few Americans read scholarly
historical works and as the historians themselves are not often willing to satisfy popular tastes, their most appreciative audience continues to be their students. Most of them, at the same time, continue
to glance over their shoulders for approval of their colleagues and
to cast covetous glances at the popularizer who sometimes pilfers
their hard-won knowledge, adds spice, and sells *his* books. Regardless
of the possible audiences most of them also go on reading and teaching history just because they like history and believe that knowledge
of it prepares them to live more humanely and their societies to act
more intelligently.

American historians, like historians in other western lands, are
not yet accustomed to an affluent society which could fully encourage every variety of serious historical study. Nor do they fully enjoy

that kind of freedom in which a scholar may pursue his search wherever it may lead. In a special sense because they are American historians, they reflect the nature and tensions of their own culture. But, at the same time, because they are historians they share the problems, limitations, and opportunities of their colleagues everywhere.

VI. Bibliographical Note on the Professional Study of History in the United States

The best sources are the books of historians in their specialized fields, their occasional essays and lectures on the study of history, and their letters and autobiographies. For this essay I have found the writings of several scholars of the first generations of professional historians (to about 1940) of special interest: Charles Kendall Adams, Herbert Baxter Adams, Carl Becker, John Spencer Bassett, Charles Beard, John W. Burgess, J. Franklin Jameson, James Harvey Robinson, and Andrew D. White. As historians became more and more conscious of their profession and of their obligations and aspirations as practitioners, they produced a voluminous literature about themselves and their work. Among the later historians (since about 1940) whose studies I have found of value are Merle Curti, Louis Gottschalk, John Higham, W. Stull Holt, Jurgen Herbst, Georg Iggers, Allan Nevins, John Snell, Arthur Schlesinger, and Walter Muir Whitehill. From my own incomplete bibliography containing about five hundred items I have selected just over fifty for the "selected list" below.

Among other sources of information are the biographies of historians written by other historians which are too numerous to list here. The *Dictionary of American Biography* (and its supplements) contains sketches of several of the best known, but there is no convenient biographical compendium for historians who are living.

The statistics on historians are never as complete or trustworthy as an exact historian would like. For this study they come chiefly from the reports of the United States Office of Education and of the American Council on Education, and the volume by John Snell and others in the selected list.

This study is also based on the publications (particularly the

Proceedings volumes), files, and inquiries of the American Historical Association and *American Historical Review* which the author had the privilege of serving from 1953 to 1963, and upon his first-hand knowledge of historians and historical study acquired during that ten-year period. The addresses of the Presidents of the Association, though of varying quality, are particularly revealing, if read as sources on the state of historical thinking.

Selected Bibliography

ADAMS, Charles Kendall, "Recent Historical Work in the Colleges and Universities of Europe and America," in American Historical Association *Papers,* vol. IV, pt. I, January, 1890; and *A Manual of Historical Literature* (esp. the long introduction), 3rd ed. New York, Harper, 1889.

ADAMS, Herbert Baxter, *The Study of History in American Colleges and Universities,* United States Bureau of Education, Circular of Information, No. 2, Washington, D. C., 1887.

AUSUBEL, Herman, *Historians and Their Craft.* New York, Columbia University Press, 1950.

BASSETT, John Spencer, *The Middle Group of American Historians.* New York, Macmillan, 1917.

BEALE, Howard K., "The Professional Historian: His Theory and His Practice," *The Pacific Historical Review,* vol. XXII (1953).

BEARD, Charles, "Written History as an Act of Faith," *American Historical Review,* vol. XXXIX (1934); "That Noble Dream," *Ibid.,* vol. XLI (1935); and *A Charter for the Social Sciences in the Schools.* New York, Scribner, 1932.

BECKER, Carl, *Everyman His Own Historian.* New York, Crofts, 1935; and *Detachment and the Writing of History: Essays and Letters of Carl Becker,* Phil L. Snyder, ed. Ithaca, N.Y., Cornell University Press, 1958.

BELLOT, H. Hale, *American History and American Historians.* Norman, Okla., University of Oklahoma Press, 1952.

BENSON, LEE, *Turner and Beard: American Historical Writing Reconsidered.* Glencoe, Ill., Free Press, 1960.

BOYD, JULIAN, "State and Local Historical Societies in the United States," *American Historical Review,* vol. XL (1934); and "Historical Editing in the United States: The Next Stage," *Proceedings of the American Antiquarian Society,* pt. 2 (1963).

BRINTON, Crane, "The 'New History' and 'Past Everything,' " *American Scholar,* vol. VIII (1939).

BUTTERFIELD, LYMAN, "Archival and Editorial Enterprise in 1850 and 1950: Some Comparisons and Contrasts," *Proceedings of the American Philosophical Society,* Vol. 98 (1954).

CAHNMAN, W. J. and BOSKOFF, ALVIN, *Sociology and History: Theory and Research.* New York, Free Press, 1964.

CAUGHEY, John, "Historian's Choice: Results of a Poll on Recently Pubblished American History and Biography," *Mississippi Valley Historical Review,* vol. XXXIX (1952).

DONNAN, ELIZABETH, and STOCK, LEO, eds., *An Historian's World: Selections from the Correspondence of John Franklin Jameson.* Philadelphia, American Philosophical Society, 1956.

ELLIS, ELMER, "The Profession of Historian," *Mississippi Valley Historical Review, vol.* XXXVIII (1951).

GOLDMAN, ERIC, ed., *Historiography and Urbanization: Essays in American History in Honor of W. Stull Holt.* Baltimore, Johns Hopkins University Press, 1941.

GOTTSCHALK, LOUIS, ed., *Generalization in the Writing of History.* Chicago, University of Chicago Press, 1963; and *Understanding History.* New York, Knopf, 1950.

HERBST, JURGEN, *The German School in American Scholarship.* Ithaca, N. Y., Cornell University Press, 1965.

HERRICK, Francis, "The Profession of History," *Pacific Historical Review,* vol. XXXI (February, 1962).

HEXTER, J. H., *Reappraisals in History.* Evanston, Ill., Northwestern University Press, 1961.

HICKS, JOHN C., "What's Right with the History Profession," *Pacific Historical Review,* vol. XXV (1956).

HIGHAM, John, with KRIEGER, Leonard, and GILBERT, Felix, *History.* Englewood Cliffs, N.J., Prentice-Hall, 1965; and HIGHAM, John, "The Rise of American Intellectual History," *American Historical Review,* vol. LVI (1951); and "Beyond Consensus: The Historian as Moral Critic," *Ibid.,* vol. LXVII (1962).

HOFSTADTER, Richard, *Social Darwinism in American Thought, 1860–1915.* Philadelphia, University of Pennsylvania Press, 1944.

———, and METZGER, Walter, *The Development of Academic Freedom in the United States.* New York, Columbia University Press, 1955.

HOLT, W. Stull, ed., *Historical Scholarship in the United States, 1876–1901: As Revealed in the Correspondence of Herbert Baxter Adams.* Baltimore, Johns Hopkins University Press, Johns Hopkins Studies, LVI, 1938; "Historical Scholarship," in CURTI, Merle, ed., *American Schol-*

arship in the Twentieth Century. Cambridge, Mass., Harvard University Press, 1953; and with KRAUS, Michael, and CAUGHEY, John, "American Historical Writing, 1900–1950: A Symposium," *Mississippi Valley Historical Review,* vol. XL (1954).

HUTCHINSON, William T., ed., *The Marcus W. Jernegan Essays in American Historiography.* Chicago, University of Chicago Press, 1937.

IGGERS, Georg G., "The Image of Ranke in American and German Historical Thought, " *History and Theory,* vol. II (1962).

JAMESON, J. Franklin, *"The American Historical Review, 1895–1920,"* *American Historical Review,* vol. XXVI (1920); "The American Historical Association, 1884–1909," *Ibid.,* vol. XV (1909); "Early Days of the American Historical Association," *Ibid.,* vol. XL (1934); *The History of Historical Writing in America.* Boston, Houghton Mifflin, 1891; and with McMaster, J. B., and Channing, Edward, *The Present State of Historical Writing in America.* Worcester, Mass., The Davis Press, 1910.

JORDY, William H., *Henry Adams: Scientific Historian.* New Haven, Conn., Yale University Press, 1952.

KRAUS, Michael, *The Writing of American History.* Norman, Okla., University of Oklahoma Press, 1953.

LEVIN, David, *History as Romantic Art.* Stanford, Calif., Stanford University Press, 1959.

MAZLICH, Bruce, ed., *Psychoanalysis and History,* Englewood Cliffs, N.J., Prentice-Hall, 1963.

NEDS, Ivy F., "A Half-Century of American Historiography, 1884–1934." Unpublished doctoral dissertation, Ohio State University, 1935.

NEVINS, Allan, *The Gateway to History,* rev. ed. Garden City, N.Y., Doubleday (Anchor Books), 1962.

POSNER, Ernst, *American State Archives.* Chicago, University of Chicago Press, 1964.

SAVETH, Edward N, ed., *American History and the Social Sciences.* New York, Free Press, 1964.

SAVELLE, Max, "Historian's Progress or the Quest for Sancta Sophia," *Pacific Historical Review,* vol. XXVII (1958).

SCHLESINGER, Arthur, and Committee, *Historical Scholarship in America, Its Needs and Opportunities.* New York, Long and Smith, 1932; SCHLESINGER, Arthur, "History," in W. Gee, ed., *Research in the Social Sciences.* New York, Macmillan, 1929; and *In Retrospect.* New York, Harcourt, Brace & World, 1963.

SHAFER, Boyd C., "History, Not Art, Not Science, But History," *Pacific Historical Review,* vol. XXIX (1960).

SHEEHAN, Donald, and SYRETT, Harold C., eds., *Essays in American His-*

toriography in Honor of Allan Nevins. New York, Columbia University Press, 1960.

SILVESTRO, Clement and WILLIAMS, Richmond D., *A Look at Ourselves* [state and local associations], Bulletins of the American Association for State and Local History, vol. II, Madison, Wisc., 1962.

SKOTHEIM, Robert, *American Intellectual Histories and Historians.* Princeton, N.J., Princeton University Press, 1966.

SMITH, Theodore, "The Writing of American History in America, from 1884 to 1934," *American Historical Review,* vol. XL (1935).

SNELL, John, PERKINS, Dexter, and Committee, *The Education of Historians in the United States.* New York, McGraw-Hill, 1962.

Social Science Research Council, *Theory and Practice in Historical Study: A Report of the Committee on Historiography,* Bulletin 54, New York, SSRC, 1946; and *The Social Sciences in Historical Study: A Report of the Committee on Historiography,* Bulletin 64, New York, SSRC, 1954.

STROUT, Cushing, *The Pragmatic Revolt in American History.* New Haven, Conn., Yale University Press, 1958.

THOMAS, Daniel H., and CASE, Lynn, *Guide to the Diplomatic Archives of Western Europe.* Philadelphia, University of Pennsylvania Press, 1959.

UNGER, Irwin, "The 'New Left' and American History: Some Recent Trends in American Historiography," *American Historical Review,* vol. LXXII (1967).

VAN TASSEL, David, *Recording America's Past: An Interpretation of the Development of Historical Studies in America, 1607–1884.* Chicago, University of Chicago Press, 1960.

WESLEY, Edgar, and others, *American History in Schools and Colleges.* New York, Macmillan, 1944.

WHITE, Morton, *Social Thought in America: The Revolt Against Formalism.* New York, Viking, 1949.

WHITEHILL, Walter, *Independent Historical Societies: An Enquiry into Their Research and Publication Functions and Their Financial Future.* Boston, The Boston Athenaeum—distr. by Harvard University Press, 1962.

WILKINS, Burleigh T., *Carl Becker, A Biographical Study in American Intellectual History.* Cambridge, Mass., M.I.T. Press, 1961.

WISH, Harvey, *The American Historian: A Socio-Intellectual History of the Writing of the American Past.* New York, Oxford University Press, 1960.

Index